CW00348293

THE
CANTERBURY
BOOK
OF
DAYS

PAUL CRAMPTON

Prominent musician of the 'Canterbury Scene', Hugh Hopper, died on 7 June 2009. Forever modest and generous, Hugh was one of the most decent blokes I've ever known and it is to his memory that this book is dedicated.

First published 2011

The History Press
The Mill, Brimscombe Port
Stroud, Gloucestershire, GL5 2QG
www.thehistorypress.co.uk

© Paul Crampton

The right of Paul Crampton to be identified as the Author
of this work has been asserted in accordance with the
Copyrights, Designs and Patents Act 1988.

All rights reserved. No part of this book may be reprinted
or reproduced or utilised in any form or by any electronic,
mechanical or other means, now known or hereafter invented,
including photocopying and recording, or in any information
storage or retrieval system, without the permission in writing
from the Publishers.

British Library Cataloguing in Publication Data.
A catalogue record for this book is available from the British
Library.

ISBN 978 0 7524 5685 0

Typesetting and origination by The History Press
Manufacturing managed by Jellyfish Print Solutions Ltd.
Printed in India

January 1st

1171: On this Friday, Henry II, still in his court at Normandy, first heard about the murder of Archbishop Thomas Becket (*see* December 29th). His initial reaction was one of shocked silence, and he withdrew himself from court. And then, grief quickly set in, with the King barely able to eat or drink. (Urry: *Becket: His Last Days*)

———•◆•———

1812: On this Wednesday, the Methodist Chapel in St Peter's Street was officially opened (*see* May 7th). The architect was William Jenkins. It replaced the 'Pepper-Box' or 'Roundhouse' Chapel in King Street, which was then passed on to the Baptists.

———•◆•———

1931: The Canterbury & Whitstable Railway officially closed to passengers on this Thursday, after just over 100 years of service. The improved bus services between Canterbury and the coastal towns were largely responsible for its decline. However, the line would continue for just over another twenty years, hauling freight services from Whitstable Harbour.

———•◆•———

2010: Police were called to a fight eight minutes into New Year's Day in Chilham. Two women had been ejected from the White Horse Inn, in the Square, when they began fighting outside. Officers were called after a large crowd gathered to watch the pair. (*Kentish Gazette*)

January 2nd

1644: On this Saturday, King Charles I wrote to the Cathedral Chapter, dispensing the newly appointed Dean, Dr Thomas Turner, from a personal installation since he could not travel to Canterbury without hazard to his person. [The Civil War was well underway, and Parliament did not much care for Dean and Chapters. Dr Turner was not able to take up his new appointment until the monarchy had been reinstated in 1660.] (*Archaeologia Cantiana*, 1930)

———— ◆ ————

1884: 'But for the liberality of Mr F. Flint, the old bridge at the Riding Gate (a tall brick arch dating from 1791) would have long continued to disfigure one of the entrances to the City of Canterbury. The new iron structure does great credit to its designer, though a few hypercritical persons – not to admire is all they know – seem to have expected something more ornate. The Town Council met on this Wednesday and resolved to recognise Mr Flint's gift in a graceful manner by placing a suitable inscription on one of the tablets on the monument on the Dane John Mound'. [The iron bridge was removed in 1970 and replaced by something even less ornate!] (*Kentish Gazette*)

January 3rd

1860: Following renovation, Canterbury's famous civic Guildhall was made available for hire on this day: 'Having been elegantly redecorated, and adapted for assemblies and entertainments of a superior character'. (*Living in Victorian Canterbury*)

————•◆•————

1913: 'Mr G.H. Delasaux proposes it would be an excellent thing if the Canterbury Town Council would dissolve their scratch fire brigade, which we can rarely see at work for the simple reason that, like the Spanish Fleet on certain occasions, it seldom happens to be in sight. The volunteer fire brigades should be amalgamated for the purpose of dealing with fires in the city and could be drilled under the supervision of the City Surveyor. Mr Delasaux's suggestion is indeed a fine one but it does not follow that the proposition will be taken up by the Council'. [Earlier in 1872, George Delasaux had been personally involved in saving the Cathedral Choir after its roof had caught fire (*see* September 3rd).] (*Kentish Gazette*)

————•◆•————

1962: 'Rubbish offer Refused' or 'Refuse offer Rubbished': An offer from Pelham Advertising to sell advertising space on the sides of Canterbury's refuse-collection vehicles, and pay the Council 10 per cent of the revenue, was turned down. (City Council records)

January 4th

1577/78: William Roper died on this day, aged eighty-two. He was interred in the family vault at St Dunstan's Church. At the same time, the body of his wife, Margaret (*see* July 20th), together with the head of Sir Thomas More, were both translated from London to Canterbury.

———◆———

1795: Much of East Kent was affected by 'The Great Snow of 1795'. On this Sunday, Fahrenheit's thermometer in the open air at Canterbury, stood at 10 degrees, well below the freezing point at 32 degrees. (*Bygone Kent*, Vol. 7, No. 5)

———◆———

1896: The *Kentish Gazette* reported the suicide of the Revd J. Parmitter, Vicar of St Mildred's Church. He was hit by a train on the Elham Valley Railway. By all accounts, he suffered years of pain from a neck injury sustained in a carriage accident, which had also resulted in attacks of 'nervous prostration'.

———◆———

1954: On this Monday, the last few rails of the closed Canterbury & Whitstable Railway were removed. The work had begun in the summer of 1953, following the railway's brief reprise to aid the flooded Whitstable (*see* February 6th). This proved to be a particularly difficult task in the Tyler Hill Tunnel.

January 5th

1795: Canterbury bookseller and amateur musician William Flackton died on this day. Born in the city, he demonstrated a talent for music at an early age and became a cathedral chorister at the age of nine. As an adult, he also composed music both religious and secular; one of his pieces, 'A Glorious Chase', was written for the Canterbury Catch Club – a male-only social society.

———◆———

1934: A proposed scheme for widening the road at St Martin's Hill at an estimated cost of £5,468 – exclusive of the cost of acquisition of the land – was the principal topic discussed at this week's meeting of the City Council. This would mean the demolition of St Martin's Old Rectory, which stood right on the edge of the road at the bottom of the hill (at No. 14). The Old Rectory and five adjoining houses were demolished in late 1936. (Crampton: *Canterbury's Lost Heritage*)

———◆———

1955: A report showed that the recent winter gales had damaged the Poor Priest's Hospital, in Stour Street, and emergency repairs were necessary. Later examinations revealed hitherto unknown roof damage that had been caused by the blast of a nearby high-explosive bomb back in 1942. (City Council records)

January 6th

1066: Following the death of Edward the Confessor, Stigand, the Archbishop of Canterbury, summoned the Witan (national council) to choose his successor. Their subsequent choice of Harold would have profound repercussions for British history (*see* November 1st). (Babbington: *Romance of Canterbury Cathedral*)

---◆---

1885: The *Kentish Gazette* reported that a very large number of parents were summoned for neglecting to send their children to school. In many cases the excuse was poverty and inability to pay school fees owing to want of employment, and in others sickness was pleaded.

---◆---

1915: Second Lieutenant Vernon James Austin, of the Royal Regiment of Artillery, was killed in France, hit in the chest by a German sniper's bullet. He was the son of Sir Herbert Austin, who founded Austin Motors. Vernon attended the King's School at Canterbury, where he was a cadet in the Officers Training Corps. His father arranged for him to be buried at St Martin's Church, in the city he loved the most. (Kent History Forum)

---◆---

1954: Plans were being formulated for Canterbury's new ambulance station to be built at Nunnery Fields Hospital. [These were never acted upon, and the ambulance station was eventually constructed in Military Road.] (City Council records)

January 7th

1888: Mr Brian Rigden, in his annual report on the weather, says: 'the year 1887 will be long remembered as the year of the great drought. There was a total absence of rain for thirty days and the total rainfall was far less than average. In Canterbury, there has been a large share of south winds, for on more than one-third of all the year's days the weather vane was pointing in that direction'.

———•◆•———

1942: On this day the Mayor of Canterbury, Alderman Charles Lefevre, announced that the Beaney Institute's vast archive of *The Times* newspaper had been given up for war salvage. He urged people to follow the example by purging their home libraries of old tomes that nobody ever read, nor was ever likely to. (Crampton: *The Blitz of Canterbury*)

———•◆•———

2005: The famous lime tree at St Lawrence Cricket Ground, Canterbury, was broken in half by high winds during this Friday night. In 1847, the ground had been built around the tree, which stood inside the boundary. If a ball hit the tree, it counted as four runs. A replacement lime tree was soon planted within the playing area to carry on this strange tradition.

January 8th

1776: On this Monday, 'there happened a great inundation [flash-flood] in Canterbury, insomuch that some persons were drowned by the vast impetuosity of the current, which overflowed across the road at the west end of Westgate Bridge, and directed its course down North Lane, with great force'. (Hasted: *Kent*, Vol. XI)

———◆◆———

1887: During choir practice at St Mildred's Church, a well-dressed young man came in through the vestry, looked about for a time and then advanced to the altar. To the astonishment of the members of the choir, he then deliberately took a small brass candlestick and immediately left the church. Some of the older choirboys pursued the man but were unable to overtake him. The stolen article was of little intrinsic value. (*Kentish Gazette*)

———◆◆———

1943: A cheque arrived this day for one guinea, accompanied by a touching letter from an eighty-eight-year-old Friend of Canterbury Cathedral: 'I am so grieved about Canterbury [having been bombed] that I feel I must make an effort and send my usual small subscription towards the funds of the Friends, remembering the happy times I spent at the Festivals and in the Cathedral Precincts and Garden of Remembrance, which I shall never see again'. (Friends' Report, April 1943)

January 9th

1855: 'Cooper Family Woes, 1': On this day, the *Kentish Gazette* reported an attempted robbery at Vernon Holme, home of Canterbury artist Thomas Sidney Cooper. A window at the back of the house was broken, but on finding protective bars behind it the burglars fled empty-handed. Apparently, the artist's two pet dogs, Trip and Tiger, slept through the entire episode. (Courtesy of Brian Stewart)

———•◆•———

1935: A man, who for five weeks had been selling 'foreign' eggs as British new laid, was sentenced to three months' hard labour at St Augustine's Sessions, Canterbury, on this Wednesday. [I can only assume that 'foreign' eggs are what one uses to make a Spanish Omelette!] (*Kentish Gazette*)

———•◆•———

1936: 'Cooper Family Woes, 2': On this Thursday, Canterbury painter Nevill Louis Cooper died after catching a chill. The death certificate also alluded to a destructive addiction to sleeping draughts. He was a well-known figure in Canterbury, always attracting attention with his bohemian and somewhat eccentric lifestyle. Although he never married, Neville was certainly 'fond of the ladies'. I am personally acquainted with one of his descendents, who still lives in Canterbury (*see* January 16th and September 13th).

January 10th

1645: On this Tuesday, at Tower Hill, Archbishop of Canterbury William Laud was executed for treason. Laud's real crime was his High-Church beliefs and fervent support for King Charles I and the Royalist cause. His beheading concluded a long period of imprisonment in the Tower and several attempts by Parliament to have him condemned. For the remaining period of the Commonwealth, there would be no Archbishop of Canterbury.

1776: On this Wednesday, antiquarian and archaeologist Bryan Faussett died in his manor house at Heppington, Street End, near Canterbury. At Oxford University, where he briefly flirted with the Jacobite cause, he was known as 'the handsome Commoner'. His collections of coins and other ancient artefacts were vast. He was buried at Nackington Church (where he had also been christened fifty-six years before), where a monument to him can be seen.

1934: A shocking tragedy occurred in St Dunstan's Street on this Wednesday afternoon when a little girl, Florence May Cooper, aged four years and eight months, was run over and instantly killed by a double-decker Canterbury-to-Whitstable bus. The child darted from behind a milk float and the bus driver had no chance of avoiding her. (*Kentish Gazette*)

January 11th

1555/56: On this day, Canterbury Cathedral 'Six Preacher', Edward Craddock, took his BA at Oxford. He was somewhat eccentric, dabbling in alchemy and spending many years seeking the Philosopher's Stone! (Ingram Hill: *The Six Preachers*)

———— • ❖ • ————

1896: On this day, the *Kentish Gazette* reported, 'St Alphege with All Saints: On Tuesday and Thursday, the children attending these Sunday schools had their winter treat at Eastbridge. On both occasions, tea was followed by a magic lantern entertainment, after which were the giving of prizes, and each child left with an orange and a packet of sweets'.

———— • ❖ • ————

1965: On this Monday evening, three as-yet unknown Canterbury musicians were thrown out of the Three Compasses pub, in St Peter's Street, for the serious crime of having long hair. The publican, Reginald Baxter, told them he was allergic to long hair and would not serve them. Those ejected were from the recently formed five-piece band, The Wilde Flowers (*see* June 24th). They were ex-Simon Langton pupils Hugh Hopper (nineteen) and Robert Wyatt (nineteen) and Herne Bay native Kevin Ayres (twenty). The band would play their debut gig later in the same week, ironically at another pub: the Bear & Key at Whitstable. (Courtesy of Hugh Hopper)

January 12th

1875: Trout fishing in the River Stour was a popular pursuit in this era, but the view was expressed that the river would contain more young fish but for the 'heavy attacks' made on trout on their way to spawn. [This was probably a reference to unlicensed fishing.] (*Living in Victorian Canterbury*)

1885: Mr Edward Garwood Hook, draper, was charged with having allowed the chimney of his premises to catch fire in consequence of not being properly swept. PC Seath said that he saw smoke and flames coming from the kitchen at Mr Hook's house. Witnesses assisted in putting it out. [His draper's shop was at Nos 12-13 St George's Street, where the former Woolworth's shop is today. His private address was No. 4 St Lawrence Villas, probably in Sturry Road.] (*Kentish Gazette*, courtesy of Tina Machado)

1985: Just a year after it was founded, the Friends of the Canterbury Archaeological Trust had raised £10,500, started a shop at No. 72 Northgate, and also attracted 380 members. At Christ Church College, on this day, the anniversary was marked with a lecture by Director Tim Tatton-Brown on the work of the Trust.

January 13th

1583: On this day, Jane Moore (née Marlowe) died in childbirth in Canterbury. She was only thirteen years old. Jane, a sister of playwright Christopher Marlowe, had married John Moore in St Andrew's Church barely nine months before. It is thought that her son died at about the same time. (Urry: *Christopher Marlowe*)

———◆———

1887: A young man employed by Mrs Andrews, butcher, Oaten Hill, met with an accident when driving in the 'New Road'. He passed a wagon and two horses – with the waggoner and a small boy walking on the pavement – when the front horse strayed against his cart and kicked out, causing it to overturn and breaking one of the shafts. The young man's hand was severely sprained and he was considerably cut around the face. ['New Road' is a reference to the New Dover Road, created as one of the new 'turnpike roads' in 1792.] (*Kentish Gazette*)

———◆———

1977: Actor Orlando Bloom was born in Canterbury on this day. He attended both St Edmund's School and King's School, where his mother encouraged him to take art and drama classes. His first television work was as an extra in three episodes of *Casualty* between 1994 and 1996. (Wikipedia)

January 14th

1812: Kent historian Edward Hasted died on this day. He was seventy-nine. He is most famous for his *History of Kent*, of which Volumes XI and XII are dedicated to Canterbury. Hasted purchased 'The Sympson House' (demolished 1813) in the north Cathedral Precincts for his mother, and is thought to have lived in St George's Street himself at the same time.

———◆———

1835: Peter Abul (thirty-one), a native of Bengal, was charged with being drunk in the High Street. PC Smith said that the prisoner went into Mrs Potter's shop and frightened her and her daughter by putting out his tongue and pretending he was dumb. In court, Mr Abul said he wasn't drunk, but had taken opium! (*Kentish Gazette*)

———◆———

1966: On this day, a compulsory purchase order for nine houses that made up Victoria Grove was published. This short cul-de-sac ran north from Hawks Lane, and was being demolished to make way for the proposed relief road (to run directly from Gravel Walk to Tower Way). The houses were demolished in readiness, but the new road was subsequently cancelled. Victoria Grove is one of Canterbury's lost streets, a car park occupying the site today. (Author's archive)

January 15th

1557: During the reign of Mary Tudor, Canterbury became a grim location for the execution of Kentish people who refused to recant their Protestant faith. In all, forty-one were burnt at the stake in a remote field off Wincheap, thereafter named 'Martyr's Field'. On this particular day, a man from Canterbury became a victim of this brutal process. He was Stephen Kemp, who lived in Northgate. In 1899 a Memorial Cross was erected on the site, listing the names of all those martyred. Within a few years, a housing development grew up around it (*see* June 19th).

———◆———

1835: 'Sir, There has been for several days at No. 17 Guildhall Street, an exhibition of models from the remains of Saxon and Roman architecture to be found in Canterbury – they are the work of a most ingenious person, a resident and, I believe, a native of the place. The self-taught artist is a shoemaker and it would be a shame for the good people of Canterbury to feel indifference for the efforts of native genius, when they are devoted to illustrate and perpetuate those mouldering records of time and events which give celebrity to their ancient City.' (*Kentish Gazette*)

January 16th

1864: On this Saturday, Nevill Louis Cooper was born at Vernon Holme, in Harbledown, to Canterbury artist Thomas Sidney Cooper and his second wife, Mary Cannon. At the time, Sidney Cooper was sixty years old. Nevill grew up to be a competent painter himself, as well as an enthusiastic tree collector. He spent a considerable amount of money beautifying the gardens at Vernon Holme and Allcroft Grange (*see* November 8th), the latter of which was also the site of his famous pinetum. (Stewart: *Thomas Sidney Cooper, see* January 9th)

1935: On this morning, the Mayor and Mayoress of Canterbury paid their annual visit to St Thomas' Hospital, Eastbridge, and presented all the Brethren and Sisters with a parcel of groceries. (*Kentish Gazette*)

1943: On, or very near this day, the two remaining pillars and arches in the north arcade of the cathedral's Victorian Library (1868) suddenly collapsed. This was a part of the building left standing after a high-explosive bomb had hit the north-east corner of it during a Second World War Baedeker raid (*see* June 1st). Fortunately, the collapse did not damage the library's west wall, which had survived from Lanfranc's monastic dormitory (1077) to its fullest height. (Sparks: *Canterbury Cathedral Precincts*)

January 17th

1876: A report on the 1876 cathedral bell ringers' annual supper stated: 'Amongst the present effective staff of ringers, there are three who took part in the last long peal, which was rung on our Cathedral bells in 1827. We allude to Mr Henry Ovenden (St Dunstan's), Mr John Small (Westgate) and Mr Edward Austin (St Stephen's) and we are glad to know that after a lapse of some 50 years, they are still hale and hearty.' (*Living in Victorian Canterbury*)

———◆———

1961: On this day, it was announced that the Archbishop of Canterbury, Geoffrey Fisher, was to resign. He had been enthroned following the sudden death of William Temple (*see* October 26th). By contrast to his predecessor, Fisher was a far more conventional, conservative character. His grounding as a rather strict private-school headmaster served him well during his period as Archbishop. Fisher was also a committed Freemason.

———◆———

1985: 'An urgent warning to parents to stop children skating on lakes and gravel pits has come from Canterbury police. The warning came after police were called to the Brett's quarry at Milton, near Canterbury (Thannington Without), by a nearby resident who saw children playing on the ice there.' (*Kentish Gazette*)

January 18th

1937: During the gale on this Monday evening, one of the poplars in the avenue near the Irrigation Farm (sewage works) in Sturry Road crashed across the road, narrowly missing a car. Luckily, the driver managed to swerve onto the pavement in the nick of time. Traffic was held up for a considerable time while the debris was cleared away. (*Kentish Gazette*)

———◆———

1958: The Council conceded there was only a faint hope left of saving the 600-year-old Fleur-de-Lis Inn, in the High Street. A firm of London developers wanted to build a new store on the site. However, apart from the Canterbury Archaeological Society, who lobbied for its preservation, there was no genuine commitment to its retention. Demolition took place a few months later.

———◆———

1963: On this Friday, the Archbishop of Canterbury, Dr Michael Ramsey, took six hours to reach Canterbury from London in his chauffeur-driven Daimler. He was due to attend the induction ceremony for the new Vicar of Sturry at 7 p.m., but became stuck in traffic on the A20 due to severe weather conditions. He finally reached Sturry well after 10 p.m., and performed his duties despite being very cold and tired. (Author's archive)

January 19th

1786: Clergyman and Canterbury historian, John Duncombe, died on this day. He wrote *An Elegy to Canterbury Cathedral* and edited the second edition of Gostling's *Walk*, as well as being a poet. He, nonetheless, cut a somewhat eccentric figure in the Cathedral Precincts, being described as 'neglected in his person, and awkward in his manner; a long face with only one eye, and a shambling figure; his pocket stuffed with pamphlets'. [He sounds fine to me!] (Ingram Hill: *The Six Preachers*)

———◆———

1872: In the Blean Workhouse, a legitimate female child (no name recorded) was born to John and Margaret Cock, from the St Gregory's parish, Northgate. (Author's archive)

———◆———

1938: Mr A. Graham Porter gave a lantern-slide lecture at the Slater Memorial Hall (adjacent to the Beaney) on this Wednesday, on the subject of communication between bees. He told how the hum of bees was carried on the air in much the same way as wireless waves, and bees could keep in contact with each other from as far as four miles apart. [Older Canterbury citizens will be able to tell you how the 'hum' of the tannery was also carried on the air at this time.] (*Kentish Gazette*)

January 20th

1810: On this Saturday, Samuel Streeting was committed to St Augustine's Gaol, charged upon the oaths of William Silk, Robert Blanch and others, with having stolen from out of the barn of the Revd Allen Fielding, Hackington, a sack marked 'A.F.' and about two bushels of beans, the property of the said Allen Fielding. Also committed was John Warner, a notorious character, for stealing from the same barn. [The 'County' gaol in Longport, completed in 1808, replaced the one situated in St Dunstan's Street.] (*Kentish Gazette, see* February 29th)

———◆———

1846: On this Tuesday, Revd William John Chesshyre became a 'Six Preacher' of Canterbury Cathedral. He was already Vicar of St Martin's and St Paul's Churches, and had overseen the restoration and enlargement of the latter. He also created the parish of St Gregory's in the early 1850s, in response to the vast amount of military housing recently built in the area. He became a Canon Residentiary in 1858, but died less than a year later at the relatively young age of fifty-four. (Derek Ingram Hill: *The Six Preachers*)

———◆———

1955: On this Thursday, demolition work began on the Riding Gate Inn to enable the construction of a roundabout. (Crampton: *Canterbury Then and Now*)

January 21st

1409: By his will, dated this day, Henry IV desired to be buried in Canterbury Cathedral. He left all arrangements to his cousin, Thomas Arundel, who happened to be the Archbishop. Henry did not die until 1413, but poor health prompted the writing of an early will. He was buried on the north side of the Trinity Chapel (*see* August 21st) opposite the Black Prince, whose son, Richard II, Henry IV had deposed some years before. Henry's widow, Queen Joan, joined him there in 1437. (Cathedral Chronicle, 1976)

———•◆•———

1733: 'For some months past, most of the inhabitants in Canterbury and the suburbs have been dangerously ill with a flying distemper, which at once attacks them with shakiness and chillness in their heads and all over their limbs, whereby great numbers of inhabitants have been carried off. Like distemper rages all over the country.' (*Kentish Post or Canterbury Newsletter*)

———•◆•———

1958: A Hastings solicitor, arriving late at Canterbury Court after having driven cross-country through the snow, apologised to the judge and added, 'Now I know what Dr Fuchs must have felt like when he met Hillary at the South Pole'. The judge replied, 'I had the same thought myself!' (Author's archive)

January 22nd

1690: Sir Edward Masters was buried on this day at St Paul's Church. His memorial tablet reads: 'In memory of Sir Edward Masters… and his wife Dorcas… by whom he had 20 children, of whose conjugal love, paternal care, constancy at the Church and sacraments, peaceableness and sobriety, and exemplary charity, all that knew him are so many witnesses.' (St Paul's Church Guide)

⸺◆⸺

1885: At the Sidney Cooper School of Art, St Peter's Street, Canterbury, distribution of prizes won at a recent art examination took place on this Thursday. The Dean occupied the chair, whilst an address was delivered by Sir Frederick Leighton, President of the Royal Academy and himself a great painter. (*Kentish Gazette*)

⸺◆⸺

1944: An air raid took place at dawn on this Saturday morning. Incendiary bombs were scattered across the St Dunstan's Suburb. Properties in London Road and St Dunstan's Street were gutted, whilst St Dunstan's Church received minor damage. However, by far the biggest fire took place at the premises of Barrett's in St Peter's Street. A single incendiary bomb destroyed the entire complex because of difficulties the fire brigade had in gaining access, and also problems in lifting the fire hydrant manholes. (Crampton: *The Blitz of Canterbury*)

January 23rd

1785: On this day, one of Canterbury's first Sunday schools began in St Alphege Church under the auspices of the Revd George Herne. He described one of his parishes, Northgate, as 'poverty itself' and on that first Sunday, he found the 120 children who turned up to be 'very ragged and disorderly'. He further claimed that many hadn't been inside a church since the day they were baptised. (*Bygone Kent*, Vol. 2, No. 9)

———— • ◆ • ————

1888: During an archaeological dig in the cathedral's East Crypt on this Monday, workmen uncovered a hitherto unknown collection of bones. They formed the skeleton of an adult male, with a skull that showed signs of significant trauma. In addition, the stone coffin in which they were found was close to the spot where Becket's body had lain from 1170 to 1220. The discovery sparked an intense debate about the fate of Becket's remains (*see* September 7th). (Butler: *The Quest for Becket's Bones*)

———— • ◆ • ————

1963: The results of a survey of the cast-iron Riding Gate footbridge showed that it was unsound and should be demolished. A section of the adjacent City Wall had collapsed only few months before. The bridge was finally dismantled in 1970 (*see* January 2nd). (Author's archive)

January 24th

1684: A letter dated this day was sent by Archbishop Sancroft to the Master of St John's Hospital, authorising him to demolish the dormitory. At this time, the building was almost exactly 600 years old. Pulled down at about the same time was much of the original chapel, the present chapel being a surviving fragment of it. Some walls of the dormitory survived, however, and for the following 300 years, became largely neglected and ivy-covered, with lean-to sheds employed against it. A full survey of the remains took place in 1984. (CAT Annual Report, 1983/84)

───────◆◆───────

1931: On this day, the Dean of Canterbury Cathedral, Dick Sheppard, announced his decision to resign after less than two years in the role. He had become a popular national figure as Vicar of St Martin-in-the-Fields, London, after his services were regularly broadcast on the BBC throughout the 1920s. However, in accepting the position of Dean, he had probably taken on too much. Dick suffered from bouts of crippling depression, punctuated by short periods of bright optimism and gaiety – all symptoms of bipolar disorder. (Sparks *et al*: *Canterbury Cathedral*)

───────◆◆───────

1944: The first 'Bevan Boys' arrived for work at Chislet Colliery on this day. (Llewellyn: *Hersden*)

January 25th

1795: At eight o'clock this Sunday morning, the cold was so intense in Canterbury that the mercury in Fahrenheit's thermometer, exposed in the open air, sunk 2 degrees below 0, or 34 below the freezing point. It finally exploded with the cold (*see* January 4th). (*Kentish Register*, courtesy of Tina Machado)

1836: On this Monday, a young woman was cleaning windows on the second floor of her master's house in Castle Street when she lost her hold and fell into the street. She was instantly taken up, but in a few moments expired, having dreadfully fractured her head. (*Kentish Gazette*)

1952: On this Friday, the new Woolworth's store in Canterbury was open. It was the first new shop to appear in St George's Street following the devastation of the Blitz ten years earlier. Before the official opening time, a massive queue formed outside which also snaked round across the adjacent building site. My grandmother, Violet Crampton, was in the queue and recalled that when the doors finally opened, she was swept around the store by sheer weight of numbers, barely able to place her feet on the ground, let alone stop to buy anything! (Crampton: *Canterbury 1945 to 1975*)

January 26th

1567: The Dean of Canterbury, Nicholas Wotton, died on this day at the age of sixty-nine. Following the Reformation, he became the first Dean of the new 'Dean and Chapter' at Canterbury (*see* April 8th) despite being a Catholic. He survived this difficult period by being Protestant in a professional capacity while continuing his Catholic faith in private. He also spent much time abroad. Wotton's elaborate tomb, showing him kneeling at prayer, can be found in the Trinity Chapel of Canterbury Cathedral. (Ryan: *The Abbey and Palace of St Augustine's*)

1875: At Canterbury Police Court, John Constable was charged with gambling by playing at 'pitch and toss' on a Sunday afternoon. (*Living in Victorian Canterbury*)

1935: The Drill Hall [now the Westgate Hall] was the scene on this Saturday afternoon of a happy gathering of 1,053 little ones, on the occasion of the annual Northgate Poor Kiddies Treat. Actually, there were 700 children from the Northgate area and 353 from other parts of the city. [The Northgate area was crowded with hundreds of terraced houses originally built in the early nineteenth century for soldiers – and their families – stationed at the nearby infantry barracks.] (*Kentish Gazette*)

January 27th

1501: The Archbishop elect of Canterbury, Thomas Langton, died on this day, just five days after being chosen. Perhaps the excitement of securing the role was too much for him? (Wikipedia)

———•◆•———

1939: Despite the 'peace in our time' of the Munich Agreement (*see* September 29th), the country continued to prepare for war with Germany. On this day, some 110 Canterbury school teachers canvassed the city to establish households that would be able to take in evacuated children. This exercise had originally been carried out at the time of the Munich Crisis, but the data quickly became out-of-date as some 169 households had since fled Canterbury. (*Bygone Kent*, Vol. 7, No. 9)

———•◆•———

1966: On this day, Canterbury architect Anthony Swaine won an award for his restoration of the late seventeenth-century house at No. 20 King Street. At one time, it had been a pub called the Farriers Arms. (Author's archive)

———•◆•———

2009: Holocaust Memorial Day was marked by an event held at the Westgate Hall. This year's theme was 'Stand Up to Hatred'. The free event was opened by the Lord Mayor and included poster displays, music, films, presentations, poetry, a quiet area for reflection and a talk from a Holocaust survivor. (www.hmd.org.uk)

January 28th

1874: On this Wednesday, Mary Caldwell was born at No. 52 Palace Street, Canterbury. As Mary Tourtel, she would go on to create the much-loved Rupert Bear character. (Stewart: *The Rupert Bear Dossier, see* November 8th)

———— •◆• ————

1889: A well-known local character, 'Bob Ridley' or 'Bob the Bellman', whose patronymic (family name) was Hatton, died at his father's residence in Cossington Road, Canterbury, on this Monday. Frequenters of the Canterbury Cricket Ground will remember the deceased as the bellman during Cricket Week. A few seasons back, a subscription was raised to buy Bob a new bell, which he had used regularly ever since. (*The Kentish Note Book*)

———— •◆• ————

1985: 'Canterbury is becoming cluttered with signs, City councillors heard on this Monday. Therefore, the Public Works Committee decided not to spend £525 on "temporary" signs to the new Marlowe Shopping Arcade. But the committee did approve spending £1,200 on nine pedestrian and eight traffic signs to the Marlowe Theatre. Councillor Alan Collyer said the Council was getting "a little Marlowe mad". "Everything from pubs to hairdressers are being labelled Marlowe," he said, "We're getting to the point where we start off to the theatre and end up getting a haircut!"' (*Kentish Gazette*)

January 29th

1750: On this day, John Wesley came to Canterbury for the first (recorded) time. As yet, there was no 'Methodist Society' or church in the city, so meetings were held in a variety of odd locations, including a farmhouse on the outskirts and a house in the Cathedral Precincts. For this visit, Wesley preached in an 'Antinomian' meeting house in an alley (locally known as 'Godly Alley'), off Lamb Lane. Today, Lamb Lane is the part of Stour Street from Beer Cart Lane to the High Street. The alley was probably Spratts Square, near Greyfriars, cleared as slums in 1938.

———•◆•———

1883: The Canterbury Ragged Sunday School had their usual year's treat with a magic lantern entertainment. Toys, fruit and money were provided, enabling each child to have a substantial tea and an article of clothing. [The Ragged School movement was established in the 1840s by patrons such as Lord Shaftesbury, Thomas Barnardo and the Archbishop of Canterbury, to provide free education to the poorest in society.] (*Kentish Gazette*)

———•◆•———

1971: On this Friday evening, Canterbury Scene group, Soft Machine, came home and played at Darwin College in the University of Kent, Canterbury. (Bennett: *Out Bloody Rageous*)

January 30th

1807: On this day, former Canterbury Mayor and well-known tycoon James Simmons was buried in a vault in St Mildred's churchyard. He had died in London on January 22nd. His white stone monument can still be seen, but has weathered to the extent that it is no longer legible. (Panton: *Canterbury's Great Tycoon*)

1926: On this Saturday evening, the Theatre Royal in Guildhall Street closed its doors for the last time. Patron Thomas Sidney Cooper had heavily subsidised the theatre to ensure its survival. After his death, son Nevill took over the burden, spending an estimated £10,000, but he finally tired of this expenditure. The building was later demolished for a new Lefevre's store. (Stewart: *Thomas Sidney Cooper*)

1933: 'The initial work on the site of Canterbury's new cinema in The Friars is making excellent progress. The cinema will be fire proof.' [This claim stood up well during the night of 1 June 1942, when a number of incendiary bombs clattered onto the cinema's roof with no harmful effect. However, a few penetrated the roof and burst into flames in the auditorium below. Luckily, a seventy-year-old firewatcher, Mr B. Wells, managed to extinguish them.] (*Kentish Gazette*)

January 31st

1885: On this Saturday, a wedding took place at a nearby village (probably Chartham). As the loving couple crossed the South Eastern line, they had to pass close to a locomotive at the level crossing (next to the station). The engine driver, in a vein of humour, suddenly opened the pet cocks (emitting a loud hiss of steam), which startled the bride so much that the next day a child was born to her, but lived no longer than twenty-four hours. The funeral took place on the Monday. Thus, a marriage, a birth and a death occurred within a short space of three days. (*Kentish Gazette*)

1913: 'Dear Sir – We are glad to be able to announce that the Kent and Canterbury Hospital is now free from scarlet fever, and that we are in a position to receive in-patients as usual. Will you please make it known that we are in want of the following: Old linen and calico, warm left-off dressing gowns, night gowns for children, and a set of baby's clothes, and we should be very obliged if any of your readers would kindly help us with a fresh supply. – Yours truly, Arthur J. Lancaster, Secretary' (*Kentish Observer*)

February 1st

1690: On this day, Archbishop of Canterbury William Sancroft was suspended and deprived of the See for not recognising William of Orange as King. It was not the first time this Archbishop had directly challenged the monarch. In 1687, he petitioned against James II's Declaration of Indulgence, which gave religious freedom in England. This greatly assisted in bringing the Catholic James II down. Ironically, although William Sancroft was happy to accept his Protestant successor William as regent, he still felt bound by his oath of loyalty to James and was therefore removed.

———◆———

1985: Complaints that an advertisement for the Canterbury-produced Sindy doll was sexist and offensive have been dismissed by the advertising industry's watchdog. Forty complaints were received about a poster headlined 'Miss August, Playmate of the Month', but the watchdog body has accepted an explanation from Pedigree Toys of Market Way. The company's group product manager, John Mitchell, said, 'It's all a storm in a teacup'. The row blew up after posters showed Sindy dressed in spotted blouse and jeans, lying on the beach beside a radio. [Canterbury's Pedigree factory closed in the 1980s and was demolished for a housing scheme.] (*Kentish Gazette*)

February 2nd

1642: Anti-Royalist, Puritan-extremist iconoclasts gained entry to the cathedral at night and vandalised the recently installed baptismal font. This would not be the first time that such damage was caused during the Civil War period (*see* August 26th; for the fate of the font, *see* September 11th). (Sparks *et al*: *Canterbury Cathedral*)

———•—•———

1894: Mr Henniker Heaton, in his address at the recent 'smoking concert' at Canterbury, had stated that in Constantinople, a man is entitled to twenty wives. Sheikh Muhammad Yehya of Ghazipur, India, has now responded. He said that though the Moslem religion does allow plurality of wives, it limits the number to four. Moreover, the Prophet hedged this permission round with conditions so numerous and so stiff that 'it is next to impossible for human effort to carry them out honestly'. (*Kentish Observer*, courtesy of Tina Machado)

———•—•———

1955: PC Slater was called to Guildhall Street, where he found a car parked over the pad that actuates the traffic lights. A queue 100yds long had already built up. Half an hour later, an American woman, Mrs Mitzi Mabus, returned quite unaware of what she had done. In her defence, she said it was her first visit to Canterbury. (Author's archive)

February 3rd

AD 619: On this day, the Archbishop of Canterbury, 'Laurence of Canterbury', died after about fifteen years in the role [some records show the date as the 2nd]. Laurence arrived in Kent at the same time as his predecessor, Augustine, in AD 597. It was also Augustine who consecrated him, before he died, to ensure continuity of their Christian mission. Laurence was made a saint after his death. However, he is not to be confused with St Lawrence (of Rome), after whom the Medieval Hospital and Cricket Ground along Old Dover Road were named.

1910: The annual Brewster Sessions for the City of Canterbury were held at the Guildhall on this Thursday when there were five licences reported by the police on the ground of redundancy, being: the Gun Inn – St Dunstan's; the Wheatsheaf – Pound Lane; the Lord Nelson – Knott's Lane; Tally Ho – Clyde Street; and the White Swan – Northgate. Of these, only one was renewed: the Gun in St Dunstan's, the remainder being referred to the Compensation Authority. [The Gun Inn only reopened for two years and today the building is an Indian restaurant. The Tally Ho also reopened and is still trading today!] (*Kentish Gazette*)

February 4th

1938: 'We are asked by Canterbury City Police to make an appeal for old boots. Unfortunate men tramping the country in search of work frequently call at the police station and, in many cases, are pitifully shod. It would be doing a real kindness if cast-off boots were sent to the station (in Pound Lane) so that such men can be helped on their way.' (*Kentish Gazette*)

———◆———

1955: On this Friday, Canterbury allotment holders appealed to the Council to help combat the problems caused by eelworm in the city. Eelworms are especially known for damaging potatoes, hence the disruption caused on allotments.

———◆———

1959: The Council will support appeals for the abolition of tax on bus fuel oil, so long as East Kent pass on the benefit of any savings to passengers. (City Council records)

———◆———

1966: The Ministry of Defence has offered to sell to the Council thirty-four acres of land at the Old Infantry Barracks (off Sturry Road). The sale would be with vacant possession, except for four married officers' quarters, which the Ministry wants to keep for four years. [This area would later be redeveloped as the Brymore Housing Estate.] (City Council records)

February 5th

1426: On this Sunday, an escaped prisoner sought sanctuary by hiding behind the railings of Archbishop Chichele's tomb. The monks were able to appeal to the same Archbishop for the man's removal, as Chichele had erected the tomb well before his own death, which did not occur until 1443 (*see* 28th February). The good brothers were evidently deeply upset by the disruption this incident caused. (Geddes: *Tomb Railings in Canterbury Cathedral*)

1833: The Canterbury & Whitstable Railway has rendered so much benefit and such great advantages to the city and its neighbourhood that it ought to receive the fullest encouragement of every tradesmen, and one sentiment alone should actuate all its inhabitants – to afford it that support that a liberated and enlightened public would not fail to give for advantages already received and likely to occur from it. (*Kentish Gazette*)

1958: The City Council accepted a tender for the demolition of twenty-one old houses that stood along the north side of New Ruttington Lane. This marked the resumption of slum clearance in the city, after the interruption caused by the Second World War. The previous demolition programme had been halted in 1938. They came down the following year. (Crampton: *Canterbury Suburbs and Surroundings*)

February 6th

1759: On this Tuesday, the Mayor of Canterbury Leo Plomer issued the following notice: 'If any one shall give information to [me] against any person who, without leave in writing, shall take, kill, or destroy any fish within the liberties of the city, then that informant shall be paid by the Chamberlain, upon conviction of every person offending in the day-time: ten shillings; and in the night-time: twenty shillings.' (*Kentish Post*)

———•◆•———

1846: On this Friday, the South Eastern Railway's new line from Ashford to Canterbury (West) first came into public use. The line hadn't yet been extended through to Minster Thanet, nor had Station Road West been properly laid out; however, a connection to the Canterbury & Whitstable Line could finally take place (*see* December 1st).

———•◆•———

1953: On this Friday, the Canterbury & Whitstable Railway temporarily reopened in the wake of the floods that had devastated the North Kent coast. The line through Whitstable and Herne Bay had been put out of action due to the encroaching sea, and so the closed railway from Canterbury became a lifeline to an area cut off in both directions. (Hart: *Canterbury & Whitstable Railway*, *see* December 1st and February 28th)

February 7th

1786: On this day, the *Kentish Gazette* reported: 'One night last week, some villains entered the house of Mr John Fleet, in Turn-Again-Lane, Palace Street, from whence they stole about three guineas in gold, and some silver, which was deposited in a small box, in a chest of drawers; also four silver teaspoons and a silver tablespoon.'

———◆———

1902: Thomas Sidney Cooper, probably Canterbury's greatest ever painter, died on this day, aged ninety-eight years. He had suffered from attacks of bronchitis for years, but this time it proved fatal. His funeral service was conducted in the cathedral, and he was laid to rest in the graveyard at St Martin's Church. (Stewart: *Thomas Sidney Cooper*)

———◆———

1962: The Council declared their intention to tackle the problem of the numerous abandoned cars to be found across the city. (City Council records)

———◆———

1969: On this day, the former Canterbury & Whitstable Railway *Invicta* locomotive was moved from its position outside the Riding Gate, to a new site in the Dane John. A massive low-loader was used, even though the journey was only a matter of a few yards. The move was necessary because of the construction of the ring road. (Butler: *Canterbury in Old Photographs*)

February 8th

1338: 'Saved from Gaol': A pardon was granted to John Atte and John de Bromesdon, Brothers of the Greyfriars in Canterbury, for having rescued Thomas Sauvage and John Wydour. In what was probably an act of mercy, the monks had rescued the felons – both of whom had been sentenced to death – while on their way to execution. Later the same month, John Nichol, Rector of All Saints' Church, Canterbury, was also pardoned for his part in the same rescue. (Cotton: *The Greyfriars of Canterbury*)

1859: 'Committed to Gaol': The following were reported to be 'in the Gaol of Canterbury': John Henry Whyman, late of St Margaret's Street, Canterbury, greengrocer and employed in Her Majesty's Dock Yard Chatham; also Robert Thomas Couling, late of the Bell Tavern, High Street, Canterbury, out-of-business. (*London Gazette*, courtesy of Tina Machado)

1935: Miss Macfarlane's annual bridge and whist party, in aid of the funds of the RSPCA, took place in Canterbury on this Friday and, as in previous years, proved an unqualified success. There were thirty-eight tables and, as usual, a number of valuable prizes; while the lavish tea, generously provided by many friends of the cause, was daintily served and greatly appreciated. (*Kentish Gazette*)

February 9th

1555: Six Preacher of Canterbury Cathedral, Rowland Taylor, was burnt at the stake for his reforming Protestant beliefs. He had been Domestic Chaplain to Archbishop Cranmer, who met a similar fiery fate. (Derek Ingram Hill)

---◆---

1881: In the Blean Workhouse, an illegitimate female child was born to Caroline Wanstall of the parish of Blean. No name was recorded. (Author's archive)

---◆---

1959: While a field on Mr John Holdstock's Supperton Farm, Wickhambreaux, near Canterbury, was being ploughed on this Monday, the plough caught in the fin of a container of incendiary bombs. The police were informed and, during the following day, a bomb-disposal squad disinterred the container in which there were about 170 incendiaries. Most of them had detonated on impact, but a few were still live. [A Me. 109 had crashed at Wickhambreaux on 7 September 1940.] (*Kentish Gazette*)

---◆---

1962: It was announced that smallpox vaccinations would be held at the Central Clinic (Poor Priests), Stour Street, until the end of February. This would give an opportunity for members of the public to boost their vaccination if they intended to go abroad this summer. [Smallpox was eradicated worldwide in December 1979.] (Author's archive)

February 10th

AD 704: This is the feast day for French female St Austrabertha. In medieval times, it is said that her skull was one of the many holy relics kept at Canterbury Cathedral. (Author's archive)

———•◆•———

1880: Sold on this day for £150 were three early nineteenth-century cottages at Nos 1-3 Knott's Lane, Canterbury. They were described as being of brick, plaster and tile, with a yard at the rear. [The houses were demolished in 1938.] (*Bygone Kent*, Vol. 1, No. 12)

———•◆•———

1888: The mystery skeleton discovered in the Eastern crypt (*see* January 23rd) was re-interred in the same location. In the interim, the bones had been photographed and carefully examined. By now, there was much press interest in the find, particularly given the extensive and compelling, yet circumstantial, evidence that these were the remains of Thomas Becket. (Butler: *The Quest for Becket's Bones*)

———•◆•———

1936: A fierce blaze at Blean on this Monday morning destroyed a fine old thatched barn at Butler's Court Farm, owned by Mr Albert Price of Victoria Dairy. A spark from the chimney of the adjoining cottage is believed to have fallen on the thatch. (*Kentish Gazette*)

February 11th

1835: On this Wednesday, a numerous meeting of 'The Commission of Pavement' was held in the Guildhall, when Alderman Brown's proposition for 'macadamising' the High Street was lost by a majority of thirty-two against fourteen. A proposal to appoint a committee to consider the subject was 'negatived' by a majority of twenty-nine against nineteen. [The 'macadam' road surface was developed in the 1820s, initially with the aggregate being laid without a binding agent.] (*Kentish Gazette*)

1870: Acting upon the recommendations of Mr James Reid, one of the honorary surgeons at the Kent and Canterbury Hospital, Eliza Webb, was admitted on this day, for an operation 'which could not be satisfactorily undertaken at her own home', but with 'her husband being in a small way of business at Petham, a donation was promised from him to reimburse expenses'. (*Archaeologia Cantiana*, 1988)

1931: On this Wednesday night, the old windmill at Waltham, near Canterbury, was blown over in a gale. Known as 'Cloke's Mill', it dated from the 1850s, but hadn't worked for about thirty years when it was destroyed. In 1979, the surviving brick base of this smock mill was being used as a garage.

February 12th

1810: An unfortunate event occurred this Monday morning to a young man of the name of John Neighbour, who acted in the capacity of 'boots' at the Fountain Inn (St Margaret's Street) in this city. Having gone into one of the rooms, it is supposed he took a loaded pistol belonging to a gentleman who was about to depart on his journey when, for some accidental cause, it went off and almost instantly killed him. (*Kentish Gazette*)

1844: The Matron of the Kent and Canterbury Hospital, Mrs Ann Banfield, found the following 'illegal' foodstuffs in the lockers of patients: Maria Wright – some plum cake; Ann Baldock – two crumpets; Elizabeth Morris – two uncooked sausages; Sarah Sayers – three small cakes; and Mary Stone – some cheese. (Marcus Hall *et al*: *Kent and Canterbury Hospital*)

1856: A complaint about the schoolmaster at the Canterbury Union Workhouse (Nunnery Fields): 'The master [of the Guardians] reported that complaints had been made to him by several boys that Corporal Punishment had been inflicted upon them by Mr Varley… in that he had hit them with a ruler, and made them stand in the corner with nothing on but their shirts, outside his bedroom door!' (*Living in Victorian Canterbury*)

February 13th

1884: During this Wednesday night, a fire broke out in a stable lodge and other outbuildings belonging to Mr S. Collyer at Blean. One Mr Glover immediately set off on horseback to give the alarm at Canterbury, and the Kent Brigade with their engines were on the scene with praiseworthy dispatch, a team of four greys from Mr Burton's well-known stables being employed. [The 'Kent' Brigade was based at No. 29 High Street, and the 'City' Brigade at the Corn Exchange, Longmarket.] (*Kentish Gazette*)

———•◆•———

1952: This Wednesday saw the opening of the public enquiry into the City Council's Post-war Redevelopment Plan. Conceived by the City Architect, Hugh Wilson, it envisaged the construction of a ring road, two cross-city relief roads, and the comprehensive redevelopment of the Blitzed parts of Canterbury. However, the main bone of contention was the huge amount of compulsory purchase required. Although the plan was finally approved, lack of funds would soon prove a problem (*see* November 3rd). (City Council records)

———•◆•———

1992: Human error resulted in two tigers escaping from their enclosure at John Aspinall's Howlett's sanctuary, Bekesbourne, whilst open to the public. Luckily, they were rounded up within half an hour. (Author's archive)

February 14th

1650: Commissioners appointed by Parliament came to the city in order to survey and value the estate 'of the late Dean and Chapter of the Cathedral Church of Christ in Canterbury' (*see* April 30th). Houses in the North and South Precincts – many converted from former monastic buildings – were included in the valuation. Also surveyed were the cloisters, the water tower, the treasury, the audit house and the Dean's library and chapel. Whilst the houses were deemed suitable for re-sale or rent as dwellings, the other structures were solely valued for demolition material, such as the lead on the roof. If this wasn't bad enough, an even more horrifying proposal was looming (*see* July 9th). (*Archaeologia Cantiana*, 1937)

———•◆•———

1883: The Post Office reported that the number of Valentines delivered in Canterbury on this Wednesday was larger than in former years. (*Kentish Gazette*)

———•◆•———

1984: Whilst workmen were cutting a trench in the basement of the travel agent's at No. 9 High Street, they revealed the well-preserved remains of a Roman portico: an open gateway with columns supporting a triangular pediment. This was thought to be part of the forum complex, one of the principal public buildings of Roman Canterbury. (*Archaeologia Cantiana*, 1984)

February 15th

1896: 'Kindly grant me an inch of your valuable space in which to protest against the cathedral yard being turned into a practise ground for lady bicyclists. On Wednesday afternoon, a feeble old lady was nearly knocked down by one of several cyclists who were riding at a furious pace in front of the south-west porch, and the only apology offered was: why don't you keep out of my way'. (*Living in Victorian Canterbury*)

1935: A fourteen-year-old boy, formerly employed by a Canterbury newsagent, admitted stealing seven pints of milk from outside houses. The chief constable said there had been many such offences and police officers in plain clothes had been sent out to try and detect the offenders. The lad was given a good character and a clergyman, who found him a good situation, said that the trouble was that the boy did not have enough to eat early in the morning, and stole milk on that account. He was bound over for two years. (*Kentish Gazette*)

1985: The ancient wooden barn at Vale Farm, near Broad Oak, having been carefully dismantled, was transported to a museum at Maidstone in advance of the proposed reservoir.

February 16th

1534: On this day, the meagre possessions of the condemned 'Holy Maid of Kent', Elizabeth Barton, were valued and an inventory made. A few items were purchased by the Prioress of St Sepulchre's Nunnery in Canterbury; the rest was considered to be 'mere junk', consisting of clothing and a few trinkets. (Neame: *The Holy Maid of Kent*, *see* December 7th)

1565/66: On this day, Thomas Rolf granted the buildings of the former Greyfriars Friary to Sir William Lovelace, MP for Canterbury. It had been a private house for about twenty-five years, and was very much larger than the small, single building to be found today. William was the grandfather of the poet Richard Lovelace. (Cotton: *The Greyfriars of Canterbury*)

1985: Canterbury's annual Carnival Queen Selection Dance flopped this Saturday evening. Only four of the twelve girls entered turned up, one judge failed to arrive and the public was indifferent. 'We are all bitterly disappointed,' admitted Chairman Mr Selwyn Gauden, 'but, at the same time, we are pleased with the quality of the carnival court'. The new Miss Canterbury is nineteen-year-old Amanda Gillmore, an accounts clerk from Downs Road. All four girls entered were placed by the judges! (*Kentish Gazette*)

February 17th

1936: Those who attended the annual dinner of the Canterbury Male Voice Choir at the County Hotel this Monday evening experienced an enjoyable and successful time, which was completely harmonious in more ways than one. (*Kentish Gazette*)

◆

1967: On this day, a Canterbury Scene group, the Soft Machine, released their first single, 'Love Makes Sweet Music'. Written by Kevin Ayres and sung by Robert Wyatt, the record was produced by ex-Animals Chas Chandler. That night, the band played the UFO (Underground Freak Out) Club for the first time. The intense, largely improvised instrumental music they performed that night was in marked contrast to the R&B-influenced pop of their single, which sadly failed to reach the charts. (Bennett: *Out Bloody Rageous*)

◆

1992: The design for the proposed Whitefriars Development Scheme became subject to competition, with four rival proposals put out to public consultation. This eleven-acre part of Canterbury's south-east quadrant had been subject to extensive bombing during the Second World War, although by no means as much as is sometimes suggested. Until about 1999, the Whitefriars area was occupied by largely unloved Modernist buildings, with wide roads originally made to encourage traffic into the city – a trend no longer considered desirable. (Crampton: *Yesterday's Whitefriars*)

February 18th

1123: On this day, William de Corbeil was consecrated as Archbishop of Canterbury. During his incumbency, the See of Canterbury finally gained primacy over the Archbishopric of York. William was also responsible for building the tall castle keep at Rochester and for finishing off the enlarged eastern arm (choir) of Canterbury Cathedral.

◆

1516/17: By his will dated this day, William Geffrye gave: 'To the Friars Observants (Greyfriars) of Canterbury: 20s, that they celebrate and say obsequies for me and my parents'. He also gave 6s 8d (being one-third of a pound) to the Black Friars and Austin (White) Friars for the like. (Cotton: *The Greyfriars of Canterbury*)

◆

1967: A warning to spectators at Kingsmead Stadium to behave themselves was issued by Canterbury City Football Club chairman, Councillor Ben Bennett. This followed 'scenes' outside the dressing rooms when fighting broke out after the Canterbury vs Ramsgate game. 'I feel it is a disgrace to have men, yes men, fighting between themselves over a silly incident or two on the field of play'. Mr Bennett went on to urge that participants 'be sportsmen and gentlemen: less swearing and bad comments to the officials of the game, particularly from the stand!' (*Kentish Gazette*)

February 19th

1885: This Thursday evening, the sergeant-majors of the Canterbury Cavalry Depot entertained Sergeant-Major Eaton at a dinner at the Saracen's Head Hotel, on the occasion of his promotion to the rank of riding master. [The Saracen's Head was a late seventeenth-century hostelry that stood at the east end of Burgate. It was demolished in 1969 to make way for the second stage of the city's ring road.] (*Kentish Gazette*)

1942: Warship Week in the city had raised £360,011 – as of this day – towards the £460,000 needed to pay for HMS *Clare*, and thus allow the destroyer to be adopted by Canterbury and Bridge-Blean districts. HMS *Clare* was an ex-USA destroyer, built in 1920, which had been taken out of store and transferred to the Royal Navy under the Lease Lend Agreement of 1940. The money raised in the National Savings campaign at Canterbury paid for its refit. HMS *Clare* survived the Second World War and was scrapped in Ayrshire during 1947, barely five years later.

1945: Military control of the Elham Valley Railway was withdrawn on this day and normal services resumed. However, the line would only last for another two years.

February 20th

1880: The Revd Edgar Henry was ordained as the first minister of the proposed St Andrew's Presbyterian Church at Wincheap Green. The foundation stone for the new building was laid in the same year. [Sadly, the redundant building was demolished in 1973.] (Taylor: *The Free Churches of Canterbury*)

———◆———

1911: On this day, the Electric Picture Palace opened in St Margaret's Street. Previously the building had been both a music hall and auction mart. The new cinema lasted for less than two years.

———◆———

1937: On this day, the *Kentish Gazette* reported: 'It will soon be compulsory for every petrol pump to be equipped with a clock which, operated by the pump mechanism, shows petrol delivery in gallons and is proof from outside interference. To meet this need, Canterbury motor engineer Mr Marcel Hallet has fitted his own pumps – and some others – with clocks of his own construction. His clocks register accurately up to twelve gallons and are easily reset to zero by the touch of a lever'. [Before the Second World War, Hallet's operated from No. 26 St Dunstan's Street with at least two petrol pumps affixed to the front of the 'garage', which had no forecourt!]

February 21st

1173: On this day, former Archbishop of Canterbury Thomas Becket was declared a saint and martyr by Pope Alexander III. Miracles ascribed to Becket were being recorded within hours of his death, notably by those people of Canterbury who had eagerly soaked up the Archbishop's blood with rags, whilst his body still lay there on the flagstones. It was claimed that diseases and infirmity had been cured by those who had either touched or ingested the blood.

———◆———

1759: On this day, a new high-speed 'post coach' service was announced to run from Canterbury to London. Beginning the next week, it would set out daily at seven o'clock in the morning from the King's Head. The return journey was planned to reach Canterbury at six in the morning. Horses would be changed at Sittingbourne, Rochester and Dartford. [The King's Head, at No. 32 Northgate, closed in the 1950s.] (*Kentish Gazette*)

———◆———

1866: 'Vernon Grange', at No. 35 Old Dover Road, was purchased by Thomas Sidney Cooper on this day. He never lived in it himself. The property has the curiosity of a rooftop pond and a Judas tree in the front garden. (Stewart: *Thomas Sidney Cooper*)

February 22nd

1785: 'Last Tuesday night, passed through this city on his way to town – Mr Blanchard, the celebrated aeronaut – where he intends to make an experiment in his air balloon.' (*Kentish Gazette*)

1844: William Chandler, aged ten from Sturry, was admitted to the Kent and Canterbury Hospital on this day, suffering from an injury to his face following an accident with gunpowder. Treatment lasting twelve days resulted in a 'cure', and he was removed by his father on March 5th. (*Archaeologia Cantiana*, 1988)

1943: The Regal Cinema, in St George's Place, reopened on this Monday following repairs to extensive damage sustained in the daylight attack of 31 October 1942 and during a follow-on raid the next day. The cinema's flattened ballroom was never replaced (*see* October 8th) thus giving the building's frontage a somewhat asymmetrical appearance. (*Bygone Kent*, Vol. 6, No. 12)

2009: On this Sunday the Hairy Bikers, Si King and Dave Myers, stopped off in Canterbury as part of their quest to find the true tastes of Kent for their new television series. In this endeavour, they sampled sausage pastries at Tiny Tim's in St Margaret's Street, but finally settled on cooking Dover sole for the programme.

February 23rd

1537: Thomas Cromwell's planned Suppression of the Monasteries first impacted significantly on Canterbury. On this day, religious houses with an income of less than £300 were the first to be dissolved, and two such places in Canterbury qualified. They were St Sepulchre's Nunnery at Oaten Hill and St Gregory's Priory in Northgate. Both subsequently became private houses. (Tatton-Brown: *Canterbury: History and Guide*)

———◆———

1886: On this Tuesday, the *Kentish Gazette* reported that Esther Baker, a young woman, was summoned for breaking windows and glasses at the property of Edmund Tucker, landlord of the Falcon Inn, St Gregory's, during the previous week. The prosecutor said she had promised to pay for the damage and not to return to the premises. Consequently, the charge was withdrawn. [The Falcon, at No. 26 Artillery Street, must have been relatively short-lived. By 1910, the building had been sub-divided into flats. It was demolished in about 1968.]

———◆———

1962: Construction of Friday's new greengrocery wholesale warehouse, off St Andrew's Close, began on this day. Once opened, the warehouse boasted a large supply of venom antidotes, due to the likelihood of poisonous spiders being uninentionally brought in via crates of exotic fruit, such as bananas.

February 24th

1917: On this Saturday, the *Kentish Gazette* reported on a Council meeting: 'Councillor Dean referred to the blue lights, which were placed along the high pathway in the Old Dover Road, and proposed that they might be introduced to other parts of the city without danger. Councillor Stone said he couldn't understand where the danger came in. It was well known that whenever an air-raid warning was given, it was merely a question of touching a button and the lights were put out!' [Councillor Stone, or 'Stonie', was a Council member continuously from 1899 to 1957, the year in which he died when aged ninety-four.]

1967: Following considerable pressure from both the public and Council authorities, Minister of Transport Barbara Castle finally announced plans for the bypassing of villages such as Bridge, Boughton and Dunkirk on the A2. To achieve this, a dual carriageway from Brenley Corner at Faversham to Dover, via Canterbury, would be constructed.

1973: On this day, Soft Machine played the Rainbow Theatre in London, sharing the bill with fellow Canterbury Scene group Hatfield and the North, as well as eccentric song-smith Ivor Cutler and ex-Bonzo Roger Ruskin Spear. (Bennett: *Out Bloody Rageous*)

February 25th

1892: 'An Announcement': 'During winter evenings, Mr Gilson gives lessons to amateurs in legerdemain (i.e. conjuring tricks) and sleight-of-hand, including tricks with and without apparatus, card, coin and handkerchief conjuring, etc. Terms very moderate and proficiency guaranteed. Apply St George's Bazaar, Canterbury.' (*Kentish Gazette*)

1928: In view of the imminent demolition of the Catholic church at Hackington and all the associated buildings (i.e. the former Hales Place mansion and, later, St Mary's College), burials in the church from either era were all carefully exhumed. And then, on this day, they were re-interred in a radial pattern around the tiny chapel and former dovecote building, only 300 yards away. [This tiny consecrated building can still be found off Tenterden Drive today.]

1963: As a British Road Services employee was driving an articulated lorry, minus its trailer, in The Parade, Canterbury, a sack barrow fell from the back and struck the rear wheel of a cycle, which was being wheeled in the gutter. Having later been fined £5, the driver said he was sorry it happened but blamed the uneven road surface, which caused the back of his vehicle to jerk up so that the barrow fell off. (Author's archive)

February 26th

1564: On this day, future playwright Christopher Marlowe was baptised at St George's Church, Canterbury. The date of his actual birth is not recorded, but could have taken place on any date in the preceding three months. A plaque commemorating the event can be seen on the church's surviving clock tower today. The font, in which this christening took place, also survived the June 1942 bombing, albeit in pieces. In the aftermath, sections of the font's base were rescued by the cathedral archivist, Dr William Urry, and taken to the archive in a wheelbarrow.

1811: On this Tuesday, Thomas Marsh, a husbandry servant of William Hammond Esq. at Swarling, near Petham, was conveyed to Kent and Canterbury Hospital with a fractured leg, a consequence of having fallen under a wagon loaded with corn, the wheel of which passed over it. (*Kentish Gazette*)

1965: An advance party of the 1st Battalion, The Queen's Own Buffs, under commanding officer Lieutenant Colonel H.B.H. 'Blick' Waring, flew to British Guiana on this day. The party, which included the adjutant Capt. James Shephard of Canterbury, flew from London Airport and landed at Georgetown. [Guyana gained independence from the UK in May 1966.] (Author's archive)

February 27th

1783: This Thursday morning at about 9.45 a.m., a remarkable phenomenon of great brightness was observed by many people in the cloudless sky above Chilham, near Canterbury. It was in the form of a semi-circle about 45 degrees in diameter – being rather larger than a halo for which it was mistaken by many. It was beautifully variegated with colours of the rainbow and continued to be visible for near an hour. (*Kentish Gazette*)

———— •◆• ————

1981: The obituary of Canterbury historian and cathedral archivist Dr William Urry appeared in *The Times* on this day. Being a native of Northgate, an ex-pupil of Kent College and a wartime Buffs veteran, Urry's Canterbury credentials couldn't have been better. His posthumously published works on Thomas Becket and Christopher Marlowe are invaluable sources that have been quoted from in this book. Urry was plagued by serious health problems in the last twenty years of his life and, finally, he was denied the long happy retirement in Canterbury that he had been keenly anticipating.

———— •◆• ————

2003: Current Archbishop of Canterbury, Dr Rowan Williams, was enthroned on this Thursday. Of Welsh descent, he has demonstrated himself to be a man of both liberal and tolerant attitudes. (Wikipedia)

February 28th

1439: From this day, 'ordinations are to be held in the Infirmary Chapel [of Christ Church Priory] by the Bishop of Ross, acting for Archbishop Chichele, who is growing old and feeble'. (*Archaeologia Cantiana*, 1925)

———◆———

1935: On this Thursday, a monster whist drive was held at the Territorial Drill Hall under the patronage of the Mayor and Mayoress of Canterbury, Councillor and Mrs F. Wood. The event was in aid of the memorial in the new Kent and Canterbury Hospital. [At the time, construction of the new hospital in South Canterbury had just begun. Presumably, mention of the 'memorial' was a reference to the Foundation Stone – *see* July 12th.] (*Kentish Gazette*)

———◆———

1953: On this Friday, the very last train on the Canterbury & Whitstable Railway is thought to have run, following the line's temporary reopening in order to carry supplies to flood devastated Whitstable (*see* February 6th). The dismantling of this historical railway began that summer (*see* January 4th). (Hart: *Canterbury & Whitstable Railway*)

———◆———

2008: Health inspectors discovered poor standards of food hygiene and kitchen practice in many Canterbury city-centre pubs and restaurants. 'Do you want flies with that?' (Mostly the *Kentish Gazette*)

February 29th

1604: Archbishop of Canterbury John Whitgift died on this day. He was a noted anti-Puritan, and was said to be very close to Queen Elizabeth I.

1784: On this Saturday, the *Kentish Gazette* reported that one John Walkin was committed to St Dunstan's Gaol by Thomas Heron Esq. This was on the oath of Mr W. Amos and Walkin's own confession of having stolen one silk 'handkerchief' and a pair of Worsted stockings, both found in his possession. [At this time, the 'County' gaol was situated in St Dunstan's Street, not far from the Roper Gate, whereas the 'City' gaol was still housed at the Westgate.]

1956: Plans for a new bridge at Grove Ferry were unveiled by the Bridge-Blean Rural District Council. Hitherto, all vehicles wishing to cross the River Stour at this location had to use a manually operated flat-bottomed raft.

1992: A psychic fair was held at Canterbury College, New Dover Road, on this Saturday and the next day. Organised by 'Mind Matters', the fair featured crystal readings, palmistry, tarot readings, clairvoyance and astrology. The Saturday fair was followed by a concert of 'new-age' music! (Author's archive)

March 1st

1837: On this Wednesday, the *Kentish Gazette* reported, 'the framework of the new clock to be erected on St George's Church in this city has been raised during the last week under the superintendence of Mr John Hacker, one of the church wardens. The weight of the frame, made of iron, is about 23cwt and is supported by a figure well carved in stone'.

———— • • ————

1955: On this day, 'Norman' made his first appearance in Canterbury for many years. Not Norman Wisdom or even Norman Tebbit, but an ancient Romanesque or Norman column which had been uncovered in the undercroft of the old Guildhall, during the second phase of its demolition. The stone pillar had survived from a very early building phase, probably the twelfth century. Consequently, it survived the demolition and was incorporated into the cellar of the new shop on the site. (Crampton: *Canterbury's Lost Heritage*)

———— • • ————

1961: At a Council meeting on this day, it was agreed that perfume-dispensing machines would be installed in the ladies' conveniences in Castle Row and at the Westgate Gardens boating lake. It was also announced that some unwanted Egyptian and Peruvian pottery was to be sold off by the museum. (City Council records)

March 2nd

1955: 'Not Chuffed!': At a meeting on this day, the Council refused permission for the Co-op to use the City Arms on their new building (in St George's Street). However, they saw no problem in permitting the use of Canterbury's famous 'Three Choughs' on the float for the city's Carnival Queen. (City Council records)

---◆---

1962: 'Feasey's Trouble!': 'The car was only 18in over the white line marking the end of the restricted area,' wrote Cyril Child of Faversham when, on this Friday, he sent a guilty plea to Canterbury Magistrates Court. Inspector Feasey said the car was not only left for half an hour in the Rose Lane restricted area, but was also barely 1ft from a 'No Waiting' sign. (Author's archive)

---◆---

1974: The Yehudi Menuhin Music School played a concert at the Cathedral Chapter house on this day. The ensemble featured a young Nigel Kennedy on violin. (Author's archive)

---◆---

1985: Road users are being urged to make way for the new Canterbury fire engines, which use an American-style 'yelp' siren rather than the traditional two-tone horn. 'The sirens are supposed to give drivers a better idea of where the engine is coming from,' said Station Officer John McCall. (*Kentish Gazette*)

March 3rd

1539: Sir Christopher Hales wrote to Thomas Cromwell over a dispute surrounding the occupation of the recently dissolved Greyfriars. One Thomas Spylman wanted it for a house, whereas a Mr Batherst needed it for cloth-making premises. Subsequently, Spylman prevailed and Batherst leased part of the former Blackfriars instead. (Cotton: *The Greyfriars of Canterbury*)

1933: When a number of Aylesham residents were fined for using their wireless sets without licences, it was stated that Post Office authorities had visited 400 homes in the village. Mr A.K. Mowll, prosecuting, said they were very difficult cases to discover because as soon as news went out that a PO representative was in the district, people immediately disconnected their sets. (*Kentish Gazette*)

1950: On this Friday, the *London Evening News* reported: 'A tumbledown tower is holding up a £1,000,000 redevelopment scheme in Canterbury.' The City Council had always wanted rid of the remains of St George's Church (*see* June 16th) but now it was preventing the realignment of St George's Street. Finally, the tower alone was retained but the Council refused to contribute towards the cost of its restoration.

1965: A suggestion that Cow Lane be renamed was rejected. (City Council records)

March 4th

1611: The Archbishop of Canterbury, George Abbott, was enthroned on this day. The *Chambers Biographical Dictionary* describes him as 'a sincere but narrow-minded Calvanist'. (Wikipedia)

1833: On this Saturday, a meeting was held at the Guildhall for the purpose of petitioning Parliament to support 'Lord Apsley's Bill' to restrict the labour of children in factories to ten hours daily and prevent children under nine years of age being so employed. [The Factory Act of 1833 was actually championed by the MPs Anthony Ashley-Cooper – later the 7th Earl of Shaftesbury – and Michael Sadler.] (*Kentish Gazette*)

1874: Born at the Blean Workhouse on this day, to Ann Austin of the parish of St Dunstan's, a legitimate male child – no name recorded. (Author's archive)

1942: The Mayor, Alderman Charles Lefevre, announced that around 1,500 indoor Morrison shelters were now being distributed in Canterbury. He also stressed the need for continued vigilance. The city had not been bombed for well over a year, and Tugboat Annie (Canterbury's main air-raid siren) had remained silent. However, the Mayor warned that the city was still in the front line and not immune from further attack (*see* June 1st). (Crampton: *The Blitz of Canterbury*)

March 5th

1798: In the St Dunstan's parish in Canterbury, Mr T. Chaplain (a shopkeeper), his wife and three children each took what they thought was cream-of-tartar and brimstone as a physic. [This was once a popular cure for constipation.] Tragically, sugar-of-lead was used in the mixture instead of cream-of-tartar, and all but the youngest child subsequently died 'through excessive vomiting'. (*Maidstone Journal*)

———◆———

1835: On this Thursday evening, the third City Subscription Ball took place at Bellingham's Assembly Rooms. The attendance was more numerous than on the previous occasions, there being about 150 present. The dancing went off with great éclat. [Hasted makes mention of the Assembly Rooms being near St Mary Breadman Church – demolished in 1900 – so this could be a reference to the building later known as the 'Foresters' Hall', which is now part of Nasons.] (*Kentish Gazette*)

———◆———

1958: Details for the new season in the 'Canterbury and District Bat and Trap League' were announced on this day, with twenty-nine teams expected to take part. The 'White Hart' and the 'Old City' had dropped out, but new to the league were the 'Mill House', the 'Gate Inn' and the 'Two Brothers'. (Author's archive)

March 6th

1883: The weather has been comparatively mild in Canterbury for some time past, but on this Tuesday, a very disagreeable change took place. The atmosphere became very cold and the biting wind that blew throughout the day was accompanied by occasional falls of snow. (Author's archive)

1935: A cat picking its way daintily and unconcernedly across the road dislocated traffic in Guildhall Street this Wednesday afternoon. To avoid a nine-fold fatality, a brewery lorry, about to negotiate the corner, came to a shuddering stop, brakes squealed from the following cars – and then the traffic lights turned red! A bus then mounted the pavement into Guildhall Street and the chaos extended into the main street. The last sighting of the cat was a slowly waving tail disappearing with feline indifference to the trouble it had caused. (*Kentish Gazette*)

1957: Planning permission was refused for the erection of 160 houses in Sturry Road, twenty in Hollow Lane, fifty in New Dover Road, twenty-three in Old Dover Road and twenty in Spring Lane. In each case, the proposed building site fell within an area restricted to agricultural use only, as well being on land proposed for Canterbury's green belt. (City Council records)

March 7th

1956: A demolition order was made against the following old houses in Canterbury: No. 25 Castle Street, Nos 2, 7 and 8 Black Griffin Lane, No. 19 Abbott's Place, Nos 14 and 15 Victoria Row and Nos 16 to 19 London Road. (Author's archive)

———•◆•———

1962: Proposals submitted by William Lefevre Ltd to expand their existing premises were opposed by the City Council on this day: specifically, the demolition of Nos 4 and 5 Sun Street – considered to be of special architectural interest – and their replacement by a new building. An application to build a loading dock in Sun Yard was also refused. (City Council records)

———•◆•———

1976: Automatic lifting barriers were installed at the St Stephen's Road railway level crossing on this day. Barriers at the St Dunstan's crossing had been provided just under five years before (*see* July 19th). The gates at the Sturry level crossing were replaced in 1974. (Mitchell and Smith: *Branch Lines around Canterbury*)

———•◆•———

1985: On this day, British Home Stores opened in the newly built Marlowe Shopping Arcade. Joining them in the complex would be Principles, Miss Selfridge, Top Shop, Top Man, Solo, the Early Learning Centre, Mothercare, Tube shoe shop and Culpeper's, the herbalists. (*Kentish Gazette*)

March 8th

1696: On this day, Fynch Rooke Esq. was killed in a duel in the 'North Holmes', near St Martin's Church. He fought with Ensign Anthony Buckeridge, who also died in the field. (Hasted: *Kent*, Vol. XI)

◆

1834: There is now in the possession of Mr Davey in the High Street, Canterbury, a hard-crystallised substance, found in the interior of an oyster this week by one of his daughters. Several gentlemen have seen it and opinion seems to prevail of it being a real pearl. It was found in one of the common oysters from Whitstable, and is about the size of a thrush's egg. (*Kentish Gazette*)

◆

1872: On this day, Dr Alfred Lochee reported that Sarah Doughty was not a fit patient for the Kent and Canterbury Hospital, as she was 'out of her mind'. (*Archaeologia Cantiana*, 1988)

◆

1956: On this night, the Canterbury 'Civil Defence Corps' assisted in the demolition of an old cottage in North Lane as a training exercise. Other CD exercises were held in abandoned cottages in Gas Street. The voluntary Civil Defence Corps was formed in 1948, in response to the threats of nuclear war. They were finally stood down in 1968.

March 9th

1641: A report submitted to the House of Commons on this day first considered the abolition of Dean and Chapters, including at Canterbury. This is surprisingly early in the sitting of the Long Parliament, and the King, Charles I, was still in London. Nevertheless, this proposal, together with the imprisonment of Archbishop Laud in February that year (*see* January 10th) clearly shows that Parliament was already revealing their Puritan credentials.

———————— • ◆ • ————————

1777: William Gostling, writer, historian and Minor Canon of Canterbury Cathedral died on this day. He was eighty-one. His major work was *A Walk in and about the City of Canterbury*, which was produced in the last years of his life. The book was revised and reprinted in 1825. He was resident in the Cathedral Precincts (*see* December 31st) and therefore knew them intimately.

———————— • ◆ • ————————

1936: Canterbury butchers were in the novel position of being without lights – the illumination sort, of course – at their annual dinner at the County Hotel this Monday evening. Just as the lamb cutlets and peas were about to be served, the room was plunged into darkness by the failure of the electricity due to the main fuse blowing out. (*Kentish Gazette*)

March 10th

1379: King Richard II granted a licence, on this day, for the purchase of the ground to build the new Holy Cross Church. Hitherto, the church had been located in chambers above the old Westgate (which had existed since Roman times) but this was currently being completely rebuilt as a purely defensive building. The new church would be placed alongside the rebuilt gateway, just inside the line of the City Wall.

———◆———

1885: On this day, the *Kentish Gazette* reported that the Dean and Chapter of Canterbury have decided to issue another appeal to churchmen generally for further subscriptions towards the fund for providing the cathedral with a new organ. The amount received is about £1,600 and as soon as £2,000 is guaranteed, the order will be given for the building of the new instrument.

———◆———

1963: Cyril Kent admitted using a car without an excise licence at Harbledown. In his defence, Kent explained his dilemma: his car had been stolen and damaged in a crash, breaking his rear nearside quarter light. Until his insurance company approved the repairs, he couldn't get a test certificate, and without that, he couldn't get an excise licence.

March 11th

1914: The very first bus service between Canterbury and Faversham – today's No. 3 – began on this day. (Woodworth: *East Kent*)

———◆———

1933: The Kent County Plan makes reference to the proposed road (A28) from Milton Bridge to Westbere Butts: to bypass Canterbury and Sturry (to the north), and it appears that inquiries of the county surveyor have elicited the reply that he is still unaware when the project will be put in hand. The suggestion is made that when the question of the city boundary has been settled, more may be heard of the northern bypass. [This road was never built, despite the Westbere Butts being built to face the proposed new route – i.e. with its back to the existing A28!] (*Kentish Gazette*, *see* March 20th)

———◆———

1975: Whilst returning from a 'fling' in Canterbury, a student from Eliot College, at the university, trampled on the roof of a parked Volkswagen in Whitstable Road for a dare, causing £57 worth of damage. Upon waking sober the next day, Mr R. was so remorseful that he voluntarily called on the car owner and offered to pay for the damage. Consequently, he was let off with a conditional discharge. (Author's archive)

March 12th

1810: Various petty thefts of lead from copings and pipes have lately been committed in the vicinity of this city, and during this Monday night, a leaden urn was stolen from the front of Mrs Webb's house at St Thomas' Hill. From the weight and make of the article, it is impossible that any one person could have carried it away. (*Kentish Gazette*)

1888: During alteration in St Anselm's Chapel of Canterbury Cathedral, a twelfth-century wall painting of St Paul was discovered. (Friend's Report, 1932)

1965: It was reported that the East Kent Road Car Co. had won their long-standing battle with Canterbury City Council. They wanted to demolish five old cottages on the north side of North Lane to expand their premises. For their part, the usually 'demolition-obsessed' Council wanted to place a Preservation Order on them. Finally, the Minister of Housing decided the cottages were of insufficient historical interest for such an order to be granted. This was not the end though, for the City Council got their revenge the next year by refusing the company's formal application for demolition. In turn, East Kent threatened to reduce bus services if they couldn't expand their depot.

March 13th

1839: At a meeting of the Commissioners of Pavement on this Wednesday at the Guildhall, the important and long-required alteration in the houses adjoining St George's Church was unanimously determined upon. About forty commissioners were present, with the Mayor in the chair. [The heyday of the commissioners was during the last quarter of the eighteenth century, *see* April 23rd.] (*Kentish Gazette*)

———•◆•———

1885: On this day, a memorial service for General Gordon took place at Canterbury Cathedral. He had been murdered in Khartoum on January 26th. On the same day, a silver lime tree was planted to his memory in the south-west corner of Canterbury Cemetery. [The tree, with its memorial plaque, was still there in 1985 when this article was written.] (*Bygone Kent*, Vol. 6, No. 10)

———•◆•———

1924: During an archaeological dig at St Augustine's Abbey on this day, an ancient burial cross, made of lead, was found in the south aisle of the Norman church (completed *c.* 1091). The inscription reads: 'On the eleventh of March 1063, departed out of this life Wulfmaeg, sister of Wulfric the Abbot.' Therefore, the lead cross related to a burial made in the earlier Anglo-Saxon abbey. (*Archaeologia Cantiana*, 1925)

March 14th

1713: The records of the Baptist Church in Canterbury for this day proved that being a Nonconformist was a serious (and rather miserable) business: 'the question is raised whether any Gospel church can or ought to bear with any of their members who educate their children in the art of dancing and playing on all sorts of music, on any pretence whatever'. (Taylor: *The Free Churches of Canterbury*)

———•◆•———

1833: On this Tuesday, upwards of 250 children belonging to the charity school, and other children, were regaled at the Royal Oak great room with roast beef and plum pudding. Upon this occasion, they sang two psalms and the national anthem and were severally presented by Mr Halcomb with an orange. [The Royal Oak, in Longport Street, became a victim of the Blitz on 1 June 1942. Today, the site is part of the car park.] (*Kentish Gazette*)

———•◆•———

1986: On this day, the terms of the 'Treaty of Canterbury' became binding in both French and English law. Signed by Margaret Thatcher and Francois Mitterrand at Canterbury Cathedral on February 12th, this treaty agreed to the terms governing the design, financing, construction and operation of the proposed Channel Tunnel.

March 15th

1684: On this day, two drawings were made illustrating a proposed external route from the south Cathedral Precincts to the cloisters. These were largely for Archbishop Sancroft, because an entry would need to be made through his palace wall to make this possible. Hitherto, the only way from Christ Church Gate to Green Court Gate, via the cathedral's west end, was through the nave. (Sparks: *Canterbury Cathedral Precincts*)

———•◆•———

1783: 'Run away this Saturday, George Godwin (aged twenty), apprentice to Joseph Salmon, carpenter, at Canterbury. He wears his own dark hair, is of a pale complexion and about 5ft 6in high. Whoever harbours or employs the above apprentice, after this notice, will be prosecuted as the law directs. If Godwin returns, he will be forgiven.' (*Kentish Gazette*)

———•◆•———

1948: On this Monday, Mary Tourtel, creator of Rupert Bear, died in Canterbury aged seventy-four (*see* June 27th). A few days earlier, she had collapsed in the street from a brain tumour when going to meet a friend for lunch. She passed into a coma and never regained consciousness, dying in Kent and Canterbury Hospital. Mary is buried, together with her husband Herbert, in St Martin's churchyard. (Stewart: *The Rupert Bear Dossier*)

March 16th

1232: On this day, 'John of Sittingbourne', a monk of Christ Church Priory, was elected by his peers to be Archbishop of Canterbury. Unfortunately, this was quashed by a somewhat fussy Pope Gregory IX; the second of three nominations to be so rejected. In John's case, he was probably deemed too close to the cathedral monks, and would therefore side with them in all matters.

———•◆•———

1684/85: On this day, William Roper was buried in the Roper Family Vault, in St Dunstan's Church. Also Mistress Margaret Lowe Roper who 'at ye same time was put into ye vault with him'. [There were once two burial vaults beneath the Roper Chapel: one was completely back-filled in the nineteenth century; the other – containing the head of Sir Thomas More in a wall niche – has been excavated several times.] (St Dunstan's notes)

———•◆•———

1786: This week was committed to His Majesty's Gaol in this City, Francis Bell, on a strong suspicion with having feloniously and burglariously broke and entered the dwelling house of Thomas Hayward in the parish of St Mary Bredin, and stealing thereout: a tea-kettle, a tin kettle, a pot and a sack, his property. (*Kentish Gazette*)

March 17th

1605: Katherine Marlowe, mother of the murdered playwright Christopher Marlowe, died on this day. Her husband, John, had died only weeks before, on January 25th. Both were buried in St George's churchyard. (Urry: *Marlowe and Canterbury*)

1807: It was reported that Alderman James Simmons had financed the construction of four houses in London Road for the poor of the St Dunstan's parish. He died on January 22nd that year so probably never saw their completion. These properties are likely to be those ordered for demolition in 1956 (*see* March 7th).

1907: On this day, the Rising Sun in Sturry Road was destroyed by fire. It was only nineteen years old at the time. After reconstruction, the pub continued to trade until closure in 1975. The building then became a women's refuge.

1937: When a lorry driver was stopped by PC Coatsworth for exceeding the speed limit, he said, 'I was not exceeding the limit and I have two alibis!' This was part of the evidence given at St Augustine's Sessions on this Wednesday. The chairman remarked, 'I should have thought one [alibi] would be sufficient!' The two alibis did not obviate a fine. (*Kentish Gazette*)

March 18th

1938: On this day, Barrett's new premises were opened in St Peter's Street to replace a building destroyed by a fire only four months before. This was one of Canterbury's few art-deco buildings and displayed many architectural elements typical of the style. Sadly, it was all but destroyed in another fire, during an incendiary bomb attack (*see* January 22nd). (Barrett's archive)

———— ◆ ————

1964: The City Council defended their application to demolish the nine old houses of St Stephen's Fields (opposite The Causeway) by means of compulsory purchase. The houses were pulled-down in 1967 to make way for a new Barrett's depot.

———— ◆ ————

1977: The *Kentish Gazette* reported, 'Opponents of the City Council's Rosemary Lane multi-storey car park plan are chilling the champagne to celebrate its death. It is expected that a Kent County Council committee will turn down a traffic management application from the City Council. If the plan is thrown out, it seems certain the city's controversial car park will be killed off'. [In the event, the car park was built, but the screening of it by houses on three sides considerably lessened its brutal impact upon the adjacent castle keep.]

March 19th

1883: ''Ello...'': At a meeting of the Canterbury Watch Committee, Mr T. Cross called attention to the annoyance caused by children who, under the pretence of selling flowers, begged in the principal streets. Superintendent McBean said the police did all they could in the matter. They frequently took the flowers and threw them in the river.

———◆———

1958: ''Ello...'': The new chief inspector, A.G. Keech, gave us the benefit of his 'three month's observations' on what was wrong with Canterbury in an uncompromising diatribe. Of motorists, he said they were responsible for a 'dangerous disease' of 'selfishness and bad manners', and the only solution was to abolish all parking in the city-centre streets. Of pedestrians, he objected to 'youths from the West Station, walking three or four abreast along the pavement,' concluding: 'I am not going to walk off the pavement into a bus for the children of Canterbury, or anyone else'. (*Kentish Gazette*)

———◆———

1963: ''Ello; what's goin' on 'ere then?'': A young man from Glen Iris Avenue was stopped by a police officer in St Peter's Street, who had noticed that the registration numbers painted on the front mudguard of his motorcycle had flaked off. (Author's archive)

March 20th

1934: During this month's meeting of the General Purposes Committee of the Canterbury City Council, Councillor S. Palmer suggested the city was a dangerous place for shoppers owing to the heavy volume of traffic passing through it. Palmer moved that they should request the Roads Survey Committee give urgent consideration to the proposed Northern and Southern bypass roads. (*Kentish Gazette, see* March 11th)

1950: On this Monday, Alderman Stanley Jennings purchased the large house known as Hall Place at Harbledown. He had been renting the place since 1942, when the premises of his printing business in St George's Lane were destroyed in the June Blitz. Before long though, Jennings had managed to re-establish his business at its new Harbledown home. In about 1974, part of the grounds to Hall Place was lost to the Harbledown bypass. Jennings sold Hall Place to Wiltshier's in 1992. (Osborne: *Harbledown Heritage*)

1987: On this Friday, the Queen, in the company of the Duke of Edinburgh, came to Canterbury to open Cathedral House. Situated in No. 11 The Precincts, the building had been extensively renovated to become the administrative offices for what was, by then, the largest cathedral enterprise in this country. (Cathedral Chronicle, 1987)

March 21st

1556: On this Wednesday, Archbishop of Canterbury Thomas Cranmer was burnt at the stake in Oxford for heresy and treason. Cranmer was pivotal in the formation of the Church of England, and editor of the *Common Book of Prayer*. However, he was also a compromiser, forever walking a tightrope between the religious conservatives and radical reformers, who both attacked him. In Canterbury, he ensured that the transition from the old Christchurch Priory to the new Dean and Chapter went as smoothly as possible, appointing Canons and Six Preachers, of both the conservative and reforming persuasions. With a return to Catholicism under Mary Tudor, Cranmer was imprisoned. Having been sentenced to death, he was then compelled to make several recantations and forced to watch colleagues being executed. However, despite these statements against his conscience, Mary was determined to make this elderly man suffer. As the flames rose, Cranmer dramatically withdrew his recantations and plunged the hand that had signed them into the fire first, to 'punish it'.

1786: On this Tuesday, the Assizes for Canterbury ended at the Guildhall when Samuel Cartwright, for stealing a heifer – the property of Miss Overand, of Acomb – received a sentence of death. (*Kentish Gazette*)

March 22nd

1556: Cardinal Reginald Pole was consecrated as Archbishop of Canterbury, whilst the ashes of Thomas Cranmer were still warm (*see* March 21st). However, the Catholic Pole had good reason to despise the Church of England and its instigators. In 1532, Henry VIII had offered to make him Archbishop of York if he supported his divorce from Catherine of Aragon. Pole refused and went into exile. Later, Henry had most of his family brutally executed. Under Mary Tudor, Pole fully supported the wholesale burning of Protestants (*see* January 15th) but he didn't have long to reverse all of Archbishop Cranmer's reforms (*see* November 17th).

❖

1939: A defendant, summoned for speeding at St Augustine's Sessions, Canterbury, wrote that the officer who stopped him (PC Coatsworth) was so courteous that he thought he'd met one of the new 'courtesy cops'. However, his solicitor, Mr C.A. Gardiner, admitted it would probably make no difference in the amount of the fine. In this, he was proved correct! [In 1935, the Church Assembly had urged more courtesy on the roads, a sentiment supported by the AA. In 1937, the first 'courtesy cops' appeared in national pilot schemes.] (*Kentish Gazette*)

March 23rd

1959: The imminent twinning of the cities of Canterbury and Rheims was delayed due to the French Mayor losing an election. The new Gaullist Mayor said he needed a short time to settle in first. In the end, this delay lasted three years (*see* May 12th). (Author's archive)

———•—•———

1960: 'Small Shop Fire': During this Wednesday, fire broke out in the upper storey of a Frank Lyons Television and Radio Shop, at No. 78 Broad Street. Two fire tenders were summoned to tackle the blaze, which was quickly brought under control. Later, dramatic pictures appearing in local papers prompted the proprietor to ask for a declaration to be published, saying he was still open for business as usual! (Crampton: *Canterbury Suburbs and Surroundings*)

———•—•———

1963: 'Big Shop Fire': On this Saturday night, a fire broke out in the rooftop Grace and Favour restaurant of the recently opened Riceman's store in St George's Lane. This was barely thirty minutes after late-night diners and restaurant staff had left the building. Luckily, the fire brigade managed to save all the trading floors below, although there was some water and smoke damage. The rest of the shop reopened within days as repair work got underway. (Crampton: *Yesterday's Whitefriars*)

March 24th

1568: On this Sunday, Cardinal Odet de Coligny, a Huguenot convert and refugee, died whilst lodging at Meister Omers in the Cathedral Precincts. In fact, he was en route to Dover and a return to his native France, but succumbed to a mystery illness. Poisoning was suggested, but never proved. The cardinal was interred in a temporary tomb within the Trinity Chapel to await carriage to France, but this never took place and he is still there today. In 1990, this 'temporary' tomb played a role in another Canterbury mystery (*see* August 14th).

———— • ◆ • ————

1681: The Archbishop issued a decree uniting certain parishes in Canterbury. They were: St Paul's with St Martin's; St Mary Breadman with St Andrew's; Holy Cross with St Peter's; and St Alphege with St Mary Northgate. (Hasted: *Kent*, Vol. XI)

———— • ◆ • ————

1884: This year, 'Thomas Sidney Cooper sent four pictures to the Royal Academy exhibition. The private viewing took place on this Monday at his picturesque residence, Vernon Holme, near Harbledown. During the afternoon, many of the Canterbury elite arrived and received a cordial welcome from the venerable and talented artist who, we were glad to observe, appeared to be in excellent health'. (*Kentish Gazette*)

March 25th

1644: On this day, Canterbury Cathedral was formerly sequestrated by Parliament. Captain Thomas Monins of Dover was duly appointed treasurer-general of the estates. Although the Dean and most of the Residentiary Canons were absent by this time, the actual Dean and Chapter was not being abolished (*see* March 27th). For now, this was effectively a 'change of management' at the cathedral. However, more drastic moves would follow after the establishment of the Commonwealth (*see* April 30th). (Sparks *et al*: *Canterbury Cathedral*)

1885: 'Richard Dadds requests us to say that when convicted by the Canterbury magistrates, he did not say he would rather pay the fine than pick oakum. He said he wouldn't mind going to prison if he could have some oakum to pick; he finds the time hangs heavily on him when employment is not found for him.' [Oakum is loose fibre obtained by untwisting old rope: work that was given to prison inmates. It was used in waterproofing wooden ships.] (*Kentish Gazette*)

1933: The controversy over the unprotected state of the Nailbourne Stream, opposite Barham Post Office, has now been settled by the erection of black and white guard posts by the KCC. (Author's archive)

March 26th

AD 668: On this Thursday, Archbishop of Canterbury Theodore of Tarsus was consecrated. Although the cathedral had been firmly established by this time, St Augustine's Abbey was still considered the more important of the two. Consequently, it was at the latter that Theodore established his school. Here, astronomy, ecclesiastical computus, astrology, medicine, Roman civil law, Greek rhetoric and philosophy were taught, as well as the use of horoscope.

1885: Between three and four o'clock this Thursday afternoon, information reached Canterbury that a serious fire had broken out at Tile Lodge Farm (on the Hoath Road, north of Sturry).

1935: A party of seniors from Sturry School had a unique opportunity of studying the electrical equipment of a modern cinema during this Tuesday morning, when they visited the Regal Cinema (St George's Place), by the courtesy of the manager, Mr S. Wickenden. (*Kentish Gazette*)

1951: On this Monday, the Marlowe Theatre in St Margaret's Street was opened. It was converted from the 1927 Central Picture Theatre by the addition of a vast rear extension built behind the stage area. The Marlowe also made a great asset out of the cinema's mock Tudor foyer building. (Crampton: *Canterbury's Lost Heritage*)

March 27th

1643: On this day, a Parliamentary ordinance ordered the sequestration of the estates of all Dean and Chapters who had supported the King, Charles I, at the outbreak of the Civil War. There was no doubt that Royalist Canterbury would be included. In 1641, complete abolition had been suggested (*see* March 9th) but now, with a war to win, such moves would have to be postponed. (Sparks *et al: Canterbury Cathedral*)

———◆———

1783: On this Thursday was committed to His Majesty's gaol in St Dunstan's James Lumsden, a private in the 21st Regiment of Light Dragoons, for a violent assault on William Jull of Ickham. With a drawn broad sword, he cut him across the elbow, and several times more when he was on the ground. As a result, Jull was obliged to submit to the amputation of his arm. Lumsden is to be tried for the offence at the next Quarter Sessions at the Old Castle. It is said that the above assault was in consequence of Jull having in his possession some unaccustomed goods. [The trial would actually be held at the Sessions House, built in 1730, which was situated opposite the castle.] (*Kentish Gazette*)

March 28th

1833: On this Thursday, a man calling himself 'Sir William Courtenay' was arrested at the Rose Inn for swindling Thomas Stroud, a waiter there. The fantasist, John Nichols Thom, or 'Mad Tom', suddenly turned up in Canterbury in September 1832, and by the sheer power of his presence and skill as an orator first convinced people that he was 'Count Moses Rothschild' and then 'Sir William Courtenay'. Having set up base at the Rose Inn, in The Parade, he not only contested the general election of that year, but also started up his own newspaper, *The Lion*. He failed in both ventures, but still managed to convince people of his credibility. Upon his arrest, he was taken to gaol at the Westgate for this and other charges. However, such was his following at the time, particularly amongst the poor of Canterbury, that on the 30th a riot broke out in response to his incarceration and troops were called into Canterbury to quell it. (Rogers: *Battle in Bossenden Wood*)

❖

1915: During this evening, a terrific snowstorm accompanied by 80mph winds took the top and sails off the windmill at Kingston, near Canterbury. It never worked again. (Finch: *Watermills and Windmills*)

March 29th

1808: The hedges, and especially those growing in warm situations and nigh to brooks, will be found, on inspection, are so largely stored with the repositories of caterpillars that unless attention be paid to them before they escape from their webs, by those most interested in their destruction, we are persuaded they will have to look in vain for the foliage of those useful plantations during the ensuing summer. [Almost 200 years later, the same manifestation was observed in hedgerows across the Canterbury area.] (*Kentish Gazette*)

1883: Archbishop Edward White Benson was enthroned at Canterbury Cathedral on this Thursday. Earlier, a single ticket for this occasion was being offered for sale through *The Times* at some £5.

1929: On this Thursday morning, the 'Thanington Poisoning Tragedy' took place. A couple from Tyneside had entered a suicide pact and drank Lysol [a disinfectant] on allotments near Thanington Court Farm. The couple had fallen in love but, he being married, they could not pursue their relationship. Margaret Dawson died that day, but Ralph Pattison recovered. He was subsequently sentenced to death for her murder, which was later commuted to a life sentence. (Courtesy of John Viner)

March 30th

1669: Canterbury historian William Somner died on this day. He was seventy. His crowning achievement was *The Antiquities of Canterbury*, published in 1640, the first full-length history of the city. A staunch Royalist, Somner intervened during the Roundhead troops' orgy at the cathedral in 1642 and rescued its valuable archive. He lived in Castle Street and was buried at St Margaret's Church.

———————————•◆•———————————

1833: During the week, we have had rather more 'doing' in all descriptions of fine hops – without any alteration in prices. The frosty weather has put a complete check on the plant. A fortnight since, the bine had every appearance of being early. Now the probability is we shall be later than usual. Although often referred to as a 'vine', the hop is technically a 'bine', for unlike vines – which use tendrils and suckers for attaching themselves – bines have stout stems with stiff hairs to aid in climbing.

———————————•◆•———————————

1902: Appearing before Mr T. Wacher (Chairman) and Mr H.G. Sadler, Alfred Yeoman was fined 10*s* and cost of 13*s* 6*d* for ill-treating a mare on this day, by riding it while in a lame condition. The case was proved by Sergeant Jackson. (*Kentish Gazette*)

March 31st

1554: Catholic Nicholas Harpsfield, a biographer of Sir Thomas More, was made Archdeacon of Canterbury, replacing Edmund Cranmer, the married brother of the imprisoned Archbishop (*see* March 21st). He welcomed Cardinal Pole to the See, but was deprived following the death of Mary Tudor and later died in prison. (Albin: *Thomas More and Canterbury*)

———◆———

1867: On this Sunday, a wedding took place within Canterbury's Jewish community. Sophia, eldest daughter of Mr Nathan Jacobs of Sun Street, married Daniel Mitchell. The ceremony was performed by the rabbi of the city's Hebrew congregation at the family home, followed by an evening ball held in Mr Jacobs' large warehouse, also in Sun Street, where dancing was kept up with much spirit until an early hour. (*Living in Victorian Canterbury*)

———◆———

1934: In regard to the appointment of lavatory attendants etc for which the age limit was fifty, Councillor Knowles urged that this should be raised to sixty as there were a number of ratepayers over fifty who were quite capable of undertaking the work. [Sadly, we no longer have public lavatories in Canterbury, let alone lavatory attendants! No wonder people are forced to adopt 'continental methods' for relieving themselves, however anti-social!] (City Council records)

April 1st

1928: On this day, an unfortunate incident befell Archbishop Cosmo Gordon Lang who, as distinguished guest, was attending a ceremony for the Blessing of the Rood at St Simeon's Church, near Canterbury. As he stood to give the solemn address, a boy from the choir placed a new patent rubber device, known as a 'whoopee cushion', on the still-warm pew, and within inches of the purple-clad posterior. Upon resuming his seat, his Grace's serene countenance quickly turned to one of consternation as a loud 'report' was heard to reverberate around the ancient rafters. The miscreant remains unidentified. (*Memoirs of Miss Avril Ineptus*)

———◆———

1933: On this day, the *Kentish Gazette* reported: 'The Sturry annual parish meeting recorded that if all went well, a supply of current to Fordwich and Sturry would be available in the summer. The cost would not be more than 8*d* per unit, but might be less if residents took up the matter with enthusiasm and many had electricity installed'.

———◆———

1964: The head postmaster thought that some confusion may arise from calling the new cul-de-sac off St Stephen's Road 'St Stephen's Close', and suggested that 'Blore Close' be more suitable. The Council took no action. (City Council records)

April 2nd

1835: The members of the George and Dragon district meeting of the Canterbury Conservative Club dined together on this evening. Charles Pout Esq., late Alderman of this city, presided. By all accounts, the evening was passed in the utmost harmony and joviality. [The George & Dragon Inn was an attractive three-storey timber-framed structure of probable sixteenth-century date. It was demolished in the 1890s to make way for the Beaney Institute.] (*Kentish Gazette*)

———— • ◆ • ————

1938: On this Saturday, a fire broke out at Kent College, situated between Canterbury and Rough Common. During a hockey match, flames were seen coming from one of the dormitories. Whilst waiting for the fire brigade, the players formed a bucket chain on the main staircase. Much of the building's top floor was gutted and the tower collapsed, never to be replaced. In the aftermath, the nearby St Edmund's School offered emergency accommodation. (Wright: *Kent College*)

———— • ◆ • ————

1963: Two twelve-year-old Canterbury boys did not fancy their school dinner, so they walked into Victor Value's store and stole a bar of fruit-and-nut chocolate. At the Juvenile Court on this Tuesday, one boy was fined £1; the other was given an absolute discharge. (*Kentish Gazette*)

April 3rd

1883: The Medical Officer – Mr F. Wacher – reported that a person at Cold Harbour was suffering from typhoid fever. [Frank Wacher was Canterbury's Medical Officer of Health for fifty years between 1878 and 1928. He died in 1935, aged eighty-two years.] (*Kentish Gazette*)

———•◆•———

1928: Demolition of the stripped Hales Place mansion began on this day. Although gelignite was used to bring the walls down, it was hoped that as many bricks as possible could be salvaged for re-use. (Author's archive)

———•◆•———

1933: Victim of a hopeless passion for a girl who did not return his love, Frederick William Taylor (aged twenty-one), of No. 11 St George's Terrace, committed suicide at Highland Court, Bridge, where he was employed as a carpenter. He was found shot through the heart. His funeral took place at St George's Church, and he was laid to rest at Canterbury Cemetery.

———•◆•———

1963: The Canterbury Society asked if Nos 29-36 St Radigund's Street could be withdrawn from a compulsory purchase order, so that they might be renovated and preserved. The request was refused, as their demolition was necessary for the proposed ring road. [They were pulled down in about 1966.] (City Council records)

April 4th

1540: On this Thursday, the Christ Church Cathedral Priory finally surrendered to the Crown. Other religious houses in Canterbury had fallen in the autumn of 1538, but now the priory's 'stay of execution' was over. The last Prior, Thomas Goldwell, was pensioned off, as were some of the monks, but others were found positions in the New Foundation by the compassionate Cranmer (*see* April 8th). Following its surrender, the cathedral was 'de-cluttered' of all remaining shrines and relics (*see* April 10th) although the principal Becket tomb had already disappeared (*see* September 7th).

1910: A class of instruction for junior officers of the Yeomanry opened at Canterbury on this day. Major H.F. Fraser, 21st Empress of India's Lancers, was appointed commandant and Lieutenant D.W. Godfree, of the same regiment, the adjutant. (*Kentish Gazette*)

1962: At a Council meeting on this Wednesday, the installation of traffic lights at the Westgate, to control the junctions of Pound Lane and St Peter's Place, was discussed. (City Council records)

1965: On this Sunday, the last pint was pulled at the Freemason's Tavern in St Margaret's Street. The pub was being torn down for the proposed cross-city relief road (*see* January 14th). (Author's archive)

April 5th

1173: The Abbot of Bec Abbey in Normandy, Roger de Bailleul had been elected as Archbishop of Canterbury to succeed Thomas Becket. However, on this day, he turned the job down and was duly absolved. Roger clearly had no wish to raise that particular poisoned chalice to his lips.

—◆—

1886: Mary James, a little old woman who stated she belonged to Faversham, was charged with being drunk and disorderly at Canterbury Police Court. PC Hawkes deposed to having arrested her in St Dunstan's Street. The prisoner was fined 1s with costs 6s 6d. (*Kentish Gazette*)

—◆—

1990: The massive archaeological investigation at the Longmarket site began on this day. This took place following demolition of the unloved Modernist development of 1961. It was the largest dig site within the City Walls to become available for some years and hopes were high. In the late 1940s, the famous Roman pavement had been discovered on one side of the same area. In the event, the digging of cesspits and wells over a long period of medieval occupation had destroyed much of the earlier Roman levels, leaving only isolated patches of archaeology and a collection of cellars to be interpreted. (Canterbury Archaeological Trust)

April 6th

1881: On this Wednesday, the Simon Langton Boys' and Girl's Grammar Schools opened for the first time at The Whitefriars. Originally known as the 'Middle Schools' they were designed to be just that: a bridge between the free charity schools of the poor and the prestigious, fee-paying King's School; effectively middle schools for the middle classes. Boys and girls were given almost equal status in the same complex, although the sexes were strictly segregated.

———•◆•———

1955: On this day, the City Council decided that peafowl would not be re-introduced to the Dane John in spite of their popularity during the area's Victorian heyday. [The peacock is the male bird of the peafowl species.] On a happier note, in 2010 guinea fowl have recently been introduced to the Green Court, which is part of the King's School.

———•◆•———

1965: The Council announced that the old city police station in Pound Lane would become a music school, but only temporarily as its eventual demolition would be required for the third and final stage of the ring road. [Thirty-five years later, the school is still there and this part of the ring road has been long-since cancelled.] (City Council records)

April 7th

1524: John Roper, former 'General Attorney' to Henry VIII, died on this day. He was buried at St Dunstan's Church, Canterbury, where the family had a small chantry. However, John's son, William Roper – future son-in-law and biographer of Sir Thomas More – decided to build a new chapel in honour of his father. Adopting the latest Tudor style and the use of brick, it was ready the next year.

◆

1833: On this Wednesday, Mr Plumptre presented a petition from Canterbury for the abolition of slavery. It was hoped that notwithstanding the clamour that had been raised against the bill introduced by an honourable baronet, it would be persevered in and passed into law. [John Pemberton Plumptre represented East Kent for twenty years, from 1832 to 1852. He was a fervent supporter of the Slavery Abolition Bill.] (*Kentish Gazette*)

◆

1961: On this day, Canterbury City Council agreed to approach British Railways with a view to purchasing a steam locomotive. The one in question was 'School's Class', No. 30933 and was named *King's Canterbury*. It was about to be displaced by electrification in Kent. In the event, the deal floundered and the locomotive was subsequently scrapped.

April 8th

1331: The longest-ever serving Prior of the Cathedral of Christ Church, Henry of Eastry, died on this day, aged ninety-two, 'having ruled the house with much prudence and success for nearly forty-seven years'. It is thought that Bell Harry is named after him.

———•◆•———

1541: On this day, the New Foundation at Canterbury Cathedral was formally set up, with the establishment of the Dean and Chapter and the King's School. Duly installed were the Dean (*see* January 26th) twelve Prebendaries (or Canons Residentiary) and Minor Canons. Unique to Canterbury would be the college of Six Preachers, appointed directly by Archbishop Cranmer. They would be outsiders, preaching in the new spirit of the Church of England, and a counter-balance to the rest of the New Foundation, which consisted of many re-employed 'monastic-style' clergy from the dissolved priory (*see* April 4th).

———•◆•———

1933: The report on the RSPCA dogs' home at Harbledown, Canterbury, by the superintendent, Mrs De Vere, showed that altogether forty-one dogs were received, of which seven were destroyed, two died and, more happily, homes were found for thirty-two. [The dogs' home was situated at Wingate Hill, now part of Upper Harbledown.] (*Kentish Gazette*)

April 9th

1649: Royalist-supporting poet Richard Lovelace was released from prison for the second time. He then sold all the remaining family properties, including the Greyfriars at Canterbury. Incarceration had inspired the poem 'To Althea, from Prison', with its famous line: 'Stone walls do not a prison make'.

1861: The Committee and teachers beg to solicit the friends of the Ragged School for subscriptions to enable them to establish a weekly Ragged School in Canterbury so that these children may be properly instructed. [The Sunday Ragged Schools had already been established.] (*Living in Victorian Canterbury*)

1927: 'Wool prices in Canterbury': There was a steady 'tone' on this market – Kent teg (sheep in its second year) fleeces were quoted at 15*d*; ewe (female) and wether (male) fleeces at 14*d*; half-breed fleeces at 16*d*. (*Kentish Gazette*)

1954: Thefts of books have been taking place from both libraries at the Beaney Institute. As a result, the reference library is to close when there is insufficient staff and a metal grid that had been removed from some bookshelves is being replaced. A list of stolen books has also been circulated to bookshops and auctioneers in the city. (Author's archive)

April 10th

1540: On this day, Archbishop Cranmer and five other commissioners produced a detailed inventory of all the valuable plate and vestments that still remained in Canterbury Cathedral, following the recent surrendering of Christ Church Priory to the Crown (*see* April 4th). In all, some 850 items were listed, both large and small, although certain manuscripts were allowed to remain.

———— • ◆ • ————

1937: In his parish magazine for April, the Vicar of St Dunstan's, the Revd E.A. Miller, wrote, 'What a pity that good music does not attract people nowadays; the heathenish noises of jazz seem to be preferred'. He was indignant at the treatment afforded an orchestral concert recently given in the parish, the audience not being as large as he thought the performance deserved. (*Kentish Gazette*)

———— • ◆ • ————

1940: A Me. 109 was shot down during an attempted raid on Canterbury by a Spitfire from No. 74 Squadron. It crashed at Frost Farm, St Nicholas-at-Wade, 5 p.m. The pilot was killed. (*The Blitz Then and Now*)

———— • ◆ • ————

1965: Following a suggestion from a member of the public, Council officials are to suggest a suitable location for a tree to be planted in memory of the late Sir Winston Churchill. (City Council records)

April 11th

1070: On this day, the last Saxon Archbishop of Canterbury, Stigand, was finally deposed having survived the Norman Conquest for over three years. He died in prison two years later.

1447: A frequent visitor to Canterbury, Cardinal Henry Beaufort died on this day. In his will, he left the considerable sum of £1,000 to the cathedral, most of which would be spent on rebuilding its central tower. This work would see the demolition of the Norman Angel Steeple and its replacement by the familiar Bell Harry Tower. (*Archaeologia Cantiana*, 1940)

1927: On this day, the first 'City' bus routes for Canterbury were introduced. They were: Whitstable Road to Old Dover Road; Wincheap to Sturry Road; and London Road to St Martin's Hill. (Woodworth: *East Kent*)

1936: 'The demolition of workshops and old cottages, which formed the dangerous bottleneck and blind corner in Broad Street has, besides exposing a further extent of the ancient City Wall, revealed the archway of the old Queningate.' [The blocked Roman Queningate can be seen in the City Wall, just to the north of the stairway leading up to the 'modern' access into the Cathedral Precincts.] (*Kentish Gazette*)

April 12th

1833: Having been released from Westgate Prison on bail for charges of theft and perjury (*see* March 28th) 'Sir William Courtenay' spent a few days in London, but this seems to have been engineered to allow him the occasion of a 'triumphant return to Canterbury'. Having given plenty of notice, he reached Harbledown, to be received by 'the tag-rag and bob-tail of Canterbury'. 'Courtenay' then took rooms at the Old Palace, as he was clearly no longer welcome at the Rose Inn. His trial would be next (*see* July 1st). (Rogers: *Battle in Bossenden Woods*)

———•◆•———

1885: On this Sunday, a very interesting ceremony was witnessed when the old chain Bible of Canterbury Cathedral was replaced in the position it originally occupied, upon what is known as Cranmer's Desk in the north-east aisle of the cathedral. (*Kentish Gazette*)

———•◆•———

1942: On this Saturday, 'Spitfire Week' was launched in Canterbury. Fundraising activities were numerous. They included the Northgate First Aid post organising the laying of a mile-of-pennies outside the Beaney Institute, and two 'Spitfire' football matches on the Brett's Sports Ground between Canterbury and the Royal Engineers. Many children also gathered and sold bunches of primroses. (Crampton: *The Blitz of Canterbury*)

April 13th

1838: A faculty on this day permitted the Rectory House, in White Horse Lane and belonging to St Mary Breadman Church, to be pulled down, 'the said house being much out of repair, situate in one of the narrowest streets of the City and surrounded by paupers' dwellings.' [The church itself, in the High Street, would be demolished in 1900. Nothing of it remains.] (Woodruff: *Canterbury Parish Registers and Records*)

———◆———

1875: St Thomas' Roman Catholic Church in Burgate officially opened on this day. It was built on the former burial ground of St Mary Magdalene Church, which had recently been demolished, with the exception of the tower that still survives today.

———◆———

1977: 'The way has been cleared for speedway to continue at Kingsmead Stadium. The City Council's Planning Committee recommended by six votes to three that permission be granted for the next five years. Meanwhile, the season is due to start at Kingsmead at the weekend, when Canterbury Crusaders meet Red Star Prague, the strong Czech touring team.' [According to the Canterbury Crusaders' website, the last speedway match at Kingsmead was held on 31st October 1987 against Rye House.] (*Kentish Gazette*)

April 14th

1733: Whereas Sarah West, wife of John West, of the parish of Barham near Canterbury, has separated from her said husband six months since by agreement and she, having run him in debt to several persons since the said separation. This is to give notice that her husband will not pay her debts, or debts which have been or shall be contracted by his said wife. (*Kentish Post or Canterbury Newsletter*)

———◆———

1808: Several swallows were, for the first time this season, observed on the wing near Canterbury on Tuesday last; and on this Thursday, the notes of the nightingale proclaimed anew the approach of summer. (*Kentish Gazette*)

———◆———

1902: A testimonial: 'I, the undersigned, have been suffering from acute sciatica, neuritis and rheumatic gout of a most painful character for seventeen weeks. The usual medical treatment was tried but failed to afford relief. I was then induced by Dr T.S. Johnson to undergo the Dowsing Radiant Heat and Light treatment from which I have derived the greatest comfort and relief.' Emma Fill, No. 33 St George's Place. [Bathing in electric light could be had at 'Oswald House', No. 1 Watling Street. The building was demolished in about 1951.]

April 15th

1795: On this Wednesday, 'a remarkable fine fat ox was slaughtered by Mr Hercules Giles, butcher, in Canterbury, which weighed 85 score and 14 pounds, exclusive of the fifth quarter; and the loose fat 11 score and 4 pounds'. A very handsome bullock, of the Kent and Sussex breed, it had been 'fatted' by John Goddard of Westenhanger. Sadly, Hercules didn't have long to spend the profits of his purchase, dying the same year on November 29th. (*Kentish Register*, courtesy of Tina Machado)

———◆———

1884: The extensive premises in Stour Street, occupied by Messrs Alfred Neame & Co., soap & candle manufacturers, narrowly escaped being destroyed by fire on this morning. When the men went to breakfast everything was apparently safe, but when the foreman returned he found that some barrels on the ground were on fire. The damage is estimated at £50. [In 1898, the Post Office bought the factory, and later built a telephone exchange on the site.] (*Kentish Gazette*)

———◆———

1965: On this Thursday, the Queen, accompanied by the Duke of Edinburgh, came to Canterbury to distribute the Royal Maundy money. At the cathedral, she was escorted by the Archbishop, Michael Ramsey.

April 16th

1806: Mr C. Abbot, of Canterbury, in passing the corner of Lamb Lane [Stour Street today] into the High Street yesterday came into contact with the wheel of a hand-cart, which jammed him against the wall with such violence as to occasion his death this day. (*The Gentlemen's Magazine*, courtesy of Tina Machado)

———— • ◆ • ————

1936: On this Thursday, two families were rendered homeless by a fire which gutted two thatched cottages at Gravel Castle Hill, Barham, near Canterbury. The outbreak was apparently caused by burning soot falling from one of the chimneys onto the thatch. (*Kentish Gazette*)

———— • ◆ • ————

1939: Whilst a hole was being excavated in the garden of the Municipal Offices at the Dane John, for the purpose of building a subterranean ARP Control Room, a Roman pottery kiln was discovered. (*Archaeologia Cantiana*, 1940)

———— • ◆ • ————

1967: Two boys found some detonators near Whitehall Railway Crossing during this Sunday evening. Stephen Dearing (aged sixteen), of No. 17 Priest Avenue, aimed at one detonator with his catapult and hit it. As a result of the explosion, he received head injuries and was taken by ambulance to Kent and Canterbury Hospital, where he needed several stitches. The other boy, Timothy Coupland, was not hurt. (Author's archive)

April 17th

1534: On this day, Sir Thomas More was imprisoned for refusing to sign the 'Act of Succession', which gave priority of the Protestant children of Anne Boleyn over the Catholic Princess Mary, from Henry VIII's first marriage. On the same day, the ever-mediating Archbishop of Canterbury, Thomas Cranmer, wrote to Thomas Cromwell asking if More be allowed to swear a modified version of the oath. Thomas More also had a crisis of conscience with the 'Act of Supremacy' (*see* June 3rd and April 20th).

———◆———

1886: One evening last week, a curious demonstration took place in Canterbury. A Salvationist named 'Lord' led a procession of about 100 boys from Stour Street to the police station and back. The boys sang the hymn 'We Shall Win', and evidently intended their proceedings as a manifestation of displeasure at the recent persecution of Salvationists. [The Salvation Army faced furious opposition from the brewing and licensing trade, who were losing business because of the Army's opposition to alcohol and their specific targeting of the frequenters of public houses. The opposition soon formed a group: 'The Skeleton Army'. As a result, Salvationists were abused both verbally and physically.] (*Kentish Gazette*)

April 18th

1795: Died in Canterbury on this Saturday, after a sudden decline in her condition, Miss Sarah Pout, aged twenty-five, daughter of Mr William Pout, upholsterer. She bore a tedious and painful illness with the most Christian patience and resignation, and her kind and amiable disposition will be long remembered by her friends and acquaintances. (*Kentish Register*, courtesy of Tina Machado)

———◆———

1882: On this day, the ancient Duke of York pub, adjacent to the Riding Gate, was given over to the Council for demolition. This would make room for the Riding Gate itself to be pulled down and replaced with an iron bridge (*see* January 2nd). Up until 1969, the pub site was used to display the *Invicta* locomotive.

———◆———

1885: On this day, Mary Barbara Felicity Hales (Sister Mary Clare) died in penury at Sarre Court, near Birchington. The Carmelite nunnery she was attempting to build at Hackington remained incomplete, never rising above the first floor (*see* August 3rd).

———◆———

1967: A meeting of the Canterbury Coffee Pot Club was held this Tuesday evening in a room over the Nag's Head in Dover Street. A talk on 'Nigeria' was promised for the next gathering. (Author's archive)

April 19th

1012: On this day, the Archbishop of Canterbury, Alphege, was brutally murdered at Greenwich by his Viking captors. He had been captured after Vikings had laid siege to Canterbury from 8-26 September 1011. His martyrdom took place after Alphege had refused to allow himself to be ransomed (*see* June 9th).

———— • ◆ • ————

1357: On this day, the Black Prince, together with his prisoner King John II of France – captured at the Battle of Poitiers – came to Canterbury on their way back up to London. Here, they both visited the Becket shrine and made their offerings. (Cathedral Chronicle, 1976)

———— • ◆ • ————

1884: On this Saturday, the great conservation demonstrations were held in Canterbury. The widespread wearing of primroses by both men and women indicated the great and growing strength of conservation in the district. (*Kentish Gazette*)

———— • ◆ • ————

1966: On this Tuesday, a thirteen-year-old boy, who ran away from home, told Canterbury Juvenile Court how he found work and lodgings in London and finally met up with a beat group. The boy had been brought before the court as he was said to be out of his parents' control and he also faced a motoring offence committed before he ran away. (Author's archive)

April 20th

1434: On this Monday, Elizabeth Barton and her five male supporters were taken from the Tower of London to their place of execution at Tyburn (*see* December 7th). It is likely that Sir Thomas More watched the departure of the 'Holy Maid' and her companions from his room in the Tower (*see* April 17th). Unlike the five men, Elizabeth was spared the torments of being hanged, drawn and quartered, and was allowed to hang until she died; a process that itself would have taken some minutes. (Neame: *The Holy Maid of Kent*)

———◆◆———

1508: The tomb of St Dunstan in Canterbury Cathedral was opened to settle a dispute with Glastonbury Abbey, who also claimed to have the saint's remains. To the delight of Archbishop Wareham and the Christchurch monks, they found the proof they needed. Within two sealed coffins was a third bearing the plate: '*Hic Requiescit Sanctus Dunstanus Archiepiscopus*'. From inside the coffin, his skull was retrieved to be shown as a relic and the rest re-buried. (Hasted: *Kent*, Vol. XII)

———◆◆———

1935: The Mayoress of Canterbury, Mrs Frank Wood, organised the annual street collection on behalf of the Kent and Canterbury Hospital Maintenance Fund, which took place on this Saturday. (*Kentish Gazette*)

April 21st

1109: Archbishop of Canterbury Anselm died on this Wednesday. He succeeded the great builder Archbishop, Lanfranc, and himself began a great extension of the cathedral's eastern arm. During his reign, Anselm clashed with two kings, William Rufus and Henry I, over the same problem that would later plague Henry II and Becket, i.e. the power struggle between Church and State. As a result, Anselm was twice forced into exile. His body is thought to still lie beneath the floor in the cathedral chapel that bears his name.

•◆•

1826: A child called Turmaine, whose parents resided in the parish of St Dunstan's, has died from hydrophobia [rabies], after being bittern by a dog some sixteen weeks previously. (*Maidstone Journal*)

•◆•

1934: A tragedy of mental illness was revealed at an inquest held at the Municipal Offices this Saturday, concerning the death the previous day of a married woman from Littlebourne Road, Canterbury, who was found dead as the result of gas poisoning. The shocking discovery was made by her husband on his return to dinner. (*Kentish Gazette*)

•◆•

1961: The Council briefly entertained the idea of siting the new public swimming pool in the Dane John. (City Council records)

April 22nd

1547: On this day, Philippa John, the last Prioress of St Sepulchre's Nunnery (*see* February 23rd) was buried at St George's Church. In her will, she referred to Henry VIII as 'Supreme Head in Hell'... with 'Hell' crossed out and 'Earth' substituted.

———◆———

1884: During this Tuesday morning, an earthquake was felt in the city and also across most of North-East Kent. In Canterbury, Miss Kingsford of Barton House, Barton Mill, on the Sturry Road, while in the bedroom at the top of the house, heard a low rumbling noise and was so alarmed that she rushed downstairs. (*Kentish Gazette*)

———◆———

1954: The new Barrett's store, on the corner of St George's Street and Rose Lane, was opened on this day by television magician, David Nixon. He was able to conjure up quite a large crowd of onlookers. (Crampton: *Yesterday's Whitefriars*)

———◆———

1960: A mysterious hum that had troubled many people across Kent was now being heard by people in Canterbury. Mr Colin Weaver of The Close, Downs Road, said that he and his wife had been woken by it at 4.30 a.m. William Deedes, MP for Ashford, raised the matter in Parliament but was unable to solve the mystery. (Author's archive)

April 23rd

1787: On this day, the Canterbury Pavement Commissioners issued their first order. Their prime objective was to 'un-clutter' the streets and provide modern Georgian thoroughfares suitable for the new age of turnpikes and stagecoaches. Many old buildings would be sacrificed as a result. (Panton: *Canterbury's Great Tycoon*)

◆

1833: 'It is said that a case has been submitted to an eminent barrister to advise the rated inhabitants of Canterbury on the liability of the Corporation to provide a gaol for this 'City'; and respecting the 'County' rate, which has of late years pressed so heavily upon the inhabitants.' [The 'City' gaol had already expanded from the Westgate into part of a new building next door in 1829. The 'County' rate was to pay for the gaol in Longport, first opened in 1808.] (*Kentish Gazette*)

◆

1942: On this Thursday, Archbishop William Temple was enthroned in Canterbury Cathedral. He was a larger-than-life married man, who was decidedly left-leaning politically; quite unlike his ultra-conservative predecessor, Cosmo Lang, who was also a 'confirmed bachelor'. Author of several books and a voracious reader, despite being terribly short-sighted, Temple had earlier helped to mediate in the General Strike of 1926.

April 24th

1538: Henry VIII issued an extraordinary writ: 'To thee, Thomas Becket, some time Archbishop of Canterbury' – whom he knew full-well had been dead for 368 years – 'to appear within thirty days to answer to a charge of treason, contumacy, and rebellion against his sovereign Lord, King Henry II'. Henry clearly thought that Becket didn't deserve the sainthood he'd been blessed with, all the devotion he had as a result and, more to the point, the riches his tomb in Canterbury Cathedral possessed. On the other hand, if Becket had appeared in spirit form to answer those charges, then the King may very well have revised his opinion. (Home: *Canterbury, see* June 10th)

1899: On this Monday, the first-ever bus service began between Canterbury and Herne Bay, using a six-seater wagonette based on a Daimler motorcar chassis. The return fare of *2s 6d* was quite competitive with other means of travel at the time, but despite this the service did not survive for long. (Woodworth: *East Kent*)

1970: Canterbury Chamber of Trade has complained that people using the new multi-storey car park in Gravel Walk are experiencing difficulty in finding their way into and out of the building. (*Kentish Gazette*)

April 25th

1633: Charles White was appointed a Six Preacher of Canterbury Cathedral on this day. He was married twice: firstly to Mary, daughter of Siriack Rucke of Boughton-in-the-Blean, on 19 June 1628, and secondly to Frances May, spinster of Canterbury, on 17 February 1630. He died in 1647. (Ingram Hill: *The Six Preachers*)

1906: On this Wednesday, the Dean and Chapter offered some duplicate books from their vast library for sale by auction. This, and one other sale, yielded £553 17s 9d, which was duly 'invested' in London, Brighton & South Coast Railway stock! (Sparks *et al*: *Canterbury Cathedral*)

1935: On this Thursday, over 1,500 live trout made an eighty-mile road journey to Fordwich. They were to form part of the annual restocking quota of the Canterbury & District Angling Association. The fish were conveyed in a special motor tank containing oxygenated water, and showed no signs of car sickness. (*Kentish Gazette*)

1960: On this Monday, Canterbury Old Age Pensioners Club celebrated its eightieth anniversary with a tea and concert at the Red Cross Centre (in Lower Chantry Lane). Mr E.W. Evans, chairman for a second year, presided. The decorated tables made a fine show as members entered the hall. (*Kentish Gazette*)

April 26th

1793: On this day, the original Kent and Canterbury Hospital at Longport opened its doors to admit the first patients. Interestingly, as building work neared completion, rumours circulated that the hospital might not open due to inadequate funds. This led to Major Robert Brownrigg seeking to hire the building as barracks. The request was instantly rejected. (Marcus Hall *et al*: *KCH 1790 to 1987, see* June 9th)

———◆———

1933: A fierce blaze during this Wednesday night partially gutted the Methodist school in St Peter's Grove. When over 320 children, many with their mothers, arrived at the school gates, they found policemen guarding the ruins. Only splendid work by the firemen prevented the flames spreading to the adjoining Methodist church. The damage is estimated at between £3,000 and £4,000. [A 1980s plan to relocate the school to an area in Whitstable Road, opposite Westgate Court Avenue, came to nothing.] (*Kentish Gazette*)

———◆———

1962: 'Man Stops at Halt Sign': Driving a moped in Bekesbourne Road, Bridge, during this Thursday evening, John E. Carr, of No. 4 St Lawrence Close, Canterbury, ran off the road and into a 'Halt' sign. The sign was damaged but Mr Carr was not hurt. (Author's archive)

April 27th

1810: 'An Announcement': 'Any person who can advance from £1,500 to £2,000, wishing to engage in the 'Millering' business in Kent – now carrying on to the extent of 100 sacks of flour per week, with a good connexion for the sale of the whole – will be treated with by addressing a letter (post-paid) to A.B. at the King's Arms Printing Office, Canterbury. The Mill has sufficient power and is in complete repair to manufacture 150 sacks of flour per week in the shortest water time, lying well for the London Market, that the trade may be considerably extended.' (*Kentish Gazette*)

———•◆•———

1950: 'Elham Valley Railway, 1': On this day, the Harbledown Junction signal box, which had once controlled the meeting of this railway with the Ashford to Canterbury main line, officially closed for good. This now-lost building briefly featured in the 1944 Powell and Pressburger film *A Canterbury Tale*.

———•◆•———

1955: 'Elham Valley Railway, 2': The metal bridge that had once carried this line over the River Stour at Whitehall was dismantled on this day. At the time though, both brick buttresses and the embankments either side were retained. Today, that on the river's north side still survives.

April 28th

1642: The inscription of a portrait that hung in the old Guildhall: 'Henry Robinson, of this City, who by deed [on this day] gave £100, the interest of which is yearly to be paid to a young Freeman [someone eligible to vote] who was put out [nominated] by the overseers of the poor'. (Gostling: *Walk*)

———◆———

1904: On or near this day, the full proposals of the Canterbury & Herne Bay Light Railway Co. were published. Formed in 1903, this company envisaged the construction of a 3ft 6in tramway system in a circular route that also took in Whitstable. Starting in Broad Street, Canterbury (opposite the Saracen's Head pub), the line followed Military Road and then Union Street before leaving the city via Sturry Road. Sadly, this idea never left the drawing board. (Author's archive)

———◆———

1960: During the past few weeks, further interesting discoveries have been made relating to the history of Canterbury's City Wall in the course of excavations carried out near the 'White Cross' bastion (adjacent to Pin Hill, near the East Station). The work has been under the direction of Mr Frank Jenkins, with the assistance of Mr Lawrence Lyle and Mr P. Woodfield. (*Kentish Gazette*)

April 29th

1808: On this day, the *Kentish Gazette* carried the following report: 'Several of the principal barley growers in this neighbourhood have called a meeting of the proprietors and occupiers of lands on which barley is grown. We have no doubt that similar meetings will be held in other towns to express their sentiments and to petition Parliament that the great agricultural interests of the kingdom may not be too hastily sacrificed to the advantage of the possessors of colonial produce.'

1966: A large compulsory purchase order was issued on this day involving houses in the Northgate area, namely in Alma Place and Notley Street, together with those remaining in Artillery Street and Artillery Gardens. This was the last 'slum clearance' order of this type, before the tide turned in favour of retention and modernising old properties. (Author's archive)

1967: On this day, Canterbury Scene group Soft Machine played the much-hyped '14-hour Technicolour Dream' at Alexandra Palace, together with Pink Floyd, Frank Zappa, The Move, Susie Creamcheese, and just about anyone who had anything to do with the 'Summer of Love'. (Bennett: *Out Bloody Rageous*)

1973: On this day, his twenty-eighth birthday, Hugh Hopper played his last gig with Soft Machine. (Bennett: *Out Bloody Rageous*)

April 30th

1649: With the Civil War now won, the Commonwealth could turn their attention back to ideas first formed at the beginning of the 'Long Parliament'. As long ago as 1641, the concept of getting rid of Dean and Chapters was first mooted (*see* March 9th). And now finally, on this day, a Parliamentary Ordinance formally abolished them all, including that at Canterbury. This would be acted upon in 1650 (*see* February 14th). (Sparks *et al*: *Canterbury Cathedral*)

———◆———

1965: Canterbury City Council is to be asked to terminate the present catering contract at the new Technical College at the end of the year, and to invite fresh tenders to be submitted. During the past few weeks, both staff and students have been boycotting the refectory against increases in the prices of coffee and snacks. The proposal was agreed. (City Council records)

———◆———

2009: 'A young Canterbury couple fear they might have contracted the deadly swine flu virus after returning sick from holiday in Mexico with several symptoms of the virus. The pair, aged twenty-two and eighteen, were yesterday still quarantined at their homes in Canterbury and taking anti-viral drugs while they anxiously waited for the results of urgent pathology tests.' (*Kentish Gazette*)

May 1st

1886: Rose Kelsey, a well-known woman in Canterbury, was charged with being drunk (*see* May 15th and September 4th). PC Ives said he was called to the Eight Bells Inn, No. 43 King Street and found the prisoner lying on the floor. She was drunk and pretended to have a fit. He was obliged to get a wheelbarrow and take her to the police station. [The Eight Bells had a notorious reputation. In 1859, the police listed three prostitutes found using it. The inn closed in 1922.] (*Kentish Gazette*)

———•◆•———

1936: On this day, a new pavilion was opened at the Simon Langton Girls' School playing fields in Old Dover Road. This was a good mile from the actual school premises at the Whitefriars. The Langton Boys' had a similar arrangement, their playing fields being at Nackington. In 1948, foundations were dug for the new Girls' School on the existing playing fields. The Boys' School would also re-site a new school on their playing fields. (Lyle: *Simon Langton Schools*)

———•◆•———

1957: Council tenants are to be allowed to use wallpaper when carrying out redecorations – provided the prior approval of the housing manager is obtained! (City Council records)

May 2nd

1883: The Canterbury Board of Guardians decided to seal a petition in favour of the 'Maintenance of Children Bill', which provides that a married woman may obtain from a court of summary jurisdiction an order for the payment by her husband of a sum according to his means, for the support of their offspring under the age of sixteen. At present, a married woman can only obtain such an order by first subjecting herself and children to the humiliation of receiving parish relief [which could mean admittance to the workhouse]. (*Kentish Gazette*)

———•◆•———

1956: 'Yes to Morris 1,000s; No to Morris Dancing': Because of the paramount importance of parking space, a request by the East Kent Morris Men for use of part of Upper Bridge Street car park has been turned down. They will be told to use the Dane John instead. (City Council records)

———•◆•———

1962: Proposals for a new road between St Stephen's Hill and Beaconsfield Road were approved on this day. When completed, it would allow traffic direct access to Whitstable Road via Forty Acres Road. However, a section of the old Canterbury to Whitstable Railway embankment would have to be removed first. (Crampton: *Canterbury Suburbs and Surroundings*)

May 3rd

1710: On this day, Lady Coventry, late of the Donjon Manor, was buried in St Mary Bredin Church. The mansion house was 'pulled down to the ground' in 1752. [It stood at the end of Gordon Road, Wincheap, where an old oast can still be found today.] (Hasted: *Kent*, Vol. XI)

———◆——

1934: On this Thursday, a collision occurred at the junction of Union Street and Military Road between a lorry owned by C. & G. Yeoman and a motorcyclist from Erith. The latter crawled from beneath the lorry with only slight injuries. His machine was extensively damaged. [Yeoman's, based at Wincheap Green, later became part of British Road Services.] (*Kentish Gazette*)

———◆——

1961: 'Going through the motions!': The foul sewer in St Peter's Place is to be re-laid at an estimated cost of £6,300. Having closely studied the matter, the city engineer reported considerable infiltration, which was causing the regular flooding of the sewer. The tannery is also to be pressed to make adequate arrangements as soon as possible for the settlement of their effluent before it is discharged into the sewer, which was again obstructed with tannery material. (City Council records)

May 4th

1955: The Mayor of Canterbury's existing salary, of £625 p.a., is to be maintained. Councillor Stone suggested it be reduced to £600, which was 'as much as anyone was worth'. The Mayor was called on to discharge numerous functions in no way related to his office. 'You cannot open a lavatory in Canterbury today without the Mayor putting the first penny in the slot.' (City Council records)

———•◆•———

1960: The Parochial Church Council wrote asking the Corporation to lay out and maintain All Saints' churchyard and St Alphege's churchyard as gardens of rest for the general public's use. The City Council replied that the proposal would be borne in mind for future consideration. (Author's archive)

———•◆•———

1985: 'Plans to open a pizza parlour outside Canterbury Cathedral have been fiercely attacked. Proposals by Pizzaland involve the conversion of the tearoom and cake shop of the Cathedral Gate Hotel – next to Christ Church Gate – into a fast-food outlet. The building is owned by the Dean and Chapter. The plan has already been described as utterly deplorable.' [Perhaps pizzas with a religious theme would have been more acceptable, for example, the 'Good King Wenceslas: Deep-pan, crisp and even'.] (*Kentish Gazette*)

May 5th

1886: Information was circulated of the disappearance of a young lady of nineteen years who had run away from home. She was recognised by an acquaintance at Bridge and found to be lodging at the village inn. The girl was described as of prepossessing appearance, and the reason given for her absconding was that she wished to evade marriage with an enamoured but unloved swain. (*Kentish Gazette*)

───◆◆───

1909: Born at the Blean Workhouse to Annie Ord, of Sturry parish, an illegitimate male child. No name recorded. The *Street Directory* of 1910 lists John Clarke Ord as a resident of Broad Oak. Could he have been Annie's father? (Author's archive)

───◆◆───

1918: A spur connecting the Ashford to Canterbury railway with the Faversham to Canterbury line at Whitehall was opened on this day. This was to facilitate movements of military traffic to and from Richborough Port. (Mitchell and Smith: *Branch Lines around Canterbury*)

───◆◆───

1965: A multi-storey car park is included in proposals for the redevelopment of the King Street-Blackfriars Street area, approved by the Council on this day. It would adjoin the planned ring road in the vicinity of St Radigund's Street (*see* April 3rd). (City Council records)

May 6th

1405: Thomas Hunden was elected as Abbot of St Augustine's Abbey, receiving benediction from Archbishop Arundel on this day. Records show that he took a journey to the Holy Land in 1412. (Hasted: *Kent*, Vol. XII)

———— • ◆ • ————

1933: The call of the cuckoo, which was reported to have been first heard in Fordwich, has now become general, and that other harbinger of summer, the nightingale, is also here. This beautiful songster has been heard in the vicinity of Giles Lane and Rough Common, and has thrilled listeners with its lovely melody. (*Kentish Gazette*)

———— • ◆ • ————

1959: The chief public health inspector reported on complaints received concerning two loaves of bread, one of which contained a length of bread-cutting blade and the other two pieces of string. Another recent incident of concern to Canterbury bakers was the discovery of a cockroach in a bread roll. (City Council records)

———— • ◆ • ————

1967: Canterbury Scene groups Soft Machine and The Wilde Flowers both played the Rag Ball at the city's Technical College on this evening. Soft Machine had just finished recording tracks for an LP that wouldn't be released for ten years. It is available today as the CD *Jet Propelled Photographs*. (Bennett: *Out Bloody Rageous*)

May 7th

1811: The stone-laying ceremony for the new St Peter's Methodist Church, in St Peter's Street, took place on this Tuesday. At this time, the Wesleyan congregation occupied a curious-looking building in King Street, known as the 'Pepper Pot Chapel'. (Author's archive, *see* January 1st)

— • —

1937: On this Friday the Mayor, Alderman Charles Lefevre, set in motion a new high-speed Cossar printing press for the *Kentish Gazette*. This enabled the size of the paper – when occasion warranted – to be increased to twenty-four pages and also greatly improved and accelerated the process of production. [The newspaper's premises were then in St George's Street.]

— • —

1941: In the early hours of this Wednesday, the Luftwaffe attacked the RAF airfields at Manston and Canterbury [the recently reopened Bekesbourne Aerodrome]. No damage was reported. (*The Blitz Then and Now*)

— • —

1965: A man who indecently exposed himself before three pupils on the playing fields of the Canterbury Technical High School for Girls (now Barton Court Grammar School) was put on probation for two years, when he appeared before Canterbury magistrates this day. The twenty-nine-year-old father of five, from Querns Road, gave an undertaking that he would undergo medical treatment. (*Kentish Gazette*)

May 8th

1754: Recorded on a stone in the external wall of the old Guildhall, adjacent to one of the city's public water-cocks: 'N.B. The above generous benefaction [i.e. the water supply] is still continued by Sir Edward Hales, Bart. 8th May 1754'. [A surviving water pump can still be seen in Longport.] (Gostling: *Walk*)

———•◆•———

1883: 'Now that the Revd E. Brailsford, having been released from prison, has resumed his duties at Fordwich Parish Church, the good that has been done in his absence is melting away. He has dismantled the choir, so carefully got together by the Revd Stuart Robson, and has in other matters so thoroughly gone back to the 'old lines' that whereas, during his absence, the church had been crowded, the congregation has now fallen back to half-a-dozen old women.' [A notorious and uncompromising Puritan, he died on 29 March 1893, aged eighty-six, and is buried in Fordwich churchyard.] (*Kentish Gazette*)

———•◆•———

2001: On this Saturday, the Honorary Freedom of the City of Canterbury was presented to architect and conservator Anthony Swaine, the artist John Ward and television producer Peter Williams. The ceremony took place at the Guildhall, formerly Holy Cross Church. (Author's archive)

May 9th

1804: From this day, the Kent and Canterbury Hospital waived one of its inadmissible categories, namely 'those who have not had either the Cow or Small Pox', to begin offering free inoculations against smallpox to the poor of the city. (*Archaeologia Cantiana*, 1988)

———◆———

1936: The Public Health Committee reported that having considered the heavy water rate, which would fall on Lower Hardres, near Canterbury, in the event of carrying through a water supply to that parish, it was decided that Mr F.V. Lee should report to the Parish Council in order to obtain the opinion of the village as to whether or not the scheme should be proceeded with. (*Kentish Gazette*)

———◆———

1942: On this Saturday, a BBC van came to Canterbury and set up in the Cattle Market. The voices of the auctioneers and other market people were recorded, as well as key figures from the life of the city. The theme of the programme being made was 'Impressions of Canterbury in Wartime', and it was broadcast soon after to overseas countries in the Empire. These were probably the last sounds to be recorded of Canterbury before the devastating Baedeker raid (*see* June 1st). (Crampton: *The Blitz of Canterbury*)

May 10th

1833: On this Friday, the magistrates committed Susanna Oliver to the House of Correction for three calendar months for professing to tell fortunes. This woman kept a notorious brothel, and there was little doubt that many poor girls were inveigled into her house under pretence of having their fortunes told, for which she used to charge 3*d* to answer an ulterior design upon them. (*Kentish Gazette*)

———◆———

1872: On this Friday, Susan Davey was denied access as an outpatient to the Kent and Canterbury Hospital as she was not 'a real object of charity', her father being considered in good circumstances as a cow keeper. Ability to pay was not the only reason to deny a patient admission. Others excluded were: pregnant women, lunatics, those with VD, vagrants, epileptics, those not clean in person or apparel… and the dying! (*Archaeologia Cantiana*, 1988)

———◆———

1952: On this Saturday, 'The Buffs (Royal East Kent) Memorial Window' in the Warrior's Chapel [or St Michael's Chapel] of Canterbury Cathedral was unveiled by King Frederick IX of Denmark, Colonel-in-Chief of the Buffs. Designed by William Wilson, and incorporating the Buffs' regimental badge, the window can be found in the chapel's east wall. (Babbington: *Romance of Canterbury Cathedral*)

May 14th

1313: Archbishop of Canterbury Robert Winchelsey died on this day. He was yet another outspoken Archbishop who fell out with the King, in his case Edward I, and was forced into exile. His tomb, placed against the far wall of the cathedral's south-east transept, became the object of much devotion and miracles were claimed. He was never canonised, but still maintained a saintly reputation. Consequently, his tomb was singled out for early destruction by the King's commissioners in their purge of the cathedral in 1540 (*see* April 4th). Although unmarked, it is likely that his bones still exist beneath the floor of the transept.

———— ◆ ————

1884: An awfully sudden death occurred in Canterbury on this Sunday evening. Mrs Eliza Coombs (aged fifty-two), living at No. 34 Lower Chantry Lane, had been present at the christening of two infants during the afternoon and appeared to be in her usual robust health. She had only returned to her home a short time when she suddenly expired. As she had been suffering from an affection of the heart, an inquest was unnecessary. [The mother of twelve children, Eliza was buried in St Gregory's churchyard on May 14th.] (*Kentish Gazette*, with additional information courtesy of great-great-granddaughter Mavis Wrightson)

May 12th

1871: In-patient Constance Emma Cuthbert was discharged from the Kent and Canterbury Hospital, with 'an expression of dissatisfaction but no definite complaint'. Name to be put into the 'Black Book'. (*Archaeologia Cantiana*, 1988)

———•◆•———

1934: In competition with over 5,000 children from schools all over Kent, the representatives of several Canterbury schools scored a marked success when they appeared at the 25th Kent Competitive Music Festival at Maidstone on this Saturday. Places were gained by the Payne Smith City Council School and Simon Langton Schools. [Payne Smith School was in Lower Chantry Lane and the Simon Langton Schools were at the Whitefriars.] (*Kentish Gazette*)

———•◆•———

1962: On this day, the off-on twinning ceremony between Canterbury and Rheims finally took place (*see* March 23rd). A deputation from Canterbury accepted an invitation from the Mayor of Rheims to attend a twinning ceremony, arranged in conjunction with a festival in honour of Joan of Arc [not the most tactful move I would suggest]. In return, the French Mayor, Monsieur Taittinger, was later invited to formally open the Rheims Way in Canterbury, followed by a lavish dinner at Tower House [although the Waterloo Tavern might have been a more appropriately 'tactful' response!].

May 13th

1834: We understand that Mr Newman, the celebrated ventriloquist, is now in this city and is about to give the citizens a very great treat. We have heard much of him (presumably by 'word of mouth'), and we must confess to have been sceptical of his powers until we had the pleasure of witnessing in a private room a specimen of his ventriloquism, when our doubts were entirely removed. (*Kentish Gazette*)

———— ◆ ————

1884: On this Tuesday, the matron of the Kent and Canterbury Hospital, Miss Aisbitt, complained of the conduct of in-patient Austin Sandy, stating that on her reprimanding him for carrying burning coals from one ward to another and dropping some on the matting – thereby burning it – he answered her in a very rude manner. Mr Sandy was cautioned as to his future conduct. (Marcus *at al*: *KCH 1790 to 1987*)

———— ◆ ————

1929: On this Monday, the Chislet Colliery Village Temporary Council School was opened in a wooden building. This was to serve the rapidly expanding mining village of Hersden. The adjacent Chislet Colliery was the closest pit to Canterbury of all those in Kent. A more permanent 'Hersden C P School' was finally opened some thirty-two years later. (Llewellyn: *Hersden*)

May 14th

1776: An old cricketing song appeared in the *Canterbury Journal* on this day: 'Come fill up the glass, ye gay sons of the plain, Let Comus and Bacchus unite in the strain; Now jocund we've played, shall loud echo repeat, That cricket's the game for the low and the great.'

— • —

1833: 'At the court of Burghmote holden on this Tuesday, it was decided that the Corporation would order that the building of a new shaft to the Abbot's Mill, and the erecting of a wall on the St Radigund's Estate, should be put out to public contract, instead of being performed as heretofore by members of the court [i.e. Corporation].' [St Radigund's Estate is probably a reference to the development of terraced houses in streets such as Duck Lane, Abbot's Place and St Radigund's Street itself, which mostly dated from this time.] (*Kentish Gazette*)

— • —

1964: On this day, a compulsory purchase order was made for the remaining pre-war buildings on the Whitefriars Development Area. These included two large Regency-period houses in Gravel Walk, a large Georgian house in Watling Street and a terrace of early nineteenth-century houses, also fronting Watling Street. (Crampton: *Yesterday's Whitefriars*)

May 15th

AD 973: Former Archbishop of Canterbury Byrhthelm died on this day. Byrhthelm had been Archbishop only briefly, during AD 959, but was soon replaced by Dunstan because he was 'too gentle to maintain discipline'.

———— ◆ ————

1873: On this day, the St Lawrence Mill in Old Dover Road burnt down. This windmill – a large smock mill – was more commonly referred to as the 'Black Mill' because of the tar that coated the external weatherboarding. Consequently, the fire was rapid and all consuming. The site of the mill was later used to form the junction for Ethelbert Road.

———— ◆ ————

1883: Rose Kelsey, a young woman, was charged with being drunk on this day. PC Mantle said that on Saturday night he found the prisoner speechlessly drunk in Westgate Grove. Superintendent McBean said she had been convicted in all the boroughs around Canterbury and has never paid a fine yet! She was fined 7s 6d and costs; in default, fourteen days. [Westgate Grove once contained the notorious Cock Inn, reputedly often frequented by prostitutes. Its name was not inspired by these ladies' job description, but rather the Cock Water Mill on the River Stour opposite.] (*Kentish Gazette*)

May 16th

1854: It is announced that a match of cricket will be played at twelve o'clock on this day at the East Kent and Beverley Cricket Ground, St Lawrence, between eleven gentlemen of the King's School, Canterbury, and a like number from Tunbridge Wells Grammar School. In order to encourage parties to pay a visit to the grounds, we find arrangements are made to furnish the public with the best of refreshments at a reasonable charge. (*Living in Victorian Canterbury*)

———◆———

1936: 'Canterbury has got a very serious housing problem, quite apart from the overcrowding problem, and everything possible should be done to encourage the provision of new houses. These are much needed for the working classes in the district to replace the obviously worn out, insanitary structures that currently exist.' [In the mid-1930s, new Council houses were being built on the Sturry Road estate – including Old Park Avenue, South Street and Reed Avenue – and as an extension to the late 1920s Thannington estate – including Cockering Road, Godwin Road and Strangers Lane. At the same time, twelve slum clearance areas were identified, the largest being in St Peter's Lane and the Kirby's Lane area.] (*Kentish Gazette*)

May 17th

1886: Arrangements have been made for the fusion of the Channel Tunnel Co. with the Continental Submarine Railway Co. Sir Edward Watkin will be the chairman of the united companies. [Watkin was also responsible for the Elham Valley Railway, opened in 1887, which he envisaged might one day form part of his Channel Tunnel rail link.] (*Kentish Gazette*)

1931: The Dean and Chapter became very concerned by the address of Lady Davidson's house in The Precincts, which carried the rather humble-sounding number '14D'. Reversion to the old name, 'Starr's House', was suggested, but fear was expressed that it might become confused with the nearby Star Brewery. (Sparks *et al*: *Canterbury Cathedral*)

1968: On, or very near, this day, Soft Machine began rehearsals with their new guitarist, Andy Summers, in Canterbury and also at Graveney Village Hall. During this process, the then roadie Hugh Hopper stood in for an absent Kevin Ayres on bass. Andy's stay with the band was brief; he walked out during a US tour in early July. [Eleven years later, Andy Summers began his route to stardom as guitarist of The Police, when 'Roxanne' reached the top twenty in the UK charts.] (Bennett: *Out Bloody Rageous*)

May 18th

1809: 'At one o'clock this afternoon, the thermometer in Canterbury was at 78°F – 2 degrees higher than the point of summer heat, an excess certainly greater than usual at the period of the year.' (*Kentish Gazette*)

———◆———

1946: On this day, Kent played their first home cricket match since the war, at the St Lawrence County Ground. The visiting team was Yorkshire. Before the match began, both teams lined up to pay their respects to those players who had fallen in the recent hostilities. (Butler: *Canterbury Revisited*)

———◆———

1960: St Margaret's Street has been slowly subsiding, it has been discovered, and on this Wednesday part of it was roped off. Mr J. Midlane, at Canterbury Estate Agency (No. 32) first noticed it when the office door kept sticking. After trying to free it without success, he got the builders in. They found that a wall in the cellar – which extended just under the road – had collapsed, and the road was gradually sinking. Now, Mr Midlane cannot use his front door and road engineers are discussing the problem. (Author's archive)

———◆———

1961: On this day, formal approval was given for the setting up of the Universities of Kent (at Canterbury), Essex and Warwickshire.

May 19th

AD 988: The Archbishop of Canterbury, Dunstan, died on this day. He was probably about eighty. His tomb in the cathedral was translated several times, but always occupied a prominent position. He was canonised in 1029, becoming patron saint of metalworkers and blind people. One of his miracles was reputed to have been when he called forth a spring of water, possibly on Old Park, to provide a supply to the religious house below. A claim by Glastonbury to have his relics was settled in 1508 when his tomb at Canterbury was opened (*see* April 20th). Thereafter, for about thirty years, his silver-clad skull was shown as a holy relic. His tomb, and probably his remains, was destroyed in the immediate aftermath of the surrender of Christ Church Priory in 1540 (*see* April 4th).

———————•◆•———————

1808: 'During this Thursday night, Mrs Waters, one of the sisters of the John Boys' Hospital [in Sturry Road] far advanced in her years, was robbed by a woman of decent appearance under circumstances as singular as they are depraved. She obtained admittance into her apartment by pretending that she was on intimate terms of friendship with her daughter, who resides in Margate.' (*Kentish Gazette*)

May 20th

1349: On this day, Archbishop of Canterbury elect John de Ufford died of the Black Death before his consecration. He was already thought to be old and infirm. A rival to his election, Thomas Bradwardine, succeeded him as Archbishop, but also died of the plague in 1349, only forty days after his consecration.

1593: On this day, Canterbury-born playwright Christopher Marlowe was arrested on the charge of atheism, which was then considered a heresy. Rather than be imprisoned straight away, he was granted bail and was then followed by an informer so that 'evidence' against him could be assembled. This probably occurred as a result of Archbishop Whitgift's purge against anyone who strayed from the doctrines of the Church of England (*see* February 29th). In actual fact, Marlowe was probably more of a 'Free-Thinker' than an atheist. (William Urry, *Marlowe Souvenir Booklet, see* May 30th)

1934: While motorcycling near the top of Littlebourne Hill, on the Canterbury to Sandwich road, on this Sunday, Joseph Graham of Herne Bay was thrown off as the result of his footrest striking the grass bank. He suffered a cut on the forehead, a bruised left eye and abrasions on the chin and right hand. (*Kentish Gazette*)

May 21st

1382: On this day, an earthquake in Canterbury damaged the cathedral's bell tower (or campanile). This tower stood separately from the main body of the cathedral, on a mound in the South Precincts. The 'Great Belfry' was damaged again in a six-hour-long storm on 27 May 1458. The exact date of the tower's demolition is unrecorded, but it had definitely gone by 1540. The cathedral's south-west tower (today's belfry) was completed in 1459 (*see* November 16th) so it is likely that the already-damaged remote bell tower was demolished shortly afterwards.

———◆———

1984: 'Villagers at Sturry, near Canterbury, are closing ranks in their battle to defeat a bypass scheme they maintain is economic madness and totally unacceptable. The City Council's backing for the building of the shorter bypass route, as soon as possible, has angered the Parish Council, tradesmen and residents. At a meeting on this Monday, residents condemned the route as "nothing more than a slip road", which would do nothing to ease the amount of traffic using village roads.' [A map of 1986 shows three bypass options, the shortest of which merely bisects the village, crossing Sturry Hill at its midpoint.] (*Kentish Gazette*)

May 22nd

1180: On this Thursday, a massive fire in Canterbury (probably in Burgate Street) threatened the cathedral, which was still being rebuilt following a similar fire that had spread to its roof (*see* September 5th). This time though, a combination of skilful fire fighting and – if accounts are to be believed – prayer saved a repeat of the disaster.

⸻ ◆ ⸻

1715: On this Wednesday, Sister Mary Browning of Canterbury's Baptist Church congregation was 'dealt with' to make her sensible of her 'evil' in going to the National Church [the Church of England] and neglecting to make good her place with them. (Taylor: *The Free Churches of Canterbury*)

⸻ ◆ ⸻

1959: 'For the first time in memory, all fixtures were completed by the Canterbury and District Football League last season, it was revealed at the annual dinner held at the County Hotel this Friday evening. Mr J.T. Tracey said that in this mercenary sort of world, when assessing the tremendous amount of voluntary service of the league's officers and measured it in time and energy, he felt very proud.' (*Kentish Gazette*)

⸻ ◆ ⸻

1982: On this Saturday the old Marlowe Theatre, in St Margaret's Street, closed for the final time. Demolition occurred shortly afterwards.

May 23rd

1844: On this day, an Act of Parliament permitted the South Eastern Railway to construct a main line from Ashford to Margate, via Canterbury (*see* February 6th).

———◆———

1945: On, or very near, this day, work started on replacing the ancient stained-glass windows of Canterbury Cathedral. Scaffolding was first placed against the west window of the nave in readiness for this long and arduous task to begin. The medieval glass had been removed for safekeeping at the time of the Munich Crisis (*see* September 28th). Examination of the remaining iron frames in 1945 showed that if the glass had not been removed, then it would have all been destroyed. (Friend's Report, 1945)

———◆———

1957: Four Council houses, which were originally to be built at Ickham, are not to be proceeded with. The Bridge-Blean Rural District Council said the scheme had been abandoned in view of the difficulties in obtaining a suitable site in the parish. The houses necessary for slum clearance in Ickham would instead be provided at St Vincent's Close, Littlebourne. [Lack of a mains water supply would have been enough to have a rural house condemned as unfit by this time.] (*Kentish Gazette*)

May 24th

1904: On this day the 'Buffs' Memorial, dedicated to the men who fell in the Boer War between 1899 and 1902 (either killed in action, or who later died of wounds or disease) was unveiled at the Dane John. The ceremony was performed by Field Marshall Earl Roberts. In July 1970, rock group Perplexity caused great offence by performing on the steps in front of the memorial.

———— ◆ ————

1936: 'Empire Day was celebrated on this Sunday by various patriotic ceremonies in Canterbury and the surrounding villages. It is a happy sign in these troublesome and anxious times to see that a healthy love for and appreciation of one's own country are being so well fostered.' [Empire Day was first celebrated in 1902 in commemoration of Queen Victoria, whose birthday this was. However, by 1958 the actual empire had largely gone, and it became British Commonwealth Day.] (*Kentish Gazette*)

———— ◆ ————

1957: On this day, concern was raised about the threat to the remaining parkland at Lee Priory, at Littlebourne near Canterbury, because of the proposed felling of some mature trees there. The fifty-room mansion had been demolished, leaving just a few outbuildings and the grounds. (Pearson: *Ghost Houses*)

May 25th

1520: On this date, King Henry VIII spent a night at the Archbishop's Palace in Canterbury, en route to the famous grand tournament of 'The Field of the Cloth of Gold' in France. (Friend's Report, 1932)

———— • ◆ • ————

1884: 'Dane John 1': Seldom has the City of Canterbury witnessed illuminations on so grand a scale as those that were seen on this night. The Dane John was lit up with thousands of small green lamps. By the generosity of the directors of the Gas Co., Westgate Towers were illuminated, as also were the Corn Exchange and the premises of Mr W. Ashenden junior, Mr Reeve, Mr K. Fullager and others. (*Kentish Gazette*)

———— • ◆ • ————

1967: 'Dane John 2': On this day, plans to build a Civic Centre (a new Guildhall) at the Dane John suddenly came to a standstill. This large Modernist office block was to form the administrative base for Canterbury, which enjoyed County Borough status at this time. However, central government had already authorised a Royal Commission on Local Government Reorganisation, therefore they refused to sanction any more spending until its findings were announced in late 1968. Subsequently, Canterbury lost its autonomous status in 1973 and was absorbed into Kent.

May 26th

1557: St Lawrence Hospital in Old Dover Road, having survived the general Dissolution in Canterbury between 1537 and 1540, was finally shut down by Archdeacon Harpsfield (*see* March 31st) when he found the place in a rundown condition. (*Archaeologia Cantiana*, 1939)

———◆———

1733: An unhappy accident happened to a bricklayer who was working at the top of a house in Burgate. A wagon going by ran against the ladder, by which accident the man was thrown down and the wagon ran over him and fractured his skull and thigh. (*Canterbury Newsletter or Kentish Post*)

———◆———

1802: From the parish register of Holy Cross Church: George McCleich, aged twenty-nine, and Thomas Dumelane, aged twenty-five, were condemned for robbery on the highway between Canterbury and Sturry on Saturday April 18th and 25th at the City Sessions. At 8 a.m. they were publicly executed at the Westgate of the city and were buried in the same grave at about 5 p.m.

———◆———

1953: Queen Salote of Tonga visited Canterbury on this day, a week before she famously attended the Queen's coronation. Whilst here, she visited the King's School and later toured the cathedral in the company of Dean Hewlett Johnson. (Butler: *Canterbury Cathedral*)

May 27th

1660: Upon the Restoration of the Monarchy and his return to England, King Charles II spent his first night at the Royal Palace at St Augustine's. And then, on this Sunday, he attended a service at the cathedral before resuming his journey to London. (Sparks *et al*: *Canterbury Cathedral*)

———◆———

1838: Following his release from Barming Asylum in 1837 (*see* October 27th), 'Sir William Courtenay's' behaviour worsened. Now believing he was the reincarnation of Jesus Christ, Courtenay held a meeting at Dunkirk in an attempt to encourage the local peasantry to rise up against the rich by exploiting resentment already being felt towards the Poor Law (*see* May 29th). (Rogers: *The Battle in Bossenden Wood*)

———◆———

1886: 'The prospect of more 'promenade music' on the Dane John is not an alluring one. In a small public garden, a band's performance can never be enjoyable unless a charge is made for admission. It is a poor compliment to the cavalry band to ask them to play to a miscellaneous collection of children.' (*Kentish Gazette*)

———◆———

1967: Whilst crossing St Stephen's crossroads on this Saturday night, two sisters were involved in a collision with a car. Both were later treated for minor injuries. (Author's archive)

May 28th

1089: The Archbishop of Canterbury, Lanfranc, died on this day. He was probably in his eighties. He became Archbishop after Stigand was disposed in 1070 (*see* April 11th). Lanfranc's first task was to completely rebuild the cathedral, which had been gutted in the Great Fire of 6 December 1067. This colossal task was completed in 1077 and, nearly a millennium later, significant elements of Lanfranc's work still remain in the present cathedral fabric. He also founded the Archbishop's Palace, St Gregory's Priory, St John's Hospital and St Nicholas' at Harbledown.

1557: On this day, Queen Mary I wrote that she soon hoped to restore one of the two great monasteries at Canterbury. (Ryan: *The Abbey and Palace of St Augustine's*)

1736: 'On this Monday, at the sign of the Cardinal's Cap in Canterbury, was fought a cock match between Canterbury and Wickhambreaux, for two guineas a battle, and three the odd. Note: there was a good 12d ordinary; and the door was but 6d.' [The Cardinal's Cap pub is in Rosemary Lane. It was rebuilt in 1820, together with a development of adjacent terraced houses. All but the pub was demolished in 1962.] (*Kentish Post or Canterbury Newsletter*)

May 29th

1838: Having attempted to rouse the locals at Dunkirk on the previous day, 'Sir William Courtenay' now assembled a 'rebel' force of farm labourers at Boughton, buying them bread, cheese and beer as an inducement. The 'mob' then went on a seemingly directionless wander around East Kent for two days, failing to recruit anyone to the cause. On their return to Bossenden Farm, near Dunkirk, a local farmer, Mr Curling, demanded that his employees return to their duties. In response, Courtenay threatened to shoot him. Curling fled to lodge a complaint with the local justices of the peace (*see* May 31st). (Rogers: *The Battle of Bossenden Wood*)

❖

1897: On this Saturday, the Prince of Wales (later Edward VII) opened the newly restored Chapter House at the cathedral. This was part of the St Augustine anniversary celebrations (Augustine arrived in AD 597). The Prince arrived at Canterbury West railway station, and the route he took was bedecked with flowers, potted plants and ferns. The *Kentish Gazette* reported the display as being 'not too gaudy' but, on the other hand, there was so much colour that 'there was a danger of the beholder going colour blind through the unaccustomed brilliancy'.

May 30th

1593: During this evening, Canterbury-born playwright Christopher Marlowe was murdered at a Deptford lodging house. Four acquaintances had been talking and drinking for much of the day, and then Marlowe and Ingram Frizer got into a heated discussion that became violent. Knives were drawn and, in defending himself, Frizer stabbed Marlowe over his right eye and he died instantly. Queen Elizabeth I pardoned Ingram Frizer only twenty-eight days later. (Urry: *Marlowe Souvenir Booklet, see* May 20th)

1919: On this day, a memorial service was held at Canterbury Cathedral for almost 500 employees of the South Eastern & Chatham Railway who had been killed in the First World War. The bereaved included the company's chairman, Cosmo Bonsor, who had lost his son in Palestine. (Hart: *Canterbury & Whitstable Railway*)

1932: The new 'temporary' children's ward at Kent and Canterbury Hospital was opened by the president of the hospital, Lord Northbourne, on this Monday. The bright and airy building was erected to provide better accommodation for the children, but also to allow their old wards in the main building to be used for paying patients. It accommodated twenty-four children, cost £1,800 and was admirably equipped with all the modern appliances. (*Kentish Gazette*)

May 31st

1792: Two officers from Customs House, Dover, followed a gentleman to Canterbury who had arrived from France. He was believed to have in his possession seditions and treasonable writings. On searching his trunk, only one packet was found, which was addressed to the president of the Constitutional Whig Club in London. (*Kentish Gazette*)

———◆———

1838: John Mears, a constable of Boughton, was sent to Bossenden Farm to arrest 'Sir William Courtenay' after his recent threatening behaviour (*see* May 29th). He took his brother, Nicholas, with him for support. On their arrival, Courtenay brutally murdered Nicholas Mears. The military were then summoned from Canterbury, and in the ensuing battle Lieutenant Henry Boswell Bennett was shot dead by Courtenay. In response, seven of Sir William's followers were killed and he himself also died in the 'battle'. (Rogers: *The Battle of Bossenden Wood*)

———◆———

1942: An uneasy air hung over Canterbury on this warm Sunday evening. Earlier, Lord Haw-Haw, broadcasting his propaganda from Berlin, warned that if Cologne were ever bombed then Canterbury would become the responding target. It was also known that other English cathedral towns had recently been bombed. Cologne was indeed attacked, in the so-called '1,000-Bomber Raid' during the previous night.

June 1st

1782: 'On this Saturday, as a maidservant of Mr Denne of Watmore Hall, Sturry, was returning home from Canterbury Market, she was stopped between Vauxhall and Sturry by a well-dressed highwayman. He leapt off his horse, carried her into a lodge hard by and, after using her extremely ill, took her purse containing 28s and rode off towards Canterbury. He had a light-coloured coat and his hair tied in a queue very much powdered.' (*Kentish Gazette*)

———◆———

1942: In the early hours of this Monday morning, Canterbury suffered the worst bombing of the Second World War. This was one of the infamous Baedeker raids, targeted on centres of historical importance. Initially flares were dropped over central Canterbury but a breeze blew them to the south-east, so it was this quadrant of the city that was targeted. Incendiaries were dropped, followed by high-explosive bombs. Firewalls were created in Butchery Lane and St Margaret's Street to stop the flames spreading westwards, whilst streets like St George's Place burnt unchecked. The cathedral had a miraculous escape, with incendiaries being manhandled off the roof, but a high-explosive bomb destroyed the library. St George's and St Mary Bredin's churches were gutted. In all, fifty people were killed.

June 2nd

AD 597: On this day, the Feast of Pentecost, St Augustine baptised King Ethelbert in the font at St Martin's Church. This was at the beginning of his Christian mission to convert England.

———◆———

1934: 'An interesting discovery has been made during excavations at Cooper's Lime Works in South Canterbury. Initially it was thought to be an underground chamber, but it turned out to be a wall built in thin red Roman bricks on a cement foundation embedded with flints.' [Cooper's was situated at the top end of Lime Kiln Road. Following its closure, the kilns were demolished in September 1965. Landfill has since eliminated much of the site.] (*Kentish Gazette*)

———◆———

1942: Barrage balloons were rushed to the city twenty-four hours after the devastating Baedeker raid for fear of further attacks. They were stationed in open areas such as the Green Court, Simon Langton playground and Miller's Field. (Crampton: *The Blitz of Canterbury*)

———◆———

1953: On this Tuesday, Canterbury began two days of celebrations for the coronation of the new Queen. As well as numerous street parties, an impressive historical pageant was held along the City Wall by the Dane John. (Crampton: *Canterbury 1945 to 1975*)

June 3rd

1162: Thomas Becket was enthroned as Archbishop of Canterbury on this day, having been personally appointed by Henry II. He was also Chancellor of England and a close personal friend and confidant to the King. The appointment was a calculated move by Henry to get 'his man' at the head of the Church, to best effect some changes in the established Church Law. When a priest transgressed, the Church was permitted to try them without reference to the Civil Law, and this frustrated the King greatly. Now though, in Henry's mind, all would be well. Unfortunately, having taken his sacred vows as Archbishop, Becket found that in all conscience he could no longer act as 'yes man' to his sovereign. Understandably, Henry felt betrayed and thus began two years of wrangling between them (*see* November 2nd). (Urry: *Becket: His Last Days*)

———— •❖• ————

1535: On this day, Sir Thomas More wrote from the Tower of London to his daughter, Margaret Roper, in Canterbury, to explain why he could not accept Henry VIII's 'Act of Supremacy', which declared the King as the head of the Church of England. As a Catholic, it was a matter of conscience for Thomas. (Albin: *Thomas More and Canterbury*)

June 4th

1783: 'Thomas Frost and Catherine, his wife, have eloped and left their children chargeable to the parish of Chartham, near Canterbury. The said Thomas Frost wears his own black straight hair, is of a brown complexion, about 5ft 7in high. He is supposed to be in Thanet, or some other part of East Kent. Catherine, his wife, is of a dark complexion, middle-sized and thought to be in Rochester.' (*Kentish Gazette*)

———•◆•———

1942: Prince George, the Duke of Kent, visited Canterbury to boost morale after the devastating Baedeker raid of June 1st. He inspected the war-torn city in the company of the Mayor, Charles Lefevre, and the Dean, Hewlett Johnson. As he walked around, gutted buildings in St Margaret's Street were already being demolished. (Crampton: *The Blitz of Canterbury*)

———•◆•———

1999: On this day, a human skeleton was uncovered by workmen in the basement of The Biz nightclub in Station Road East. Accordingly someone from the Canterbury Archaeological Trust was summoned. Unfortunately, upon arrival, he found that all the bones had been removed by the site's foreman, who claimed to be an avid *Time Team* viewer. Consequently, with the context destroyed, no information could be gleaned. (CAT Annual Report, 1999-2000)

June 5th

1781: On this day, an order was made to part-demolish the Tudor red-brick City Gate, known as the Burgate. This involved the removal of the centre section with its arches, plus all the structure above which, by this time, had become a dwelling. To remain, at least for now, would be the flanking octagonal towers.

———•◆•———

1808: During this night, an infamous and eccentric Canterbury woman known as 'Bad Betty Bolaine' died after complaining of feeling unwell. She was eighty-two. As a young woman, Betty had inherited money and, as she loved the good life and dressed provocatively, attracted many suitors as a result. However, these young men were ruthlessly exploited financially. In later life, Betty found herself rich but alone, yet she still sponged from others rather than spend her own money. (Courtesy of H.S. Cousins)

———•◆•———

1933: Bigberry Woods, near Canterbury, were the scene of a devastating fire on this day (Whit Monday), which destroyed six acres of undergrowth. The recent hot and rainless weather had made the undergrowth very dry and the flames spread quickly. The fire brigade, who were taking part in the South Eastern District Fire Brigade's Tournament, had to be summoned back from Bexley Heath! (*Kentish Gazette*)

June 6th

1786: 'James Taylor, labourer of the parish of Thannington, was convicted before Edward Toker Esq. in the penalty of 10d, charged on the oath of William Tyler, victualler, with having – on Saturday night last – been found in his gardens and there maliciously broke and destroyed eight cabbages.' (*Kentish Gazette*)

———◆———

1810: On this day, a meeting was held to discuss a proposed canal to Canterbury. Known as the 'Kent Canal', its planned route bisected St Dunstan's near the church and then ran eastwards, keeping north of the River Stour. At Grove Ferry, the canal would turn northwards and reach the coast halfway between Reculver and Birchington. The plans had petered out by 1824.

———◆———

1948: Richard Sinclair, principal figure of the Canterbury Scene, was born in the city on this day. Richard came from a long line of artistic Canterbury Sinclairs. An ancestor of his once traded at No. 101 Northgate Street as 'Richard Sinclair & Son – Photographers'. He was a founder member of the 'Wilde Flowers', and would later feature in bands such as 'Caravan', 'Camel' and 'Hatfield and the North'. Until recently Richard and his family lived in Roper Road, but they are now resident in Italy.

June 7th

1832: On this day, the *Kentish Gazette* reported: 'Two youths named Arthur Cuthbert, the younger, and Stephen Green were committed to the "City" gaol on suspicion of stealing poultry from various persons. The prisoners will undergo further examinations on Thursday next at the Guildhall, when any person who has lost poultry had better attend in order to identify their property.'

———— • • • ————

1880: Born on this day in Blean Workhouse to Emily Curd, of the parish of St Stephens, an illegitimate daughter baptised (in the workhouse) Alice, Elizabeth. (Author's archive)

———— • • • ————

1896: Born on this day in Blean Workhouse to Eliza Noakes, of the parish of Hackington, a legitimate son (no name recorded). (Author's archive)

———— • • • ————

2009: On this day a pivotal figure in the Canterbury Scene, Hugh Hopper, died after a relatively short illness. Born in Canterbury on 29 April 1945, Hugh would go on to play in the highly influential Soft Machine before quitting to produce a string of consistently groundbreaking solo albums. He married his long-time partner, Christina, only hours before his death. [*Author's note*: Forever modest and generous, Hugh was one of the most decent blokes I've ever known and it is to his memory that this book is dedicated.]

June 8th

1378: On this Trinity Sunday, the Black Prince died after a long illness. Accounts describe him as being 'bloated and distorted by disease'. Others talk of him having contracted leprosy. His will, made the previous day, directed that his body be buried in Canterbury Cathedral, in the crypt Chapel of Our Lady Undercroft. However, this 'last request' would be disregarded (*see* September 29th).

———◆———

1660: From the diary of Samuel Pepys: 'Out early, took horses at Deal. Dined at Canterbury. I saw the Minster [cathedral] and the remains of Becket's tomb'.

———◆———

1733: The vast number of people labouring under disorders of sight and hearing, that this week assembled to attend Mr Taylor, is the subject of most conversations. And among his instances of success, he recovered to sight a young gentleman who was born blind. (*Kentish Post or Canterbury Newsletter*)

———◆———

1954: At about 10 p.m. on this night, fire broke out on the third floor of Hooker's Mill, also known as Westgate Mill, on The Causeway. Being largely made of timber, the whole water mill was quickly ablaze. As a result, tenders that had been summoned from Canterbury were supplemented by those from Sturry, Bridge and finally Dover. (*Kentish Gazette*)

June 9th

1023: On this Monday, under the personal protection of King Cnut (Canute), the body of murdered Archbishop Alphege was brought back to Canterbury and solemnly buried in the cathedral (*see* April 19th). (Babbington: *Romance of Canterbury Cathedral*)

———◆———

1791: On this Thursday at noon, the first foundation stones of the new Kent and Canterbury Hospital were officially laid. The site chosen was on the north side of Longport, in an area once used as the lay cemetery for St Augustine's Abbey. (Marcus Hall *et al*: *KCH 1790 to 1987*, *see* April 26th)

———◆———

1809: During the thunderstorm about noon on this Friday, Mr Springate of Wincheap Street, Canterbury, being out on his land at Tyler Hill, was struck down by lightning, which singed his hair and, at the same time, killed a sheep close at his heels. (*Kentish Gazette*)

———◆———

1938: Pennies collected week after week by two small boys, Gordon and Ivan Carnell, enabled the whole of New Town Street (*see* November 14th) to have a sit-down tea party in the street on this Thursday to celebrate the King's birthday. The Mayor and Mayoress of Canterbury were guests of honour. (This was George VI's 'official birthday'; his real birthday was December 14th.)

June 10th

1381: On this day, Wat Tyler's rebel army marched to Canterbury. Having prayed in the cathedral and left it undamaged, they stormed over to the Archbishop's Palace, which they plundered and vandalized. However the Archbishop, Simon of Sudbury, was safe in London, at least for now (*see* June 14th). (Bateman: *Hail, Mother of England*)

1538: Henry VIII had issued a writ asking Thomas Becket to appear and answer certain charges (*see* April 24th) but as the sainted Archbishop had been dead for 368 years, it was hardly surprising he did not show up. Nevertheless, this gave the King all the excuse he needed, for on this day judgement was given in favour of Henry II. It was decreed that Becket's bones be burnt, and his world-famous shrine (with its gold and jewels) be forfeit to the Crown (*see* 31st August). (Home: *Canterbury*)

1886: On this Thursday evening, a tricycle race in connection with the Canterbury Cycle Club took place at the Wincheap Athletic Grounds. There were four entries and the race resulted: '1 – Allen (scratch), 2 – Miskin (50yd start), 3 – Solly (100yd start), 4 – Smith (50yard start). Distance one mile; time 3 minutes 45 seconds'. (*Kentish Gazette*)

June 11th

1669: On this day, Barbara, the widow of Canterbury historian William Somner, received a receipt of £100 8s following the sale of her late husband's book and manuscript collection to the Cathedral Library. She was obviously gratified that this valuable and irreplaceable collection had found a secure home (*see* June 23rd). (Sparks *et al*: *Canterbury Cathedral*)

1787: The Canterbury Pavement Commissioners issued a list of some forty properties in the main street that would need to undergo drastic alterations in order to satisfy their brief (*see* April 23rd). Consequently, protruding windows would need to be removed entirely, with others greatly reduced in size. Projecting signs were also prohibited. (Panton: *Canterbury's Great Tycoon*)

1833: 'A caution to traders': The shop of Mr Campbell, tailor, in Palace Street, was robbed of two black coats and one blue jacket at about nine in the morning by some person or persons unknown. (*Kentish Gazette*)

1951: On this Monday, the 'Canterbury Exhibition' opened on the heavily bombed Whitefriars site off St George's Street. With surviving walls from the medieval friary as its backdrop, this 'Festival of Britain' exhibition gave a history of Canterbury, as well as unveiling its future plans (*see* September 12th). (Crampton: *Yesterday's Whitefriars*)

June 12th

1836: 'The Commissioners of the Canterbury Pavement met to discuss the proposition to enter upon a new lease to supply the town lamps with gas for a period of twenty-one years. The meeting was adjourned, but it is sincerely hoped that they will come to such an arrangement as will reduce the excessive charge now made upon the tradespeople for the private supply of gas.' (*Kentish Gazette*)

———◆———

1914: Councillor Thomas Burren was summoned before the Mayor (Mr George Mount), Mr Silas Williamson and Mr E.G. Hammond at Canterbury Police Court on this Friday for keeping four carriages without having taken out licences for them. (*Kentish Observer*, courtesy of Tina Machado)

———◆———

1942: On this Friday, architect and war-damage assessor for Canterbury Anthony Swaine undertook a detailed survey of the burnt-out shell of St George's Church, which had been a victim of the terrible Baedeker raid of June 1st. He made measured drawings of the entire structure, finding it to be largely sound and capable of repair or restoration. His recommendation was that the building be 'put in splints', especially the ancient medieval tower, to await a resurrection once peace had been declared (*see* June 16th). (Author's archive)

June 13th

1555: The reading of all books written by Protestant theologian Thomas Beacon was banned under threats of severe punishment. Later, under Elizabeth I, he was made a 'Six Preacher' for Canterbury Cathedral. (Ingram Hill: *The Six Preachers*)

1625: On this Friday, King Charles I consummated his marriage with Princess Henrietta of France at the Royal Palace in Canterbury (the former St Augustine's Abbey). Having earlier met her at Dover, the Royal couple married in Canterbury that same day.

1888: During this Wednesday night, some commotion was caused by a fire in Hawks Lane. It appears that a rubbish heap became ignited in the cellar of a house occupied by ex-town sergeant Mr Wilkinson. The fire was quickly put out, the cellar being flooded up to a depth of 2ft. (*Kentish Gazette*)

1910: On this day, writer Virginia Woolf wrote to friends from The Moat House, Blean, near Canterbury. She was recuperating here in the company of her sister, the painter Vanessa Bell, and brother-in-law, the writer Clive Bell, following a major mental breakdown. To Saxon Sydney-Turner, she wrote: 'The rain falls, and the birds never give over singing, and hot sulphur fumes rise from the valleys'.

June 14th

1170: On this day, Henry II had his son, Prince Henry, crowned as his successor in his own lifetime, to ensure the Royal succession. Coronations had always been the sacred duty of the Archbishop of Canterbury, but with Thomas Becket in exile (*see* November 2nd) this was impossible. Instead, Henry coerced Archbishop Roger of York to perform the ceremony, assisted by Jocelin, Bishop of Salisbury, and Gilbert Foliot, Bishop of London. When news of the coronation reached Becket in France, he was outraged and, soon, the three participating bishops would have course to regret their involvement (*see* July 22nd). (Urry: *Becket: His Last Days*)

1381: On this day, the Archbishop of Canterbury and (more to the point) Lord Chancellor of England, Simon of Sudbury, was brutally murdered by Wat Tyler's rebel hoards at Tower Hill, London (*see* June 10th). Sudbury's Poll Tax, raised as Chancellor, had been a catalyst for the Peasants' Revolt. His severed head, with the Archbishop's mitre nailed to it, was displayed on London Bridge. His body (with a canon ball substituting for the missing head) was later buried in Canterbury Cathedral. The head was duly returned to Simon's native village, Sudbury in Suffolk, where it remains today.

June 15th

1590: On this day Margaret Marlowe, sister of playwright Christopher Marlowe, married John Jordan, a tailor, at St Mary Breadman Church in the High Street, Canterbury. She lived to be seventy-six years old. (Urry: *Marlowe and Canterbury*)

———•◆•———

1795: On this Monday, the Archbishop of Canterbury, John Moore, visited the new Kent and Canterbury Hospital in his role as its president. His Grace 'was pleased to express the highest approbation both as to the healthiness of the situation, and the cleanliness and neatness remarkable therein'. (Marcus Hall *et al*: *KCH 1790 to 1987*)

———•◆•———

1850: A monumental inscription inside St Dunstan's Church: 'In memory of the Rev. John Bowes Bunce, 49 years Vicar of this parish: he was also… Master of Eastbridge Hospital. After a lengthened term of service in his sacred calling, the duties of which he most zealously discharged, he died at Harbledown on 15th June 1850.'

———•◆•———

1933: 'The presence of a large number of butterflies has been noticed in many districts this season, so that attacks of caterpillars on plants of the cabbage tribe are not unlikely later in the year. A watch should therefore be kept for early signs of damage so that plants may be treated.' (*Kentish Gazette*)

June 16th

1833: 'Waxing Lyrical': 'Madame Tussaud's unrivalled exhibition has been the grand scene of attraction during this week in Canterbury. It would be difficult to attempt a description of this exquisite production of genius and art. The figures are inimitable – many of them attired so closely after real life and placed in such natural positions as to be indistinguishable from the visitors themselves.' (*Kentish Gazette*)

———◆———

1867: A former churchwarden of St Mildred's registered his dissatisfaction upon revisiting his church two years later: 'During my period in office, I ordered that the churchyard be planted with trees and shrubs. This was done admirably, and they were all protected by lathes and stakes. Now though, the state of the beautiful plantation is most lamentable. The whole are destroyed by forty hungry sheep having been turned into the churchyard by a butcher, and every tree has been peeled like an osier.' (*Living in Victorian Canterbury*)

———◆———

1942: On this Tuesday, the authorities attempted to demolish the gutted shell of St George's Church (*see* June 12th). Having failed to topple the tower by knocking out its south-east corner, demolition was begun from the top. Fortunately, Canon Crum noticed and personally intervened to stop it (*see* March 3rd).

June 17th

1876: 'Cathedral Fire': On this Saturday, great excitement was caused in the city by rumours that the cathedral was on fire. Workmen, cleaning the clock mechanism in the south-west tower, were using benzoline, and a lamp being used for illumination ignited it. This spilt onto the wooden floor, spreading the fire. Fortunately, hoses were promptly run from a nearby hydrant (provided since the fire of 1872, *see* September 3rd) and the blaze was quickly brought under control. Sadly though, a workman burnt in the fire died of his injuries a few days later. (*Living in Victorian Canterbury*)

———◆———

1884: 'Cathedral Ire': 'Many complaints have reached us in regard to the treatment the public receive at the cathedral on the occasion of any special service there. The scenes that take place are unseemly and are not unattended with danger. The Dean and Chapter can, with very little difficulty, remedy the present state of things, which is highly inconvenient and unsatisfactory to everyone concerned.' (*Kentish Gazette*)

———◆———

1965: On this Thursday, it was agreed that the Simon Langton Boys' Grammar School take part in an experimental physics course, sponsored by the Nuffield Foundation – the only school in Kent to be so asked. (Author's archive)

June 18th

1178: On this day, a huge meteorite 'hitting the moon' was observed by five citizens of Canterbury and recorded by the monk chronicler of Christ Church Priory, Gervase: 'The young moon was bright with its horns pointing towards the east, when suddenly, behold, its upper horn was divided in two. From the centre of this division, a burning torch sprang up, throwing flames, smoke and sparks far afield. Meanwhile, the lower part of the moon was... writhing like a snake, after which it returned to its natural condition.' (Bateman: *Hail, Mother of England*)

1808: 'Positively the last evening of horsemanship, with a great variety of other performances, will be exhibited this Saturday evening at six o'clock, in a field near St Mildred's Church. Profits arising from this event will be was given to that benevolent institution, the Kent and Canterbury Hospital.' (*Kentish Gazette*)

1914: 'While redecorating the Shakespeare Inn in Butchery Lane last week, an old painting was discovered (on the plaster) over the fireplace in the billiard room which, when uncovered, proved to be a well-preserved portrait of William Shakespeare. The portrait is no 'old master', but is probably over a century old.' (*Kentish Observer*, courtesy of Tina Machado)

June 19th

1557: On this day, a woman from Staplehurst called Alice Benden, together with six others, was burnt at the stake on Martyr's Field for their Protestant faith (*see* January 15th). Prior to the 'slaughter day', Alice had first been incarcerated at Canterbury Castle, but was then transferred to some awful place called the 'Mint Hole'. This was an undercroft adjacent to the Norman Staircase in the north Cathedral Precincts. She was then kept at the Westgate immediately prior to her death. In 1896, workmen at Martyr's Field, Wincheap, found an old pit containing many charred bones and this prompted the erection of the Martyr's Memorial in 1899.

———— ◆ ————

1792: Alderman Simmons was allowed to demolish what remained of the Water Gate, and also the adjacent City Wall at St Radigund's, to help make the foundations for the new Abbott's Mill.

———— ◆ ————

1883: 'William James Taylor, a young man, has been charged with being drunk and refusing to quit licensed premises. He was also charged with damaging a cell at the police station. The prisoner had been previously convicted seven times. He was sentenced to twenty-one days for the first offence and two months for the second.' (*Kentish Gazette*)

June 20th

1663: On this day, Prebendary John Williams of Canterbury Cathedral complained about Nonconformist 'fanatics with cudgels who frightened the countryside' in and around the city. This sort of trouble had been expected following the end of the Puritan Commonwealth period, and the restoration of the High-Church Charles II. (Sparks *et al*: *Canterbury Cathedral*)

———◆———

1941: On this day, Prime Minister Winston Churchill visited Bishopsbourne station on the military-occupied Elham Valley Railway. He had come to see the 'Bosch Buster', a large rail-mounted gun capable of hurling a 6ft shell over twelve miles as an anti-invasion weapon. When test-fired, the gun brought down ceilings and broke windows in the nearby village. (Hart: *The Elham Valley Line*)

———◆———

1969: The Eliot College Summer Ball was held at the UKC on this evening. As the advert said: '9 p.m. to 3 a.m. with bar extension. Geno Washington and the Ram Jam Band, Ainsley Dunbar and the Retaliation, The Yes, Skin Alley, and Blue Notes Steel Band with limbo dancers. With discotheque and lights. Tickets £1 single, 35/- double.' [Note The Yes way down the bill. As Yes, they would become one of the world's biggest 'prog-rock' bands.] (*Kentish Gazette*)

June 21st

1825: At a meeting of the City Council, the fate of the Westgate – the city's last remaining defensive gateway – was finally resolved, by removing the only reason to have it demolished i.e. that it was an impediment to traffic. They resolved that footpaths be formed on each side of the towers (*see* November 19th). There was also talk of roadways being built on both sides, but only the one adjacent to Holy Cross Church was completed. [A story that the Westgate was to be demolished to allow the passage of a circus is entirely without foundation!]

1833: During this Friday evening, two men, owners of a small donkey-hauled wagon, walked over Abbot's Mill Bridge, while the animals dragged the wagon, containing a child, across the stream. Being unguided, the donkeys were soon in deep water. The child immediately jumped from the cart, which was now floating, and would have surely drowned – the owners being intoxicated – but for a young man named Ellis. [Then, access across the Stour was via a narrow, wooden footbridge; horse-drawn vehicles had to use the ford alongside. The present brick bridge would be built in 1840.] (*Kentish Gazette*)

June 22nd

1164: A Bull of Pope Alexander III, issued on this day, forbade St Jacob's Hospital to take in any but lepers, for whom it was founded. This small hospital could once be found at the top end of Wincheap. Today, only a street name – St Jacob's Place – marks its existence.

———— ◆ ————

1318: On this day, some excitement was caused in the city by the arrival in custody (at Canterbury Castle) of no less a person than the grandmother of the wealthy Infanta of Kent, Juliana de Leyburn, who, together with others, had been convicted for receiving Robert Coleman (also known as) Marsh, an outlaw in the county of Kent for divers felonies. Three years after her trial, the King pardoned Juliana on a forfeit of £100. (Gardiner: *The Story of Canterbury Castle*)

———— ◆ ————

1933: At 11 a.m. this Tuesday morning, the sun was shining and Canterbury High Street flocked with shoppers, anxious to complete their purchases before the early closing. By 12.45 p.m., however, the street was deserted! A violent shower of massive hailstones was falling, with rolling peals of thunder heard and vivid lightening seen. Rain fell heavily and just over half an inch was recorded on Mr Lander's meteorological instrument in Puckle Lane. (*Kentish Gazette*)

June 23rd

1670: On this day, a fire in the cathedral's Audit House damaged or destroyed many irreplaceable books and papers, including some of the vast collection so recently purchased from William Somner's widow (*see* June 11th). It was caused by workmen mending the lead on the chamber's roof. Today, only a section of vaulting remains of the Audit House, adjacent to the Treasury. (Sparks *et al: Canterbury Cathedral*)

1770: On Tuesday last, the Archbishop confirmed 414 persons at the cathedral; and on Wednesday his grace held a visitation in St Margaret's Church for the Deaneries of Bridge and Elham, and then confirmed 1,168 persons at the cathedral. [The Archbishop was Frederick Cornwallis, who had been enthroned in 1768. He was also twin brother of the infamous Lieutenant General Edward Cornwallis; thus the twins achieved high office in both Church and State. The Archbishop died in office on 19 March 1783, aged seventy.] (*Kentish Gazette*)

1972: This day saw the release of Soft Machine's fifth album, appropriately entitled *Fifth*. It was the first LP following the departure of key founding member Robert Wyatt, and was probably the last to be considered a true Canterbury Scene record. (Bennett: *Out Bloody Rageous*)

June 24th

1652: On this day, the estate of Lady Margaret Wotton was sequestrated – this being the Commonwealth period, and she being a noted Catholic recusant. A large part of this estate was the former Royal Palace (and abbey) at St Augustine's. Upon its final return to her, Lady Wotton remarked that the place was 'in such great decay that she has a burden rather than a favour'. (Ryan: *Abbey and Palace of St Augustine's*)

1934: Between 800 and 1,000 limbless ex-servicemen, with their wives and children, took part in a 'Service of Remembrance' in the cathedral on this Sunday afternoon, organised by the St Martin Association, which maintains the welfare of limbless ex-servicemen and their dependents. (*Kentish Gazette*)

1942: A service of thanksgiving took place in the cathedral this evening, in gratitude for the building having been spared in the June bombing.

1966: This Friday, the original Canterbury Scene group, The Wilde Flowers, entered the Radio London Music Contest at the Dreamland Ballroom in Margate. With a four-piece line-up of Hugh Hopper, Brian Hopper, Robert Wyatt and Pye Hastings, they played well and came joint-first. Sadly, the promised prize of a test recording never materialised. (Bennett: *Out Bloody Rageous*)

June 25th

1783: 'It is proposed to open a commodious road from Castle Street through the Castle Green to Wincheap, and Mr Balderston has consented to part with his land for that purpose. However, a subscription is necessary to defray the expense and for the future support of the new road.' [The Worthgate once allowed access to the castle grounds, but it had been blocked up in 1548. Following this, the route in and out of town was via Castle Row, Worthgate Place and the Wincheap Gate. The 'new road' was finally completed in 1791. Sadly though, this necessitated removal of the old Worthgate, which was of Roman origin.] (*Kentish Gazette*)

———◆———

1787: On this Monday, the Canterbury Pavement Commissioners ordered that the steps up to the main entrance to the Guildhall be taken away, as soon as possible. This was part of a major undertaking to both straighten and pave the city's main street. Many ancient buildings fell victim to the process (*see* November 29th) and it was something that conservationists would doubtless balk at today. However, at the time, the transformation of the streets from medieval to Georgian was widely praised. (*Archaeologia Cantiana*, 1988)

June 26th

1727: In his will, dated this Thursday, Philip Bostock Weston left a legacy of forty marks (£26 3s 4d) to buy a silver plate for the communion table at Canterbury Cathedral. (Gostling: *Walk*)

———— • ◆ • ————

1883: On this Tuesday, the *Kentish Gazette* reported: 'An infant named Wickenden from Ivy Lane was being lifted from the floor when its head came into contact with a pair of scissors, which inflicted severe wounds. The child was taken to Kent and Canterbury Hospital at Longport (mercifully only a matter of yards away) where its injuries were attended to.'

———— • ◆ • ————

1891: A new burial ground next to the existing church at Westbere, near Canterbury, was consecrated on this day by the Bishop of Dover. (Butler: *Village Views*)

———— • ◆ • ————

1956: The site of two recently demolished cottages (at Nos 1a and 2 Pound Lane) became the subject of debate by the City Council on this day. A second-hand car dealer had been refused permission to display old cars on this tiny rubble-strewn area, and he was appealing against the decision. Refusal was maintained, but photographic evidence shows that factotum car auctions did actually take place on the site, either shortly before or just after this Council hearing! (Author's archive)

June 27th

1794: Stephen Watson (aged sixteen), in climbing upon some of the ruinous part of St Ethelbert's Tower, belonging to the monastery of St Augustine, in search of birds' nests, unfortunately fell down upwards of 30ft and broke both his thighs. He was taken up in great agonies and immediately conveyed to the adjacent Kent and Canterbury Hospital, where the fractures were set. There are favourable hopes of his recovery. (*Kentish Register*; courtesy of Tina Machado)

1808: 'During this Monday evening, the ingenious Quantrell gave his first exhibition of fireworks for this season on the Bowling Green of the Old Palace. The great variety and brilliance of his display, together with its correctness, secured to him that approbation which he generally receives.' [The former Bowling Green area is now largely occupied by Shirley Hall, being part of the King's School.] (*Kentish Gazette*)

1935: On this day, Mary Tourtel's Rupert Bear strip appeared in the *Daily Express* for the last time. She had been forced to retire due to persistent eye trouble. Mary then became a long-term resident of the Baker's Temperance Hotel, in St George's Street (*see* March 15th). (Stewart: *The Rupert Bear Dossier*)

June 28th

1758: 'An Announcement'; 'To be sold at prime cost or under, until all is sold, next door to the sign of the Two Bells in St George's, Canterbury, the remaining stock in trade of Thomas Dodd, consisting of superfine and other broad cloths, German Serges, Beaver Coatings, Duffils, Napt Bays, Shalloons, Paduafway and Mantle Serges, Worsted Demasks, Everlastings, Hair Shags, Camblets, Cambleteens, Yard Wides, and Fustians, Striped and Plain Flannels, Coach and Livery Laces, and some Whalebone.' [The Two Bells pub was indeed in St George's Street, 'not far from the gate'. It was first mentioned in 1684 and closed in around 1804.] (*Kentish Post*)

1848: St Augustine's Missionary College was opened on this day, utilising a mixture of original domestic buildings surviving from the former abbey and new ranges built in the Gothic style. With access through the medieval Findon Gate, it is occupied by the King's School today.

1963: Appearing before Canterbury magistrates on this day was a thirty-nine-year-old man who, as an accountant with the department store Riceman's, in St George's Lane, was charged with embezzling over £300 from his employers during the previous November. (Author's archive)

June 29th

1933: 'Messrs Court Bros (Furnishers) Ltd, of Burgate, have turned what was at first just an uninteresting piece of property into the ideal showrooms. Anyone will be able to stroll through the beautifully arranged garden and examine, at their ease, the displays of all kinds of furnishings that will be on view.' (*Kentish Gazette*)

1942: On this Monday, Canterbury architect and war-damage assessor Anthony Swaine personally prevented the ancient Flying Horse Inn, at Upper Bridge Street, from being demolished. On passing the pub, which Anthony knew had suffered only minor blast damage, he noticed men on the roof throwing tiles down onto the road. He asked them what they were doing, and one replied, 'Oh, we're demolishing it mate!' Luckily, at that moment, Tony saw the senior war-damage assessor, Mr Tomlinson, nearby and called him over to stop the work. (Crampton: *Canterbury After the Blitz*)

1960: At a Council meeting on this day, a councillor was accused of being sarcastic. When Councillor Wilson asked if the plans of new properties to be erected at Military Road were available, Councillor Brown replied that they were, but he did not know whether the member would understand them! (City Council records)

June 30th

AD 888: The Saxon Archbishop of Canterbury, Aethelred, died on this day. Like so many Archbishops who would succeed him, he had run-ins with the King over ecclesiastical matters – in his case, no lesser a figure than King Alfred the Great. Aethelred also had to contend with the aftermath of regular Viking raids in Kent, with Canterbury having been sacked in around AD 850.

———◆———

1884: At a meeting this Monday of the Canterbury School Board, the following report was read: 'The managers of the Board Schools are unanimous in recommending that the School Board (1) discontinue the practice of making a certain proportion of the money earned by the school part of the teachers' salaries and (2) to pay each teacher in lieu thereof a fixed sum annually'. (*Kentish Gazette*)

———◆———

1950: On this Friday, three men were sentenced to short prison terms for the theft of lead from an empty property called 'Pyrehill' at the top of Puckle Lane. Samuel Reid (aged forty-six) of No. 17 St Radigund's Street, Robert Haynes (aged fifty-three) of No. 65 Edgar Road and 'J.T.' of No. 313 Sturry Road (aged twenty-four) had all pleaded not guilty to the charges. Later, the property involved would become a Council-run retirement home. (Author's archive)

July 1st

1535: On this Monday, Sir Thomas More was tried for treason in Westminster Hall (*see* April 17th). He was found guilty and sentenced to a traitor's death, i.e. to be hanged, drawn and quartered. (Albin: *Thomas More and Canterbury, see* July 5th and 6th)

1833: On this Monday, 'Sir William Courtenay' was due to appear at the Guildhall, Canterbury, at 10 a.m. to answer the theft charge. Hundreds began to throng round the Guildhall and shopkeepers, remembering the earlier riots, promptly closed for the day. The pandemonium inside was just as bad, ultimately forcing the case to be adjourned. However, Courtenay was tried for perjury at Maidstone on July 25th and sentenced to three months' imprisonment (*see* October 27th). (Rogers: *The Battle of Bossenden Wood*)

1949: On this Friday the rebuilt cathedral organ was reopened by Sir John Stainer, who gave the inaugural recital. Work had begun as early as 1938, and some pipes were transported to the organ works of Messrs Henry Willis in Brixton, during 1940. Sadly, with work at an advanced stage, the Willis premises were destroyed in an enemy raid on 21 April 1941. All its contents, including those from Canterbury, were lost. (Friend's Report, 1950)

July 2nd

1145: Medieval Canterbury monk Gervase, a noted chronicler, tells us that on this day the church at St Gregory's Priory, Northgate, burnt down. This was part of Lanfranc's original foundation (*see* May 28th). From 1989 to 1991, a large archaeological investigation revealed burnt residues on part of the church site. The fire is thought to have heralded a major rebuilding of the priory. (*Archaeologia Cantiana*, 1990)

1521: On this day, William Roper of the manor of St Dunstan in Canterbury married Margaret, the eldest daughter of Sir Thomas More (*see* June 3rd). He was thought to have been about twenty-three at the time. William gradually became absorbed into Sir Thomas' household and, under this influence, eventually returned to the Catholic faith. Back in Canterbury, nothing remains of the Roper family house, but its ornate Tudor-brick gateway survives today.

1934: On this Monday afternoon, the first air pilgrimage to the cathedral was made. Lord and Lady Londonderry and their daughter, Lady Marie Stewart, arrived in the morning in a Hawker Moth and a Leopard Moth, the latter piloted by Flight Lieutenant Hawntrey. Lady Londonderry and her daughter remained to welcome the air pilgrims at Bekesbourne Aerodrome. (*Kentish Gazette*)

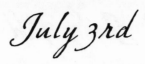

July 3rd

1733: On this Friday, a coachman was publicly whipped behind his coach for being saucy to a gentleman. (*Kentish Post or Canterbury Newsletter*)

———◆———

1883: 'We understand that the greater part of the new organ for Canterbury Cathedral will be placed in the triforium, but some portion will be over the screen in the south aisle. The idea of placing the organ over the rood screen has, we are glad to say, been entirely abandoned. The organ was opened on 30 July 1886.' (Friend's Report, 1950)

———◆———

1964: It has been announced that Canterbury Technical College is to expand its Home Management and Catering Department, previously called 'Women's Subjects'. The department deals with cookery and needlecrafts. It will continue to work at the Longport [old hospital] premises for some years, until the second phase of the Technical College is built and ready for occupation. (Author's archive)

———◆———

2001: During this night the City Arms pub, at No. 7 Butchery Lane, was badly damaged by fire. Three adjacent properties were also devastated. As this old timber-framed building was Grade II listed, great care was taken in the aftermath to record and protect what survived, to aid the rebuilding process. (CAT Annual Report, 2001-2002)

July 4th

1360: King John II of France passed through Canterbury on his return home following over three years of captivity (*see* April 19th). This time, he visited the Greyfriars and gave them 25 nobles (£8 6s 8d). (Cotton: *The Greyfriars of Canterbury*)

———◆———

1958: 'Flies Undone': The following report appeared in the *Kentish Gazette* on this day: 'Canterbury – the pivot of hellfire corner in the Second World War – is in the front line again. Its 30,000 inhabitants this time are declaring war on their own account. Every household is to spend one week in conducting a personal battle against the housefly – the common enemy on the home front. The battle cry will be "kill flies". This domestic fight is going to make modern history, for Canterbury will be the first local authority in Britain to organise a Kill Flies Week.' (*Kentish Gazette*)

———◆———

1962: The future development of the whole of the former Elham Valley Railway line, recently acquired by the Council, was being currently determined by the chief officers. At this time, the embankment immediately south of the main A28 road through Wincheap was being dug out and transported to form the embankment for the Rheims Way, adjacent to St Mildred's Church. (City Council records)

July 5th

1349: On this day, the parish of St John the Poor – whose church was 'coming to ruin' – was united with the adjacent parish of St Mary de Castro. Today, nothing remains of St John the Poor, off Marlowe Avenue, except the name of the street, St John's Lane, whose junction is opposite the site of the lost church. Only the churchyard of St Mary de Castro remains, off Castle Street. (Hasted: *Kent*, Vol. XI)

◆

1535: On this Friday, the condemned Sir Thomas More (*see* July 1st) wrote the last letter to his daughter Margaret Roper regarding his execution, which he hoped would take place the following day (*see* July 6th). By this time, More must have learned that Henry VIII had commuted the terrible death sentence to one of beheading which, although it doesn't sound like it, was a considerable act of mercy. (Albin: *Thomas More and Canterbury*)

◆

1934: William Nash, of Herne Bay, was cycling in Palace Street during this Thursday night when, in avoiding an approaching car, he swerved and struck Sydney Brown of No. 59 Northgate Street and knocked him through the window of Mr Hambley's butcher's shop at No. 20 The Borough. Fortunately, neither was hurt. (*Kentish Gazette*)

July 6th

1349: On this Friday, a soldier in Colonel Tittcombe's regiment was shot for desertion in the nether Dane John [the former moated area outside the City Wall] and was buried at the same place. (Bateman: *Hail, Mother of England*)

———◆———

1535: On this Saturday, Sir Thomas More was beheaded at the Tower of London. One account says that his family had not been given permission to witness the execution, whereas another has Margaret Roper pushing her way through the soldiers in order to kiss her father for the last time. His severed head was later displayed on a pole at London Bridge. This, however, was not the end of the tale (*see* July 20th).

———◆———

1983: A gap in historians' knowledge of old Canterbury has been filled with the discovery of some eleventh-century remains. The cellars and foundations of outbuildings connected with St Sepulchre's Nunnery were revealed during building work on two new houses in Cossington Road. The nunnery was dissolved in 1537 (*see* February 23rd). [Although no actual buildings remain today, demolition material can still be found in walls across the site, particularly those fronting Old Dover Road.] (*Kentish Gazette*)

July 7th

1220: On this Tuesday, the remains of Archbishop Thomas Becket were translated with much pomp from his 'temporary' tomb in the Eastern Crypt to a magnificent shrine designed to be the centre point of the cathedral's new Trinity Chapel. The eastern arm of the cathedral had been extensively rebuilt following the fire of 1174 (*see* September 5th).

———— • ◆ • ————

1450: On this Sunday, John Freningham, a butcher from the parish of St Andrew in Canterbury, together with others, was pardoned for having taken part in Jack Cade's rebellion. Basically, this was a rerun of the Peasants' Revolt of 1381 (*see* June 10th) albeit a little more politicised. (Cotton: *The Greyfriars of Canterbury*)

———— • ◆ • ————

1933: Many Canterbury residents recently saw and heard a Scottish piper soliciting alms in the streets. There was a sequel to his activities at a special sitting of the City Police Court when James Donnelly, of no fixed abode, was charged with being drunk and disorderly in St Margaret's Street. His associate, Donald MacDonald, of no fixed abode, was charged with obstructing PC Arnold while in the execution of his duty. Donnelly was fined £1 and the charge against MacDonald was dismissed because of insufficient evidence. (*Kentish Gazette*)

July 8th

1784: On this Thursday, the new organ in our cathedral, built by Mr Samuel Green, was opened by Dr Phillip Hayes. The placing of the organ over the entrance to the choir has produced that happy effect so long wished for by almost every admirer of this ancient and magnificent structure. This was, in fact, the cathedral's third great organ, although not everyone was a fan. Robert Lloyd described it as a 'Georgian monster' in a 'hideous and heavy case'. This particular organ did not last long (*see* July 3rd). (Cathedral Chronicle, 1986)

———— ◆ ◆ ————

1884: As Mr Ayre, the Canterbury postmaster, accompanied by his son and clerk, Mr T.F. Bing, was driving in a landau along Sturry Road on this Tuesday, one of the wheels came in contact with a roadside post. The carriage was overturned and the horse was stunned. Mr Ayre and the driver were precipitated to the ground. The former escaped with a shaking, but the driver was cut about the face and hands. (*Kentish Gazette*)

———— ◆ ◆ ————

2007: On this day, the English leg of the Tour de France concluded in Canterbury. The finishing line was on the Rheims Way, where 'Cyclists Must Dismount' signs could also be found!

July 9th

1228: The Archbishop of Canterbury, Stephen Langton, died on this day. He is most remembered for dividing the Bible into books, chapters and verses, and also for presiding over the translation of Becket's tomb in 1220 (*see* July 7th). His own tomb, in St Michael's, or the Warrior's Chapel, is half-inside and half-outside, having been pushed forward to make way for the elaborate triple-tomb of Lady Margaret Holland and her two husbands.

———•◆•———

1652: On this Tuesday, a committee was appointed by Parliament in order to select cathedrals for demolition, and it wasn't long before Canterbury Cathedral became the prime candidate. This was the most extreme in a long line of proposals, made by the Commonwealth, designed to wind down and then eradicate the principal place of worship in the Church of England (*see* February 14th). Fortunately, 'the monstrous proposal was never carried into execution'. (*Archaeologia Cantiana*, 1937)

———•◆•———

1913: On this Wednesday, the old windmill at Harbledown was demolished. It stood behind cottages at the top of Mill Lane, which is now part of the London Road Estate. The smock-type mill, having been condemned as unsafe, was pulled down by two traction engines with wires. (Finch: *Watermills and Windmills*)

July 10th

1380: On this Monday, six stonemasons at Canterbury Cathedral were given exemption from jury service for two years as they were busily engaged in the task of rebuilding Lanfranc's original nave into the lofty gothic space we know today. (Blockley: *Canterbury Cathedral Nave*)

1640: On this Tuesday, novelist, playwright and poet Aphra Behn (née Johnson) was born at Harbledown, near Canterbury. She became the first professional woman writer in English history and was buried in Westminster Abbey, although not in Poets' Corner with the male scribes. (Pearse: *Kent Women*)

1854: An early railway excursion to Hastings and Brighton took place on this Monday. Leaving Canterbury (West) at 08.50 a.m., it was due to arrive at Brighton at noon precisely. The cost was: 7s first class; 5s second class; and 3s third class. (*Living in Victorian Canterbury*)

1883: On this Thursday, while Mr Edward Green was in a stable at North Lane, Canterbury, a horse kicked him on the knee. The injury was sufficiently severe to render it necessary for him to keep to his bed for a time. A man named Stace, who was in the stables at the same time, was severely kicked in the chest by the same animal. (*Kentish Gazette*)

July 11th

1952: On, or very near, this day, four unusual cottages at Nos 10-13 Burgate Lane were demolished because they were 'unsafe'. They were unusual in being made entirely from stone. Dorothy Gardiner tells us that they originated as a single building, constructed by Mr Stephen Thornhurst in the 1550s to be used as lodgings. It is likely it was remodelled as four cottages in the early nineteenth century. Thornhurst's 'great house' had itself replaced an earlier building on the site and, presumably, re-used the stone from it. (*Archaeologia Cantiana*, 1952)

———— • ◆ • ————

1989: On this day, a planning application asked for permission to move the old farmhouse at Vale Farm, in the Broadoak Valley, to nearby Tyler Hill, brick-by-brick. This reignited the whole debate over an earlier controversial proposal to build a reservoir in the valley, which local residents of both villages thought had been quietly shelved (*see* February 15th and August 16th). (Author's archive)

———— • ◆ • ————

2000: Former Archbishop of Canterbury Robert Runcie died on this day. He is best known for two key events: officiating at the marriage of Charles and Diana in 1981, and accompanying Pope John Paul II during his visit to Canterbury Cathedral in 1982.

July 12th

1174: On this Friday, Henry II came to Canterbury to do penance at Thomas Becket's tomb (*see* December 29th). Having prayed at the Harbledown leper hospital, the King walked to St Dunstan's Church, where he stripped to his shirt prior to his barefoot walk to the cathedral. On arrival, he kissed the flagstones in the martyrdom transept where Becket's body had lain and then proceeded to his temporary tomb in the crypt. Here, the King was whipped. His act of atonement also included financial restitution to Christ Church Priory. (Urry: *Becket: His Last Days*)

———◆———

1886: On this Monday, after the 8.34 a.m. train from Bekesbourne had left the station, the steel tyre of one of the wheels of the tender broke and made a hole in the water tank. Fortunately, no breakdown occurred and the train arrived safely at Canterbury (East) station. (*Kentish Gazette*)

———◆———

1935: On this Friday, Prince George, the Duke of Kent, laid the foundation stone of the new Kent and Canterbury Hospital (*see* February 28th). The Duke then signed his autograph as 'George' into a slab of wet concrete, which would be built into the hospital's frontage. A documentary 'time capsule' was also buried.

July 13th

1220: The Archbishop of Canterbury, Hubert Walter, died on this day. Unlike many Archbishops, Walter was a friend to the monarchy – both Henry II and Richard I. He also accompanied King Richard on the Third Crusade to the Holy Land, where he helped to negotiate a peace treaty with Saladin. His tomb was the first to be placed in the new Trinity Chapel (*see* July 7th), where it can be seen today. One of the heads carved into the tomb is thought to depict the Muslim and his friend, Saladin.

1932: A memorial slab to Thomas More was laid over the steps to the burial vault of the Roper Chapel, in St Dunstan's Church (*see* January 4th). (Courtesy of Tim Tatton-Brown)

1938: A petrol pump outside Maltby's garage, in New Dover Road, was found to be on fire during this Wednesday evening. The fire brigade was called out but, on arrival, found that the outbreak had been extinguished by the prompt action of A.A. Scout, Mr Day of Tankerton and Mr Moore of Maltby's itself. [The garage, on the corner with Upper Chantry Lane, was taken over by Caffyns Ltd in 1945, who extended it in 1951.] (*Kentish Gazette*)

July 14th

AD 664: The Archbishop of Canterbury, Deusdedit, died on this day. He was the first native-born (Saxon) man to be appointed as Archbishop. His original name was 'Frithona', but he changed it to 'Deusdedit', which means 'dedicated to God'. He probably died of the plague, and was canonised shortly afterwards.

———◆●◆———

1871: Stricter rules were introduced to the Kent and Canterbury Hospital on this day, including: no smoking, drinking or playing cards. (*Archaeologia Cantiana*, 1988)

———◆●◆———

1933: 'Canterbury householders are warned against an ingenious individual who has been operating in Kent. His method is to call upon the lady of the house and inform her that her husband has ordered a fire extinguisher, on which there is 37s 6d to pay. In return for the cash, he hands over a neat parcel. Later when the parcel is opened, there is indeed a 'fire extinguisher', but in the form of a bottle of water.' (*Kentish Gazette*)

———◆●◆———

1937: On this Wednesday, the Duke and Duchess of Kent, Prince George and Princess Marina, opened the new art-deco Kent and Canterbury Hospital complex off Ethelbert Road. Archbishop Cosmo Lang, the hospital patron, was also in attendance. (Crampton: *Canterbury Suburbs and Surroundings*)

July 15th

1567: On this day, the Canterbury Burghmote Court granted permission for a company of Huguenots to settle in the city. These French Protestant 'asylum seekers' greatly enriched the life and culture of Canterbury, bringing with them their cloth-weaving skills and surnames that still resonate today, such as 'Lefevre', 'Delasaux' and even 'Martin'. The 'Strangers' were later allowed to set up a church in the cathedral crypt.

———————•◆•———————

1758: 'At the new cock-pit at Mr Moor's in Lady Wootton's Palace [St Augustine's Abbey], during the time of the races, will be fought a great cock-match, between the Gentlemen of Canterbury and East Kent, against the Gentlemen of Ashford, Hythe and Weald of Kent. They show thirty-one cocks on each side for the match, and eleven for bye-battles, and fight for five guineas a battle and twenty the main; to fight in silver weapons.' (*Kentish Post*)

———————•◆•———————

1942: On this day, the War Damage Commission inspected the cathedral (*see* June 1st) and, within days, had granted £2,000 to be spent on urgent, emergency repairs that would otherwise cause further deterioration if not tackled immediately. This included strutting up damaged walls of the Chapter House, and Great Dorter. (Cathedral Chronicle, September 1942)

July 16th

1500: On this day, a dispute between the City of Canterbury and Christ Church Priory came to a head over the ownership of a hay meadow. The field in question, called 'The Rosiers', was situated where Westgate Gardens is today. A band of armed 'citizens' stormed out of the Westgate and proceeded to threaten and 'rough up' some monks who were making hay there. (*Canterbury Mayoral Quincentenary*)

1811: On this day, regulations for the new County Prison at Longport were approved. Rule 1 was that the 'gaoler' shall 'on no account receive any fee or gratuity from strangers or others visiting the Gaol'. Rule 11 stated that the aforesaid 'gaoler' shall not 'have any benefit or advantage whatsoever from the sale of any wine, beer or other liquors, used in the Gaol'. (Courtesy of Kinn McIntosh)

1938: 'Miss Baker, of No. 56 Northgate Street, entered a BBC Discovery Competition at the Victoria Pier Pavilion, Folkestone, on this Saturday and won the first prize. She is a singer and impersonates famous film stars, including Irene Dunne and Greta Garbo.' [No. 56 was demolished in the 1950s to provide a car park for the adjacent Model Tavern pub.] (*Kentish Gazette*)

July 17th

1759: A Canterbury Cathedral Six Preacher, Thomas Rymer Junior, died on this day at the age of fifty. He was also Vicar of Shepherdswell, near Dover. As Six Preacher, he had succeeded his father, Thomas Rymer Senior. (Derek Ingram Hill)

———◆———

1954: On this day, newly built three-bedroom, detached houses on the Barton Estate were being offered for sale at 'only' £1,895. Ownership could be secured with a £200 deposit and a monthly mortgage payment of £2 4s 6d with Truscott & Collier in Canterbury High Street. Special features included a 'labour-saving kitchenette, dining recess and garage space'. (Author's archive)

———◆———

1958: An American jet plane crashed during this Thursday afternoon on the edge of a cornfield at Brenley Corner, between Canterbury and Faversham, opposite the Thanet Way Junction. It disintegrated when it hit the ground, wreckage being scattered over a considerable area. Before the crash, the pilot was seen to bale out and drift southwards towards some woods. He was later found at Fishponds, Chartham, and taken to Kent and Canterbury Hospital with minor injuries. [The exact location of the crash is now occupied by the busy interchange with the M2, which opened in 1965.] (*Kentish Gazette*)

July 18th

1783: 'An announcement: To be sold – the two freehold substantial new brick structures, tenements and premises in St George's Street, most eligible for trade, now in the occupation of Mr Stephen Richards, woollen draper and Mr Charles Austen, cutler.' (*Kentish Gazette*)

1949: During this evening, the unmarked grave in the cathedral's Eastern Crypt, possibly containing the bones of Thomas Becket, was discreetly reopened (see January 23rd). Supporters, including King's School headmaster, Canon Shirley, and cathedral archivist, Dr William Urry, were present at the exhumation. Prior to this, the identity of the bones as belonging to Becket was becoming generally accepted. The Dean and Chapter had even asked for plans for a tomb to be drawn up. In the end, further studies cast serious doubt on this assertion and the bones were reburied unmarked. (Butler: *The Quest for Becket's Bones*)

1954: On this day, the new library building at Canterbury Cathedral was officially opened. Occupying the same space as its Blitzed predecessor (*see* January 16th) the new building also incorporated eleventh-century remains of the monastic Great Dorter (or Dormitory), which had miraculously escaped the 1942 bombing. Designed by John Denham, the new library included Romanesque, Tudor and Elizabethan styles.

July 19th

1882: The tiny Presbyterian Chapel in Gas Street closed on this day, having been replaced by a vast brick-built church at nearby Wincheap Green. The chapel, built of flint salvaged from the adjacent City Wall, survived in one form or another until the early 1930s. It was then demolished as part of a scheme to de-clutter the grounds of Canterbury Castle. (Crampton: *Canterbury's Lost Heritage*)

———•◆•———

1883: Favoured by fine weather, the aquatic fete held at the swimming baths on this Thursday in connection with the Canterbury Swimming Club passed off pleasantly. The contests were watched with interest, as the excellent handicapping by Mr G.F. Finn produced some close finishes. [The open-air swimming pool was situated off Whitehall Road, in an area now known as Toddler's Cove. It closed in the late 1940s due to health concerns.] (*Kentish Gazette*)

———•◆•———

1971: On this day, automatic lifting barriers were introduced to the railway level crossing in St Dunstan's. They were only the third such set to be introduced on British Railways. Sadly, the few seconds saved from the previous system of opening and closing the gates made little difference to the traffic chaos in St Dunstan's Street.

July 20th

1535: On this Saturday, Margaret Roper rescued the head of her father, Sir Thomas More, from its pike on London Bridge (*see* July 6th). Setting sail at dawn, her boat was positioned beneath the bridge and she waited for a loyal servant to go up and shake it loose. The head is said to have landed into Margaret's outstretched apron. She soon had it set in a lead casket and carried it with her always. Upon Margaret's death in 1544, Sir Thomas' head was interred with her, at least for the time being, in Chelsea Old Church (*see* January 4th).

———◆———

1652: Canterbury Congregationalist, Sister Susan Godreyes, was suspended from communion because she had 'much sinned in going unto witches to enquire about a husband'. (Taylor: *The Free Churches of Canterbury*)

———◆———

1957: A strike amongst employees of the East Kent Road Car Co. halted all services and the bus station in St George's Lane was completely deserted. There was a good-humoured picket line at the Watling Street exit. This was part of a countrywide pay strike, where £1 per week more had been asked for but only 3s offered. Union chiefs described it as an insult. (Crampton: *Yesterday's Whitefriars*)

July 21st

1671: On this day, Meric Casaubon, Canon of the Dean and Chapter at Canterbury, was buried in the cathedral's south-west transept. He was seventy-five-years old. He had been made a Canon in 1628, at the age of twenty-nine, and became Archbishop Laud's chaplain at the same time (*see* January 10th). Being of High-Church persuasion, he was deprived of all his preferments under Parliament in 1644. However, this did not stop Oliver Cromwell asking him to write a history of the recently fought Civil War in 1649; an offer he steadfastly refused, despite much material inducement. (Friends Report, 1938)

———————◆———————

1838: An accident nearly attended with fatal consequences took place on this Saturday. John Nisbet, carter, in the employ of Mr G. Gambier of this city, had been entrusted by his master to fetch a load of laths from Dover, and on his returning with them incautiously placed himself on the top of the stack. Whilst descending the steep hill near Ewell, his foot slipped and falling, the wheel passed over his body. Surgical aid was immediately procured and he was ultimately conveyed to the Kent and Canterbury Hospital, where he now lies in a very dangerous state. (*Kentish Gazette*)

July 22nd

1170: Henry II met the exiled Thomas Becket in France. Worried that the recent coronation of his son (*see* June 14th) would damage their already strained relations, the King was in a reconciliatory mood, even promising the Regency of England to Becket if he would return. Thomas rejected this offer outright and instead complained about the coronation and the sanctions issued against him following his exile. A stalemate ensued for now (*see* October 14th). However, at about the same time, Becket wrote to the Pope asking that the three bishops who had officiated at Prince Henry's coronation be excommunicated (*see* November 24th). (Urry: *Becket: His Last Days*)

———◆———

1783: On this Tuesday, John Betts, John Shaw and John Pennington were examined by the Mayor and judges at the Guildhall for being in a riotous and disorderly manner early on the previous Tuesday morning, by breaking several knockers and by rendering useless the bell at several houses, as well as being guilty of sundry other misdemeanours. (*Kentish Gazette*)

———◆———

1967: On this Saturday, a former funeral parlour at No. 18 St Radigund's Street was gutted by fire. In June, there had been two further arson attacks in Duck Lane, then being demolished. (Author's archive)

July 23rd

1808: A criminal case is pending, in which a gentleman of extensive property is plaintiff, and a youth under eighteen years – who officiated as footman in the family, and is now a waiter in a hotel – is the defendant. The scene of the adultery is said to have been at a village near Canterbury. There are several witnesses, one of which is said to have had an occular view of the whole proceedings. (*Kentish Post or Canterbury Newsletter*)

———◆———

1873: On this Wednesday, the Dane John Estate was offered for sale by auction at the Fountain Hotel in St Margaret's Street. The estate consisted of 150 acres of farmland stretching from the moat at Pin Hill and then south across the Wincheap area. Much of this area was later redeveloped for housing, and a grid of roads with patriotic names laid out, such as: Gordon, Tudor and Victoria Roads. (The Auction Catalogue)

———◆———

1976: A Gibson guitar worth £250 was stolen on this Friday when it was left for a few minutes by a car outside Radigund's Restaurant, in Church Lane, St Mary's. The owner had briefly popped inside to retrieve some equipment and found it gone upon his return. (Author's archive)

July 24th

1733: A great number of horses are talked of to run for plates on the Barham Downs on this day, and the 25th and 26th of this instant, and besides the plates already advertised, there will be other diversions viz. ponies, Galloways and other horses to run for silver spurs, whips, saddles and money. (*Kentish Post or Canterbury Newsletter*)

1795: On this day, in-patient Mary MacMeish was reprimanded for being abusive to the nurse and other patients at the Kent and Canterbury Hospital. She was also said to be discontent with every assistance she received. (Marcus Hall *et al*: *KCH 1790 to 1987*)

1924: An inspection of the loss-making Elham Valley Railway was carried out on this day, with a view to cost cutting. This eventually led to most of the line being reduced from double to single track. (Hart: *The Elham Valley Line*)

1965: Three thirteen-year-old Scouts from the Kent College Troop, Canterbury, were rescued unhurt in Guernsey during the weekend after being trapped while climbing steep cliffs. One of the Senior Scouts, Roddy Scott, was lowered from the cliff top during the rescue. Meanwhile, one of the trapped boys, Guy Longbottom, managed to climb down and swim to safety. (Author's archive)

July 25th

1765: 'Mozart': 'On this Thursday, at eleven in the forenoon, will be a musical performance at the Town Hall, Canterbury [presumably the Guildhall] for the benefit of Master Mozart, the celebrated German boy, aged eight years, and his sister, who have exhibited with universal applause to the nobility and gentry in London. The compositions and extempore performances of this little boy are the astonishment of all the judges of music.' [The Mozart family left the city on July 31st.] (*Kentish Post*)

———◆———

1883: 'Brahms and Liszt': Joseph Lee, a soldier belonging to the Buffs, was charged with damaging a piano, the property of the proprietor of the Providence Inn, Northgate Street. A man named White, the manager, deposed to seeing the defendant go into the concert room on this day, and he then banged the instrument several times as hard as he could. John Buckle said he was told the piano had been damaged and, on examining it, found about twenty-six hammers and dampers broken and eleven wires completely wrenched out. [The Providence Inn was at No. 102 Northgate Street, on the south corner with Union Street. By 1910, the building had become a butcher's shop.] (*Kentish Gazette*)

July 26th

1884: At the County Court on this Saturday, Susan Hinds, a pauper, was charged with refusing to perform her tasks of work at the workhouse, also with breaking the door, the property of the board of Guardians, and doing damage to the amount of 7s 6d. [Two workhouses covered the Canterbury area: central and southern parishes by the Union Workhouse at the top of Nunnery Fields, and the northern parishes – including: St Dunstan's, St Gregory's and Hackington – by the Blean Workhouse at Herne.] (*Kentish Gazette*)

———◆———

1918: On this day, the First World War fighter ace Major Edward 'Mick' Mannock was shot down and killed by enemy troops. He was the highest-scoring British fighter pilot, shooting down sixty-one German aircraft. Mannock was raised in the Northgate area of Canterbury, and there is a plaque honouring him in the cathedral. In 1957, a block of flats in Military Road was named 'Mannock House'.

———◆———

1969: On this day, the last shift was worked at Chislet Colliery, near Canterbury (*see* December 10th). This was the first of the main East Kent pits to close, and most of the redundant workers moved to other mines in the area. (Llewellyn: *Hersden*)

July 27th

1863: 'Canons Fired': On this day, reforms of the Ecclesiastical Commission came into effect. At the Canterbury Dean and Chapter, the number of Canons Residentiary was reduced from twelve to six, and the old term for Canon, 'Prebendary', in use since 1541, was finally dropped. (Ingram Hill: *The Six Preachers*)

1912: On this day, the Beverley Estate at Hackington was sold by auction at the Royal Fountain Hotel in St Margaret's Street. The manor house in St Stephen's Road and eighteen acres of farmland were sold as two separate lots. Beverley House realised £450. [The site of Beverley Dairy Farm is still open land today, being the playing field across which St Stephen's Pathway runs.] (*Victorian Hackington*)

1933: 'Just before a meeting was due to start at the Friends' Meeting House on this Thursday evening, a large piece of ceiling fell with a resounding crash. Had this occurred a little later, some of those attending would probably have sustained injuries as the seats were covered with large pieces of heavy plaster.' [The Meeting House in Canterbury Lane was destroyed during the June 1942 Blitz. In the 1950s, the Quakers rebuilt it in The Friars.] (*Kentish Gazette*)

July 28th

1733: 'Alcohol…': 'The Old Rose Tavern in St George's, Canterbury, has lately been fitted up and now is in very good repair; where all persons shall find very good entertainment for man and horse. Neat wines also to be sold, viz. white at 5s per gallon or 8d per pint; red 5s 6d per gallon or 9d per pint without doors or with doors 10d a pint each. Note, I shall continue my barber's shop and wig-making by as good a hand as any in London – William Hilles.' [This was the large building on the corner with Rose Lane, later known as the Rose Hotel, which had extensive stabling facilities behind, with access from the lane. It was lost in the Blitz of 1 June 1942.] (*Kentish Post or Canterbury Newsletter*)

1913: '… and its effects'. On this Monday, Barton Gervan, a soldier with the Carabiniers, was charged with being drunk while having control of a horse in The Borough on the previous Saturday evening. PC Deal saw Gervan swaying about, and when he dismounted it was clear he was drunk and quite incapable of taking charge of the horse. (*Kentish Gazette*, courtesy of Tina Machado)

July 29th

1793: On, or very near this day, the 'muro torto' (i.e. twisted wall) was finally demolished. This was the remains of the south-west tower to St Augustine's Abbey. Hitherto, it had survived as a 30ft-high fragment, resting at a crazy angle, where attempts to undermine and then topple it had failed many years before. Much of the north-west tower, the 'Ethelbert Tower', also survived at this time (*see* October 16th).

———◆———

1833: On this Monday, a cricket match was played between twenty-two 'gentleman butchers' of Canterbury in Hopper's Gardens. The ground was visited by a large concourse of spectators who appeared to enjoy the pleasures of the day. That evening, the party partook of an excellent supper at the Prince of Orange. [This inn could once be found in the appropriately named Orange Street.] (*Kentish Gazette*)

———◆———

1913: On this Tuesday afternoon, the funeral of military veteran Thomas Caddington (aged seventy-seven), of No. 38 Union Street, took place at Canterbury Cemetery. He served with the Royal Horse Artillery and was stationed in India for some seventeen years. On returning to Canterbury, he took his discharge and was subsequently appointed canteen steward at the barracks.

July 30th

1538: On this Saturday, the Abbot of St Augustine's Abbey, John Essex (or Foche), met with thirty of his monks in the Chapter House and signed the Deed of Surrender to Henry VIII. [This was part of Thomas Cromwell's widespread Suppression of the Monasteries.] From that fateful day, the abbey, with its site and precincts and all its goods and chattels, passed into the hands of the Crown. Indeed, Henry VIII had plans for the St Augustine's Abbey site (*see* October 5th).

———◆———

1867: On this Tuesday, Canterbury painter Thomas Sidney Cooper was elected to become a Royal Academician. (Courtesy of Brian Stewart)

———◆———

1883: During this Monday morning, a milkman in the employ of Mr Rammell was in charge of a cart drawn by a mule at Northgate. Some soldiers rode down the street and the mule started to follow them. In attempting to stop the animal, the man was knocked down and run over by his own cart. (*Kentish Gazette*)

———◆———

1913: Ginnett's Royal Circus did good business on the occasion of their visit to Canterbury on this Wednesday. The turn given by Miss L. Ginnett with her cowboy pony 'Yankee' was an especially clever feature of the performance. (*Kentish Gazette*)

July 31st

1783: A few days since, the waggoners of Mr Allen, of Westbere, and Mr Goldfinch, of Hoath, were severally convicted of riding their wagons in the highway, near Canterbury, and not having some other person on foot or horseback to guide the same. They were fined the sum of 5s each. (*Kentish Gazette*)

1836: Old Palace Gardens, St Augustine's Abbey, Canterbury: Mr Stanmore (late of Canterbury Theatre) begs most respectfully to inform the inhabitants of Canterbury that these gardens will open on this Tuesday evening, under his direction. (Author's archive)

1913: 'An advert': 'The Old Canterbury Baths, Station Road West, are open 8.30 a.m. to 9 p.m. Private hot and cold baths for ladies and gentlemen 6d, 1 and 2s. These baths of specially pumped spring water will give you health. Visitors should also not miss viewing this quaint house, which is some 600 years old: admission to house and museum, 2d.' In 1906, local builder Walter Cozens dismantled this building from a site in Upper Bridge Street, and brought it to St Dunstan's. As well as the baths, the old building also housed Walter's personal museum collection. Sadly, all was lost in the bombing of the Second World War.

August 1st

1733: 'The very best plain Spanish snuff, of a most delicate flavour – truly old and desirably mellow – is now sold at the printing office in St Margaret's, Canterbury. Sold also: Dr Chamberlain's famous anodyne necklace for breeding children's teeth.' (*Kentish Post or Canterbury Newsletter*)

———◆———

1913: 'Details have been issued in the bankruptcy of Montague Frederick Charles Leech of No. 15 The Borough, tobacconist and music seller, trading as "John Ellis". The creditors to rank for the dividend represent £137 2s 11d, and the net assets are returned at £85 10s 10d. The causes of failure alleged by Leech are "want of capital and pressure by creditors".' (*Kentish Gazette*, courtesy of Tina Machado).

———◆———

1956: Fifty-one books, stolen from the library over a long period, have come into the possession of a local bookseller, who has now returned them. The police have so far been unable to obtain sufficient evidence to start proceedings. (City Council records)

———◆———

1956: Spring Lane United FC will not be allowed to play football matches on the Littlebourne Road children's playground. Whilst sufficient space is available, the touchlines would be so close to the rear gardens of adjoining houses that damage would be unavoidable. (City Council records)

August 2nd

1461: King Henry VI came to Canterbury as a pilgrim with the intention of visiting the Becket shrine. Chronicler monk John Stone writes of him being received by Archbishop Bourchier, and of processions in which Henry walked without a Crown. (Friends Annual Report, 1945)

———— ◆ ————

1913: 'The troop in the Canterbury Garrison will not, we understand, take part in this year's manoeuvres, owing to an outbreak of mange amongst the horses. The Royal Engineers, who returned to Canterbury on Saturday last, and also the Carabiniers, are encamped on the Old Park – and away from the barracks – for the same reason.' (*Kentish Gazette*, courtesy of Tina Machado)

———— ◆ ————

1961: 'A pedestrian shopping precinct has just been completed in a bomb-damaged area close to Canterbury Cathedral. A low group of modern blocks in one, two and four storeys has the cathedral as a background. The blocks are on [the site] where an early nineteenth-century covered market, the Longmarket, stood until the Blitz. Designed by City Architect Mr Berbiers, the exterior walls are in grey-brown or plumb-black bricks, reconstructed Portland stone and panels of silver grey mosaic.' [The Modernist Longmarket was demolished in 1990, *see* April 5th.] (*Daily Telegraph*)

August 3rd

1228: On this day, Walter D'Eynsham, a monk of Christ Church Priory at Canterbury Cathedral, was chosen by his fellow monks to succeed Stephen Langton as Archbishop. However, his appointment was quickly overruled by King Henry III. In addition, Walter was examined by a group of cardinals on theological matters who judged him to have 'answered badly', thus allowing Pope Gregory IX to declare him ineligible for office.

———•◆•———

1880: On this Tuesday, the contents of the large Georgian mansion at Hales Place (St Stephen's, Hackington) were put up for auction by a London firm. The last in the long line of this distinguished Canterbury family, Mary Hales, had been declared insolvent and this was the only course of action that could be taken (*see* April 18th and August 29th). (*Victorian Hackington*)

———•◆•———

1924: Following a short illness, writer Joseph Conrad died on this Sunday morning in a room above the hall at Oswalds (the old Dower House of Bourne Park), at Bishopsbourne, near Canterbury. His funeral took place at St Thomas' RC Church in Burgate, and he was laid to rest in the Catholic section of Canterbury Cemetery, to be found along Westgate Court Avenue.

August 4th

1794: On this Monday, workmen began to take down the ancient round turret attached to the south-east corner of the main tower of St George's Church. It contained a flight of stone steps to its top, crowned with a spire and handsome weathercock, useful and ornamental to the city. In 1787, an arched passage had been opened through it for pedestrians (*see* November 29th) which was supposed to have weakened the building so much that demolition was judged necessary. (*Kentish Register*, courtesy of Tina Machado)

1921: The Kent County War Memorial was unveiled on this day by the Marchioness Camden. The new memorial is the centrepiece of a site within the Cathedral Precincts, known for centuries as the Bowling Green, but now laid out as the Memorial Gardens.

1937: Passengers in a compartment of the 11.40 a.m. train from Ashford to Canterbury on this Wednesday morning had a lucky escape from serious injury when a shower of glass fell into the compartment, about three miles from Canterbury West. The six people in the compartment included two elderly ladies and a young girl who had a shower of glass down her back, but was uninjured. (*Kentish Gazette*)

August 5th

1933: Canterbury's rival art-deco cinemas both opened for the first time on this day. The Friars (Odeon) Cinema, in The Friars, was due to open on the 7th, but the date was brought forward to compete, or clash, with the opening ceremony for The Regal, in St George's Place. The former Friars became the new Marlowe Theatre in the 1980s, retaining its superb period frontage, but this was demolished in 2009 to make way for the refurbished Marlowe. The former Regal is still a cinema, but development plans currently threaten it.

1964: An application for planning permission to construct a bridge over Guildhall Street was refused on this day. This would have linked the Lefevre stores, which existed on both sides of the street, at first-floor level. (City Council records)

1980: Over seventy medieval burials have been uncovered at the west end of the old St Mary Bredin Church, during the third and final stage of the archaeological investigation of the Marlowe car park. Being an inner-city graveyard, many graves had been cut through by later burials and the diggers were sometimes faced with up to six skeletons overlapping each other. (*Kent Herald*)

August 6th

1636: On this Wednesday, Archbishop Laud wrote to admonish the Archdeacon, William Kingsley, for not living in the Prebendal house that had been allocated to him. He should have been living in No. 13 The Precincts (south of the cathedral) but he preferred to reside either at the adjacent No. 11, or at his Rectory in the village of Ickham. Kingsley further infuriated others by extending No. 13, even though he declined to actually live there. (*Archaeologia Cantiana*, 1930)

———◆◆———

1847: On this Friday, Mr W.H. Furley, one of the partners of the Canterbury Bank, High Street, wrote to the Kent and Canterbury Hospital about the problem of bed bugs, which were putting people off from being admitted: 'Surely by a more frequent periodical airing and rubbing over with some mixture, they might be kept under as in private houses'. (Marcus Hall *et al: KCH 1790 to 1987*)

———◆◆———

1939: On the main Canterbury to Whitstable Road, at the foot of Clapham Hill on this Friday, a lorry owned and driven by Spencer King from Lamberhurst Farm, at nearby Dargate, burst into flames. Gas flowing back through the cabin partition is believed to have set fire to the load of hay. (*Kentish Gazette*)

August 7th

1570: On this Friday, three-week-old Thomas Marlowe was buried at St George's Church. He was the sixth child of John and Katherine, and a brother to the dramatist Christopher Marlowe. Thomas had been baptised at the same church on July 26th, shortly after his birth. (Urry: *Christopher Marlowe and Canterbury*)

———— ◆ ————

1795: On this Monday, two women by the names of Jane Wright and Catherine Thompson were committed to the gaol (probably the Westgate) in the City of Canterbury, 'for stealing at various times a large quantity of printed cotton and other goods, from the shops of Mr James Robertson and Mr John Briggs, linen drapers'. (*Kentish Register*, courtesy of Tina Machado)

———— ◆ ————

1886: On every evening during this week, including this Saturday, the streets have been thronged with persons desirous of seeing the illuminations, which have been unusually fine. In addition to the usual lighting up of the Westgate Towers and the Corn Exchange, there was a large and splendid gas star in front of the Guildhall and the Dane John Avenue was illuminated with coloured lamps. (*Kentish Gazette*)

———— ◆ ————

1957: There will now be a copy of 'Family Planning' each month in the reading room of the Beaney Institute. (City Council records)

August 8th

1810: An affray took place in Ruttington Lane, Canterbury, this Friday evening between some soldiers of the Queen's Bays (2nd Dragoon Guards) and the populace; the former having attempted to seize a young man whom they suspected to be a deserter from the Navy. Two of the soldiers were dreadfully wounded with a large knife; the one received two severe cuts in the left breast, and the other in the abdomen. They were both conveyed to the hospital, where they lie without hope of recovery. (*The Gentleman's Magazine*, courtesy of Tina Machado)

———— • ◆ • ————

1940: With the threat of invasion by German forces looming, the Cathedral Chronicle published an article about the problems raised by false alarms of imminent invasion, not in 1940, but in 1324! In that year, Prior Eastry warned about alarm being caused by incoming refugees escaping the war between England and France over Gascony. He requested that 'no one shall be so bold, on pain of imprisonment, as to raise the common cry, or to sound trumpet or blow horn, before the people who are dwelling nearest the sea [at Dover] raise the common cry when they see the enemy on the sea and approaching land'.

August 9th

1794: On this Saturday, a thirty-ton stack of hay belonging to Mr Samuel Balderston of Westgate Court, near Canterbury, caught fire by being carried too green. By the timely assistance of inhabitants, and great activity of the military then quartered in the city, it was happily extinguished, or the consequences might have been worse had it broken out at night and communicated to adjoining stacks and barns. (*Kentish Register*, courtesy of Tina Machado)

———◆◆———

1914: On this Sunday, the Dean, Henry Wace (aged seventy-seven), spoke on 'The Christian Sanction of War' at a cathedral service. He affirmed that the new war with Germany was morally justifiable. However, this must have caused him some personal anguish, having being married for twenty years to a German woman, Cornelia Schmitz. (Sparks *et al*: *Canterbury Cathedral*)

———◆◆———

1933: The bursting of a tyre on this Wednesday caused a car – which was being driven in Sturry Road – to swerve and mount the pavement, partly overturn, strike a wall, right itself and collide with a cyclist, Frank Bolland of No. 3 New Town Street, who was knocked down. He was taken to Kent and Canterbury Hospital and temporarily detained, suffering from abrasions and shock. (*Kentish Gazette*)

August 10th

1660: On this Tuesday, the Dean of Canterbury, Dr Thomas Turner, was finally able to take full possession of the Deanery (*see* January 3rd). Having been close to Charles I, Turner suffered much during the Commonwealth period. He had most of his property seized, and also spent some time in prison. He died in October 1672 at the age of eighty-one. (Hasted: *Kent*, Vol. XII)

———◆———

1832: On this day, *The Times* reported that the Archbishop of Canterbury, William Howley, received a rough reception from the citizens of Canterbury, angry at his opposition to the Reform Act and also because of the high tithes still being exacted by the Church of England. He was booed and hissed, and had various objects, such as cabbage-stalks, hurled at his carriage. Reports say that Howley seemed quite unnerved.

———◆———

1838: The trial began on this Friday of eight men who, as followers of 'Sir William Courtenay', had been present during the carnage of May 31st. In the event two men, Thomas Mears and William Wills, were sentenced to transportation for life; William Price was sentenced to transportation for ten years; and the remainder received one year's imprisonment with hard labour. (Rogers: *The Battle of Bossenden Wood*)

August 11th

1628: On this day, Sir William Roper was buried in the family vault beneath the Roper Chapel, in St Dunstan's Church. He was the grandson of William Roper, the son-in-law and biographer of Sir Thomas More (*see* January 4th). (Tatton-Brown: *Canterbury: History and Guide*)

1871: On this Friday, Alice Amos of Chilham was refused admission as an in-patient to the Kent and Canterbury Hospital on the grounds that she was suffering from 'Primary Syphilis' (*see* May 10th). (*Archaeologia Cantiana*, 1988)

1940: 'Second World War Notebook': This was a record kept by an anonymous Canterbury clerical worker between September and December 1940. The person's office is likely to have been at the Telephone Exchange, in Stour Street. Courtesy of the Local Study Centre, this extract is extremely revealing: '4.50 p.m., Sunday. Saw a Dornier 17 brought down in Rough Common. There was a big air raid on London: saw enemy formation of forty-seven bombers, escorted by over 100 fighters'.

1991: A chronic alcoholic who burgled Cross Street Stores in St Dunstan's, on this day, was completely unable to recall the crime when his case came to court. He did, however, plead guilty and was ordered to pay £130 compensation. (Author's archive)

August 12th

AD 792: The Archbishop of Canterbury, Jaenberht (or Lambert), died on this Wednesday. Jaenberht had also been Abbot of St Augustine's Abbey. During his period of office, a dispute with King Offa saw the establishment of a rival Archdiocese at Lichfield. He greatly offended the Christ Church monks by requesting to be buried at the abbey as opposed to the cathedral.

1884: On this Tuesday, the *Kentish Gazette* reported: 'The magnificent weather, the large attendance and above all, the glorious triumph over the Australians, have contributed to render Cricket Week all that the most sanguine could possibly have hoped for. In recent years, Kent has suffered defeat in the cricket field owing to the want of a really good bowler. This year, the void so long felt has been in some measure supplied.'

1990: East Kent Bus Co. took delivery of ten new double-deckers. Five of these were allocated to Canterbury and, following a competition held at local schools, all received names. They were: 'Odyssey', 'Enterprise', 'Sir Thomas More', 'Pegasus' and 'Thomas Becket'. The names were later removed when Stagecoach swallowed up the company. The buses themselves were finally withdrawn from service in June 2010. (Courtesy of Dave Crampton)

August 13th

1783: 'An Announcement': 'Margaret Christie – scarlet and silk dyer, scowerer in Northgate, Canterbury – thanks the public for all their favours, both before and since her husband's death. She continues to execute the arts of dying and scowering in all their various branches, such as bed-furniture: cleaned and dyed to look as well as ever, gentleman's clothes: cleaned, spots taken out and the colour restored again.' (*Kentish Post or Canterbury Newsletter*)

------◆------

1936: 'Thieves, who apparently gained access via the river, broke into the warehouse of Mr D.V. Charlton – wholesale tobacconist and confectioner – in Stour Street during this Thursday night. They got away with about 70,000 cigarettes, all of one brand. Entrance was effected by smashing windows and a door at the rear of the premises. Police are confident of being able to smoke the thieves out.' (*Kentish Gazette*)

------◆------

1970: Canterbury Scene group Soft Machine played the Proms at the Albert Hall on this day. The four-piece line-up included three ex-Simon Langton Grammar School boys: Mike Ratledge, Hugh Hopper and Robert Wyatt. Before the concert, Robert was denied admission to the hall by an over-zealous doorman who refused to believe that such a 'scruffy Herbert' would be performing there!

August 14th

1837: About ten minutes before ten o'clock on this Monday night, a cry of fire was raised in this city. On inquiry, it appeared to have been emanated from a stable in Water Lane, Westgate (Linden Grove today), in the occupation of Mr Hammond, catching fire. The Kent and Phoenix fire engines were speedily on the spot and in a few minutes the flames were extinguished. [At the time, Canterbury had a number of private fire services: 'Kent' being based at No. 29 High Street and 'Phoenix' at No. 2 Upper Bridge Street.] (*Kentish Gazette*)

———— • ◆ • ————

1990: Early on this day, two young men, both ex-Foreign Legion, attempted to break into the cathedral. Later, they told the magistrates that their true aim had not been burglary, but to prove that the 'temporary' tomb of Cardinal Odet de Coligny (*see* March 24th) actually contained the remains of Thomas Becket. They claimed that this was the real reason why the French authorities – who knew of this hiding place – had never requested the return of the cardinal's body. Shortly afterwards, the *Kentish Gazette* published a letter which further deepened the mystery (*see* September 7th). (Butler: *The Quest for Becket's Bones*)

August 15th

1588: On this day, Catholic priest Christopher Buxton was executed at Canterbury for his faith. When he was led to the scaffold, he was offered membership of the Protestant Church but refused. Only thirty years before, Canterbury had been the grizzly scene of many burnings, by Catholic prosecutors, of people who had refused to give up their Protestant faith (*see* January 15th). (Green: *Saints of Canterbury*)

1914: An interesting case came before the Canterbury City Bench when George Hills, formerly of Canterbury, was charged with obtaining 6d by fraud by falsely representing himself to be a person appointed for the billeting of troops. He had been from house to house in Wincheap stating to residents that he was billeting a Scottish regiment. As a result, a large number of houses made preparations for the reception of the men and were considerably inconvenienced and were caused much anxiety. [Britain had declared war on Germany on August 4th, thus beginning our involvement in what would become the First World War, *see* September 4th.] (*Kentish Gazette*)

1945: During this night, the cathedral was specially floodlit to commemorate VJ Day, following the Japanese surrender, and thus officially ending the Second World War. (Babbington: *Romance of Canterbury Cathedral*)

August 16th

1888: Joseph Smith, a private in the 8th Hussars – wearing a good conduct stripe – was charged with stealing a ring, the property of Regimental Sergeant Major Laing of Canterbury Cavalry Depot. The prisoner had been in his quarters as his servant. Mr Cruickshank, a pawnbroker from No. 76 Northgate Street, deposed that on this Thursday the prisoner offered the ring at his shop saying it was his own, and was advanced 5s. (*Kentish Gazette*)

———◆———

1890: On this day, at the Blean Workhouse, a legitimate female child was born to Margaret Sharpe of St Gregory's parish, and a legitimate female child was born to Frances Court, of the village of Blean. In both cases, no child's name was recorded. (Author's archive)

———◆———

1976: On this day the Broad Oak Valley, north of Canterbury, was named as the site of a forthcoming free rock festival. This area was probably picked as many of the residents had recently moved out following the purchase of their land and property by Mid Kent Water in advance of a proposed reservoir scheme. The event gradually petered out and, on the day, police easily outnumbered the few 'festival-goers' who had turned up (*see* July 11th).

August 17th

1593: Canterbury gaoler and bailiff of the Westgate suburb, Thomas Arthur, died of the plague on this day. His wife, Ursula (née Moore) died of the same shortly afterwards, as did four or their five children. They were buried at St Dunstan's Church. The surviving child, Dorothy, was immediately taken into care by her aunt and uncle, John and Katherine (née Arthur) Marlowe, parents of playwright Christopher Marlowe. (Urry: *Christopher Marlowe and Canterbury*)

———◆———

1909: A curious accident occurred in St George's Street at about eleven o'clock on this Tuesday morning. A domestic servant employed at No. 4 Ethelbert Road was proceeding down the street when, opposite Mr Gambell's outfitting shop, she was struck by some bricks and debris on the shoulder and arm, which had fallen from the coping overhead. The poor girl was taken to the Kent and Canterbury Hospital and attended to by the House Surgeon. Happily, there were no bones broken but her arm was badly bruised and her wrist swollen. [Gambell & Son were at Nos 10-11 St George's Street, right on the west corner with Canterbury Lane. Their premises were lost on 1 June 1942 in the Blitz.] (*Kentish Gazette*)

August 18th

1686: Blind Canterbury preacher Francis Taylor was buried at St Alphege Church on this day. He lost his sight from smallpox whilst at Cambridge University. Being a Nonconformist, he came to favour during the Commonwealth period, becoming Vicar of St Mary Breadman's in 1647 and Six Preacher in 1655. During this time, he lived at one of the sequestrated Prebendal Stalls in the Precincts (*see* March 25th). (Derek Ingram Hill)

1875: On this day, the *Guardian* newspaper published a complaint about the garrulousness or incompetence of certain individual cathedral guides. Guided tours began in the 1850s, and proved so popular that the numbers being shown round at any one time had to be limited to thirty. (Sparks *et al*: *Canterbury Cathedral*)

1940: 'Second World War Notebook': '5:15 pm, Sunday. First bombs dropped. Nos 21 and 23 St Augustine's Road hit.' [This day saw enemy activities resumed on a massive scale. An attack commenced at 5 p.m. over Essex and Kent, tying-in accurately with the 'notebook'. No. 32 Squadron also engaged the Luftwaffe over Canterbury at 5.30 p.m., shooting down two Messerschmitt 109s: one crashed at Elmstead Court, Barham; the other ploughed into woodland at Chilham.] (*Blitz Then and Now*)

August 19th

1472: The Christ Church Cathedral Prior, William Petham, died suddenly on this day after little more than a year in office. Prior Selling succeeded him. (Hasted: *Kent*, Vol. XI)

———◆———

1884: Traction engine driver Richard Butler was summoned for having, in Lower Bridge Street, used a locomotive which did not, as far as practicable, consume its own smoke. The defendant pleaded guilty. [Steam-powered traction engines and steam rollers could still be seen on the streets of Canterbury as late as the 1950s.] (*Kentish Gazette*)

———◆———

1906: At the Blean Workhouse: born to Emma Lovell of the Staplegate parish, an illegitimate son, later baptised as Stephen. (Author's archive)

———◆———

1954: On this day, the *Kentish Gazette* published many of the old memorials and inscriptions to be found all over the doomed St Andrew's Church, just off The Parade. It was assumed that, following demolition, they would be transferred to the nearby St Margaret's Church. A marble tablet in the church porch recorded an earlier transfer: 'These monuments were removed from ye olde church of St Andrew (which stood in the middle of ye adjoining street) when that church was taken down in pursuance of the Act of Parliament... George III' (*see* December 26th).

August 20th

1764: On this day, John Wesley came to Canterbury and opened the new Methodist Chapel in King Street. This was the celebrated 'Round-house' or 'Pepper-box' Chapel, which had been built from the demolition material of St Andrew's Church in The Parade (*see* December 26th). The chapel lasted until its much larger replacement in St Peter's Street was opened (*see* January 1st). The curious King Street chapel was then passed to the Baptists and finally demolished in 1864, when their new church was opened in St George's Place.

1933: An alarm of fire reached this city on this Tuesday evening, between ten and eleven o'clock, in consequence of a haystack – the property of Mr Rammell of Sturry Court – having become overheated and taken fire. The engine was immediately dispatched and the fire brought under control without further damage. (*Kentish Gazette*)

1958: On this day, Canterbury City Council invited tenders for the erection of a new Children's Home at the Hales Place Estate. This was to replace the 'Woodville Homes' at the top end of Wincheap, which was being demolished for a development of flats. [As far as I am aware, this replacement scheme never went ahead.] (City Council records)

August 21st

1400: Royally appointed architect Henry Yvele died on this day. At Canterbury, he designed the perpendicular cathedral nave that survives in all its lofty splendour today. It is likely that he was also responsible for the Westgate Towers and the Black Prince's tomb.

1832: The coffin of Henry IV, in the Trinity Chapel, Canterbury Cathedral, was opened on this day (*see* January 21st). Ostensibly, this was to settle an age-old rumour that the royal corpse had been thrown overboard during a storm on the Thames Estuary whilst conveying it to the port at Faversham, but curiosity is just as likely a motive. Having sawn through two lead coffins, they finally saw the russet-bearded face of the King in a remarkable state of preservation. (Woodruff and Danks: *Memorials*)

1940: 'Second World War Notebook': '4.10 p.m., Wednesday. Bombs dropped on Cossington Road. Eight houses completely demolished, four killed and twenty-two injured. Two bombs also dropped at the end of Mount Road.' [On this day, the Luftwaffe flew in small raids of one or two aircraft over the South-East. Indeed, other witnesses to the Cossington Road attack saw a single enemy aircraft drop three high-explosive bombs.] (Paul Crampton and *The Blitz Then and Now*)

August 22nd

1848: The hospital weekly report announced that John Wallace, who was admitted as an in-patient, 'died whilst getting him up the stairs'. This was following an accident on the South Eastern Railway, when as a plate layer he must have been run over by a train, losing both his legs in the process. (Marcus Hall *et al*: *KCH 1790 to 1987*)

———◆———

1865: On this day, a major fire in the heart of the city destroyed much of the old Chequers of Hope Inn. The fire broke out in an upholstery business in the High Street and spread quickly through the ancient timber-framed structure. Before the conflagration could be controlled, it had reached the north side of Sun Street, destroying buildings only yards from the Cathedral Gate.

———◆———

1938: A collision occurred on this Monday afternoon at the junction of Longport Street and Lower Chantry Lane, between a car driven by William Broad of The Haven, Stodmarsh Road, and a motorcyclist, Sidney Harrison, of No. 50 Querns Road. The latter was thrown off and received cuts on the right arm and abrasions on the right ankle. [Pre-war, this narrow junction was obscured by buildings on both corners.] (*Kentish Gazette*)

August 23rd

1719: On this day, Sir Peter Gleane, Bart, was buried in the chancel (of St George's Church), who hanged himself on August 21st, but brought off by the jury as *non compos mentis* (of unsound mind), and so had a Christian burial. (Woodruff: *Canterbury Parish Registers and Records*)

1913: 'Lord Sanger's huge circus will make its appearance at the Athletic Ground, Wincheap, for this Saturday only. Afternoon and evening performances have been arranged. If the weather turns out fine, the afternoon performance will be preceded by a gorgeous procession of what is best described as a circus hippodrome and menagerie. By this visit, the city is favoured as one of the centres touched by the 1913 tour of an attractive and, in many ways, remarkable entertainment.' [The County Athletic Grounds were at the top end of Wincheap, adjacent to the premises of Robert Brett & Sons. The area is now occupied by the park-and-ride site and large shops such as Morrison's.] (*Kentish Gazette*)

1944: A Dornier bomber was shot down by anti-aircraft fire and crashed in Covert Wood, Barham, at 12.30 a.m. The four-man crew were killed and the aircraft totally destroyed. (*The Blitz Then and Now*)

August 24th

1258: The former Prior of Christ Church, Roger of Lee, died on this day. He had been appointed at a time when the relationship between the priory and the Archbishop was at an all-time low. In fact, Roger was elected Prior without Archbishop Edmund's consultation or approval. Roger resigned in 1244, but 'continued an inmate of the convent until his death'.

◆

1922: On this day, a 'freak pig' was born at Lower Hardres, near Canterbury. Mr R.J. Back, proprietor of the Granville Inn at Street End, was quick to capitalise on this 'curiosity', with its 'three eyes, three ears and two mouths' by putting out an advertisement with a photo, saying that 'the most wonderful freak in existence' could be seen at his establishment 'at any time'. (Author's archive)

◆

1967: On this day, a founding member of the Canterbury Scene group Soft Machine, Daevid Allen, was refused entry into the UK at Dover following a European tour. Upon close scrutiny of his papers, it was found that he did not have the requisite visa to live and work in the country, being an Australian citizen. Consequently, the group were forced to recruit another guitarist (*see* May 17th). (Bennett: *Out Bloody Rageous*)

August 25th

1883: As a wagonload of wheat was being carted over a level crossing on the South Eastern Railway (possibly at Whitehall) near Canterbury during this Saturday morning, it tilted over and completely blocked the up-line. The first down train was in sight, but the horses were unharnessed just in time to escape the engine, which did however take off part of the wagon shaft. A gentleman named Foreman succeeded in stopping the (up) express by running down the line, thus averting a great disaster. (*Kentish Gazette*)

———— • ◆ • ————

1942: Prince George, the Duke of Kent, was tragically killed on this Tuesday. The Sunderland flying boat, in which he was a passenger, crashed into a hillside in North Scotland. The next day, the Mayor of Canterbury, Charles Lefevre, sent a telegram of condolence to his widow, Princess Marina, on behalf of the citizens of Canterbury (*see* June 4th and July 14th). (Crampton: *The Blitz of Canterbury*)

———— • ◆ • ————

1967: On this day, five motorists were fined £5 each at Canterbury Magistrates Court. They had been caught in a new radar speed trap in the Old Dover Road during July for exceeding the 30mph speed limit. None of them were residents of the city. (Author's archive)

August 26th

1642: On this day, with the Civil War barely begun, the Parliamentary soldiers of Colonel Sandys marched on Royalist Canterbury. They gained access to the cathedral and plundered it of many fixtures and fittings. The high altar was overturned and the altar rails destroyed. Books and manuscripts of all types were torn up and the organ was despoiled (*see* February 2nd). (Sparks *et al*: *Canterbury Cathedral*)

———◆———

1888: 'The brutal murder of the old woman Rayner by Catherine Church has been the general topic of conversation during the past week. The deceased was well known in Canterbury and her sad end has caused a shock to many. The accused was little known except in the immediate locality in which she resided. Her husband is of the labouring class and when we last saw him, he appeared dejected and careworn, owing, no doubt, to the dreadful position in which his wife has placed herself.' (*Kentish Gazette*)

———◆———

2000: On this Saturday, and for the rest of the bank holiday weekend, Channel 4's *Time Team* broadcast from Canterbury. The site featured was the Blue Coat Boys Yard in Stour Street, which Wiltshier's had recently vacated and was earmarked for residential redevelopment.

August 27th

1729: An advertisement published on this day gave evidence for the existence of a windmill at the top of Dane John Mound: 'To be lett or sold: The wind-mill upon Deanjohn's Hill in Canterbury, with French stones and peaks, and other tackle to dress flower…' During the Civil War, the Mound was used as a gun platform. (Courtesy of H.S. Cousins)

* * *

1732: 'We hear from Dunkirk [near Canterbury] that on this Wednesday, there was a most terrible storm of thunder and lightening, which un-tiled several houses and did incredible damages to the churches, the like not having been known in the memory of man.' (*Kentish Post or Canterbury Newsletter*)

* * *

1931: On this day the 2nd Battalion of The Buffs, who were based at Canterbury, took over guard duty at Buckingham Palace, St James' Palace, Hyde Park and Bank of England. (Cathedral Chronicle, 1931)

* * *

1954: On this day, construction work began on the new Congregational Church in Watling Street. It would be a replacement for one lost in the 1942 Blitz. With work at an advanced stage, the official stone-laying ceremony took place on 9 March 1955. However, work was delayed in March 1956 due to a financing dispute. (Crampton: *Yesterday's Whitefriars*)

August 28th

1909: 'Opportunities for engaging in the exhilarating and popular pastime of roller-skating will soon be provided at the Agricultural Hall through the enterprise of the Canterbury Roller Skating Rink Co., which has been formed with a capital of £3,000. A splendid floor of the finest prime-rock maple has been laid down, giving a skating area of nearly 14,000ft. There is the main part for the proficient person, while for the beginner there is a practice ground reserved – probably the largest in any rink in England.' [The rink, in Rhodaus Town, was later purchased by the Canterbury Motor Co. and much of the original building still survives today.] (*Kentish Gazette* and Crampton: *Canterbury Suburbs and Surroundings*)

1940: 'Battle of Britain': 'Three Messerschmitt 109s shot down by fighters in dogfights over Canterbury: (1) Crashed and burned out south of Chartham Downs at 8.50 a.m. Pilot baled out and captured unhurt. (2) Radiator severely damaged and force-landed at Goodnestone House Farm at 9.30 a.m. Pilot captured unhurt. (3) Hit by Hurricanes of No. 51 Squadron. Dived vertically into the ground at South Barham Farm, Denton, at 9.10 a.m. Pilot baled out very low and broke a leg.' (*The Blitz Then and Now*)

August 29th

1168: On this day, there was a serious fire at St Augustine's Abbey. However, the true extent of the damage is not known. (*Collectanea Historica*)

———— • ◆ • ————

1802: Sir Edward Hales, 5th Baronet, died on this day. He had spent much of the family fortune building the Hales Place mansion at Hackington (*see* April 3rd). As a result, his son Edward, the 6th and final baronet, was soon forced to sell the property at St Augustine's (the former abbey and palace). The 6th Baronet died without issue and the family went into steep decline thereafter (*see* August 3rd).

———— • ◆ • ————

1933: Adisham Windmill, on the heights near Bekesbourne Aerodrome, burnt down on this day. The landmark mill fell victim to a prolonged drought, which had caused a nearby grass fire, and those in attendance were unable to prevent the fire from spreading to the mill.

———— • ◆ • ————

1934: The annual honey show of the Eastern Division of the Kent Beekeepers' Association was held at the Sidney Cooper School of Art, Canterbury, on this Wednesday, and was generally acknowledged as one of the best on record. The number of exhibits showed an increase over last year and the quality exceeded expectations. (*Kentish Gazette*)

August 30th

AD 832: The Archbishop of Canterbury, Feologild, died on this day. He had only been consecrated on June 9th that year and it is unknown if he lived long enough to be formally enthroned. Although he was Archbishop for only three months, his remains were venerated in the cathedral for centuries. In 1447, they were put in a chest and placed on a beam over the entrance to St Michael's Chapel (later the Warrior's Chapel) where they remained until Christ Church Priory was dissolved (*see* April 4th). (Cotton: *The Saxon Cathedral*)

1882: On this Wednesday night, Mr Secker's 'Quicksilver' coach made a delightful moonlight trip from Folkestone to Canterbury, leaving at 9 p.m. The coach arrived in the city at 10.30 p.m. (*Kentish Gazette*)

1913: In spite of the ideal weather conditions prevailing – more suitable for outdoor recreation – good audiences continue to patronise the St George's cinema. For this weekend, the special film being shown is *The Ashes of Three*, written for the cinema by American author Stewart Edward White. The cinema, in Lower Bridge Street, was taken over by the Co-op in 1934 when the Regal opened nearby (*see* August 5th). It was finally pulled down in 1961.

August 31st

1538: On this Wednesday, the last recorded pilgrimage to the Becket shrine took place. [It would be destroyed within days, *see* September 7th.] The pilgrim in question was Madame de Montrueil and the visit was recorded by William Penison, who was 'in waiting on her' by order of the Lord Privy Seal. By all accounts, she was greatly impressed by his tomb. However, when this 'gentil-woman' was offered a skull to kiss – one she was told was Becket's – she would neither kneel before it, nor kiss it. (Woodruff and Danks: *Memorials*)

1786: 'About seven o'clock on this Friday, the home of Jacob Abraham, in North Lane near this city, was broke open, and seven shirts and shifts, with about thirty pairs of stockings, were stolen thereout'. (*Kentish Gazette*)

1940: 'Second World War Notebook': '11.20 a.m., Saturday. Eight bombs dropped and three of them dropped behind and close to the office [Telephone Exchange, Stour Street?]. The GEC Depot shelter [at No. 2 Beer Cart Lane] hit and a man trapped, but all saved'. Daylight bombing was almost entirely confined to South-East England. There was also a considerable amount of indiscriminate bombing in the morning. (Paul Crampton and *The Blitz Then and Now*)

September 1st

1494: Nicholas Sheldwich of the parish of St Mary Magdalene, by his will proved on this day, gave the Friars Minor (Greyfriars) the sum of 6s 8d. He had been Mayor of Canterbury twice, and also Member of Parliament on two occasions. Nicholas married Agnes, daughter of Richard Pargate, by whom he had five children. His wife died in 1517 and was buried beside him in the lay cemetery at St Augustine's Abbey. (Cotton: *The Greyfriars of Canterbury*)

—— ◆ ◆ ——

1916: On this day, bus company the East Kent Road Car Co. Ltd began trading. It was an amalgamation of a number of smaller companies running routes all over East Kent, including 'Canterbury and District'. The first board meeting was held at the premises of Mowll & Mowll Solicitors, in Castle Street, as the new company hadn't yet acquired any premises. (Woodworth: *East Kent*)

—— ◆ ◆ ——

1934: Sixteen members of the Company of Canterbury Cathedral Change Ringers took part in the annual outing on this Saturday. The party started off from the Cathedral Gates at 2.30 p.m., the Revd Helmore (an unfortunate name for a vicar!) – who was unable to make the journey – being present to see them off. (Mostly the *Kentish Gazette*)

September 2nd

1660: On this day, William Juxon (aged seventy-eight) was nominated Archbishop of Canterbury after Restoration of the Monarchy. [The role of Archbishop had been abolished under the Commonwealth.]

———•◆•———

1768: 'To be sold by auction at 2 p.m. at the King's Head Inn, High Street: the tower of the Parish Church of All Saints', with all the timber and materials thereto belonging (except the bells, lead and clock), which will be required to be taken down with all speed, according to conditions of sale to be then produced'. [This church, opposite Eastbridge Hospital, had a bell tower that projected out into the main street. This was removed in 1769 so that the Kingsbridge, and its approaches, could be widened. The King's Head Inn was nearby, at No. 31 High Street. It closed in the early 1840s, and had become the County Hotel by 1892, albeit greatly remodelled.] (*Kentish Gazette* and Crampton: *Canterbury's Lost Heritage*)

———•◆•———

1940: Dogfights in the skies over Canterbury – two Messerschmitt 109s downed: one crashed at Nethersole Farm, Womenswold, 8 a.m., the pilot killed; the other, losing its port wing-tip, forced-landed at Tile Lodge Farm, Westbere, 5.40 p.m., the pilot captured unhurt. (*The Blitz Then and Now*)

September 3rd

1832: 'Cathedral Construction': On this day, an important ceremony of laying the first stone of the new cathedral tower took place. 'The north-west tower, when finished, will render the cathedral the finest in point of beauty.' The workmen afterwards made the church ring with their loud and hearty cheers. (*Kentish Gazette*)

1872: 'Cathedral Destruction': During this afternoon, a major fire at the cathedral destroyed much of the roof above the Trinity Chapel at the building's east end. It was caused by the plumbers' blowlamp – left while they went to dinner – igniting a quantity of twigs carried there by jackdaws for nests. The fire was tackled by the 'Kent' and 'Phoenix' brigades, together with members of the cathedral staff and some soldiers. The damage, estimated at some £3,000, could have been worse had the roof's stone vaulting not remained intact.

1881: On this day, Sidney Cooper's 'The Monarch of the Meadows' was cut from its frame and stolen. It had been purchased in 1873 by Mr John Derby Allcroft for £2,500. Negotiations were conducted via the *Daily Telegraph* for a ransom of £500, but the thieves were apprehended in January 1882 and the painting recovered. (Stewart: *Thomas Sidney Cooper*)

September 4th

1883: Rose Kelsey, a woman of abandoned character, was charged with being drunk (*see* May 1st and 15th). PC Gilbert said that about half-past nine the previous evening, he saw the prisoner lying on the pavement in Northgate Street. She was drunk and speechless and the witness obtained assistance and took her to the police station. The prisoner asked the bench to have mercy on her, as she was going to pick hops at Chilham. She was fined 20s and costs; in default one month's imprisonment. (*Kentish Gazette*)

———◆———

1914: Commencing on this Friday, the licence holders in Canterbury have been instructed to close each night during the week an hour earlier, at ten o'clock, and on Sunday nights at nine o'clock. This step was taken at the request of the military authorities, in view of the thousands of troops currently quartered in the city (*see* August 15th and September 19th).

———◆———

1940: 'Second World War Notebook': '9.20 a.m., seventeen bombs dropped; three behind and close to the office again. Three shops and a number of houses were demolished [corner of Station Road West?]. The air-raid shelter at the back of our office [Stour Street] had a direct hit.'

September 5th

1174: On this fateful day, much of the choir of Canterbury Cathedral, to the east of the central 'Angel Tower', was destroyed in a great fire. It began in the afternoon, caused by sparks from a burning thatch in nearby Burgate Street being carried on the wind to the choir's roof. Engulfed by the flames that had been fanned by a stiff south-easterly breeze, the wooden roof eventually crashed down onto the choir below, where monks were frantically trying to rescue anything that could be moved. In the crypt below, Becket's tomb remained completely intact.

———◆———

1888: The Butter Market will not be demolished after all. 'The wind has shifted', observed Councillor Wells. At August's Council meeting, some members were not in favour of repairing the structure because of the cost, estimated at being £80 to £100. Now though, that opposition has apparently disappeared. [In the event, the 'wind' shifted yet again, for the Buttermarket's building had gone by the end of the year. This was an oval-shaped open structure, with iron columns supporting a wooden dome. It covered virtually all the open space dominated today by the war memorial.] (*Kentish Gazette, see* November 13th)

September 6th

1091: On this Sunday, with solemn ceremony, the body of St Augustine was translated into the eastern apse of the recently completed Norman St Augustine's Abbey, in a stone tomb fastened with iron and lead. However, it appears that the saint was not permitted to remain there for long. Later the same night, in secret, Abbot Wydo and a few of his trusted older brethren removed the major bones from the tomb and hid them in the wall under the eastern window, employing a stone coffin specially prepared for this purpose. They went to these extraordinary lengths for fear of the holy relics being plundered by Danish (Viking) raiders. (*Archaeologia Cantiana*, 1949)

———◆———

1759: 'An Announcement': 'To be sold by auction on this Thursday and the following two days, at Mr Brook's the Sign of Sir John Falstaff, near Westgate, Canterbury: the entire stock of Mr George Hardings', glass, china and stoneware warehouse.' (*Kentish Gazette*)

———◆———

1940: In a dogfight over Canterbury, a Spitfire from No. 41 Squadron engaged a Messerschmitt 109, damaging its radiator and forcing the enemy plane to land intact at Blean around 5.35 p.m. (*see* October 12th). The Luftwaffe pilot was captured unhurt. (*The Blitz Then and Now*)

September 7th

1538: It was on, or very near, this date that Dr Richard Layton and the Royal Commissioners came to Canterbury, with the purpose of sacking and destroying the Becket shrine in the cathedral (*see* June 10th). The tomb was dismantled and all its riches seized, yielding nearly 3cwt of gold, the same in silver and countless precious stones. The spoil filled two great chests that took seven strong men to move. More crucially, the saint's bones were said to have been taken outside and burnt. Thus ended the cult of Thomas of Canterbury… or did it?

———◆———

1573: On this day, Queen Elizabeth I celebrated her fortieth birthday at the Old Palace, Canterbury, in the company of Archbishop Matthew Parker.

———◆———

1990: On this day, a letter from one 'Thomas Chough' was published in the *Kentish Gazette*. He claimed that Becket's bones had survived the destruction of 1538 and had been secretly reburied in another part of the cathedral. He further stated that this secret location is known to a handful of people in each generation who, in July (the 7th) and December (the 29th), prayed there each year for the conversion of England (i.e. back to Catholicism). (Butler: *The Quest for Becket's Bones*)

September 8th

1705: On this Saturday, Mrs Veal of Dover visited her friend, Mrs Bargrave, at her house in Canterbury (near the Cattle Market). They conversed happily from midday until 2 p.m. On the Monday, Mrs Bargrave learned that Mrs Veal had died at Dover the previous Friday, twenty-four hours before her 'apparitional' visit. (*Archaeologia Cantiana*, 1959)

❖

1888: On this Saturday, at about 4 p.m., a thirty-four-year-old widow, Georgina Byrne, left her home at No. 42a Broad Street, Canterbury, and travelled up to London. Next day, Lambeth coroner's office was notified of the death of a woman, who had been found on Blackfriars Road in an 'insensible condition' under 'mysterious circumstances'. She was taken to St Thomas' Hospital, where the house physician, Dr Luard, pronounced life extinct due to syncope (fainting!). A man, who was discovered with her lifeless form, had falsely said: 'I am her husband. I will go for a doctor.' He was never seen or heard from again. [During August and September 1888, five infamous murders took place in the Whitechapel area of London, barely two miles away from where Mrs Byrne was found. Therefore, could Georgina Byrne have been an unidentified victim of Jack the Ripper?]

September 9th

1299: On this day, King Edward I had his marriage to Queen Margaret, daughter of the King of France, blessed in the 'Martyrdom' – the cathedral's north-west transept, where Thomas Becket was murdered. The ceremony took place near the entrance from the cloister and was presided over by Archbishop Robert Winchelsey. (Hasted: *Kent*, Vol. XI)

------ ◆ ------

1788: The pavement of the principal city streets being completed, it surely behoves the Commissioners to ensure the footpaths are to be kept constantly swept. (*Kentish Gazette*)

------ ◆ ------

1940: 'Second World War Notebook': '5 p.m., heavy air-raid on Canterbury: fifty-nine bombs dropped by three bombers. Fourteen houses in Cherry Drive and Whitstable Road damaged; also in Clifton Gardens and Harcourt Drive. Three people killed in St Dunstan's Parish Hall [Orchard Street] and Miss Jordan severely injured [possibly at No. 25 Orchard Street, next to the hall]. East Kent Depot [St Stephen's Road] hit and six buses destroyed. Many bombs fell in the Cathedral Precincts, the Archdeacon's house [No. 29] got a direct hit. The Bishop of Dover's old house at the foot of St Martin's Hill got a direct hit, and Browning & Denne's yard [No. 22 St George's Place], a direct hit with three workmen killed there.'

September 10th

1938: 'Enrolments for the various services are urgently needed in order that air-raid precautions for Canterbury may be carried out both with expedition and efficiency. The greatest need is for a considerable addition to the numbers of air-raid wardens. While we still feel it is essential that work to provide bomb-proof protective shelters should receive more attention, we agree as to the need for instruction being given in anti-gas measures.' [Adolf Hitler was making territorial demands on the Sudetenland, then part of Czechoslovakia, hence the mood of impending war.] (*Kentish Gazette, see* September 29th)

———————•◆•———————

1939: On this day, vast amounts of earth were brought into the cathedral nave by lorry. The crypt had been designated an air-raid shelter for residents of The Precincts and the earth was to be moved onto the floor of the choir and its side-aisles to provide a protective cushion, should the cathedral be hit by bombs and the roof collapse. There was outrage at this proposal, but the Dean and Chapter wanted to press ahead (*see* October 13th). Concurrently, protective sandbags were also being piled around principal cathedral monuments, such as the Black Prince's tomb.

September 11th

1660: On this Saturday, Barbara, the daughter of Canterbury historian William Somner, was baptised in the restored cathedral font. This was a reward to William for having carefully saved all the pieces of the font after it had been smashed up by iconoclasts during the Commonwealth period (*see* February 2nd). (Gostling: *Walk*)

1883: On this Tuesday, 'Lieutenant Dyer and sixty-three men of the 17th Lancers left Canterbury for Portsmouth, where they embarked on board HMS *Jumma*. They are bound for Mhow in India; and owing to the prevalence of cholera in Egypt, the vessel will not pass through the Suez Canal.' (*Kentish Gazette*)

1972: On this Monday, Upper Hardres Church was badly damaged by fire. Sadly, some medieval glass was shattered and the organ destroyed.

1984: The new Sainsbury's supermarket opened on this Tuesday, just off Kingsmead Road. The building (the radical design of which courted much controversy) was constructed on a site formerly occupied by the City Electricity Works (*see* November 21st). Two hundred and forty-two full and part-time jobs were created as a result. The store was also pioneering in providing provision for disabled shoppers, with two of the twenty-three twin-bay checkouts having extra width for wheelchairs.

September 12th

1535: On this day, Prior Thomas Goldwell and the monks of Christ Church Priory all signed the Act of Supremacy (*see* June 3rd) and the Act of Succession (*see* April 17th). This is probably why the priory (at the cathedral) lasted as long as it did, whilst other religious houses in Canterbury had fallen (*see* April 4th). (Hasted: *Kent*, Vol. XI)

———◆———

1882: The Town Clerk of Canterbury has received a letter from the Dean and Chapter saying they have decided not to accede to the request of the Council that the cathedral clock should be kept to Greenwich time. They considered it rather an advantage than otherwise that 'Cathedral Time' should be in advance of the time kept at the railway stations. (*Kentish Gazette*)

———◆———

1951: The 'Canterbury Exhibition' on the bombed Whitefriars site closed on this day after a successful three months (*see* June 11th). Soon, bulldozers were called in to clear away the pavilions in order to allow the redevelopment of the south side of St George's Street. However, much to everyone's surprise, the surviving medieval walls of the old friary, much publicised as the exhibition's principal backdrop, were cleared away too, leaving just a short length surviving. (Crampton: *Yesterday's Whitefriars*)

September 13th

1178: On this day, a partial eclipse at Canterbury was taken as a bad omen by the Christ Church monks, who were busily rebuilding the eastern arm of the cathedral following the Great Fire of 1174 (*see* September 5th). Their fears seemed justified when, only a few days later, the principal architect of the new build, William of Sens, fell from the scaffolding high in the vaults and was so badly injured that he could no longer continue in the role. (Courtesy of L.L. Sims)

———•◆•———

1733: 'Matthew Elliott, mason, at the Water Lock in St Alphege, Canterbury, who has worked twenty-one years for Mr Frend, in Christ Church Yard, is now set up for himself and works and sells monuments, gravestones, paving, tables and chimney pieces of all prices.' [Waterlock Lane, now St Radigund's Street, was named after the Waterlock Gate, which once spanned the River Stour near Abbott's Mill. This largely defensive stone bridge was demolished in 1769 and replaced by a narrow wooden footbridge – see June 21st.] (*Kentish Gazette*)

———•◆•———

1924: On this day, the *Kentish Gazette* listed some of the rare conifers at Allcroft Grange, which had been collected by the late Nevill Cooper (*see* January 9th).

September 14th

1448: By a charter to the city, issued by Henry VI, it was confirmed that from this day forward, Canterbury citizens may elect their own Mayor. The first such Mayor was John Lynde. (*Canterbury Mayoral Quincentenary*)

———◆◆———

1841: Norman Saunders was discharged from hospital on this day. 'The boy appears to be of unsound mind, and so noisy that he disturbs all the patients…' (*Archaeologia Cantiana*, 1988)

———◆◆———

1884: William Watson was charged with being drunk on this Sunday evening. PC Hadlow deposed that the prisoner said he was a stranger to Canterbury and his foot had been crushed by being run over by a wagon. He was fined *2s 6d* with costs. (*Kentish Gazette*)

———◆◆———

1968: Soft Machine split up following their last USA gig supporting the Jimi Hendrix Experience. Exhausted roadie Hugh Hopper returned to Canterbury via Portugal, Kevin Ayres fled to Ibiza amidst clouds of self-doubt, and a disillusioned Mike Ratledge returned to London to write new material in peace. Robert Wyatt, however, remained in the States, and adapted some old tunes into two suites with new lyrics, which would prove useful, as the band would soon reform with Hugh on bass to replace Kevin. (Bennett: *Out Bloody Rageous*)

September 15th

1808: 'About four o'clock this Thursday afternoon, a fire broke out in a hop-oast called the Nunnery Oast, in Dover Lane [Dover Street today], occupied by Joseph Royle Esq. which by prompt assistance was in a short space of time got under, after burning the cloth and floor, and from the means employed to extinguish the flames, damaged a small proportion of the hops. The fire was considerably dampened in the first instance by water, which was kept constantly in case of accidents, a judicious precaution that should in all similar cases be adopted.' [The damage must have been worse than first thought, for the oast would soon be extensively rebuilt, *see* September 25th.] (*Kentish Gazette*)

1940: 'Enemy planes engaged in the skies over Canterbury': 'The petrol tank of a Messerschmitt 109 fighter set alight. It crashed and burned out at Adisham Court, near Bekesbourne, 12.09 p.m. The pilot baled out and was captured badly burned. A Dornier 17 bomber, on its way to London, attacked by several RAF planes. Crashed in flames and exploded in trees on Alcrofts Farm, Sturry, 12.40 p.m. Three of the crew were killed, two were captured.' (*The Blitz Then and Now*)

September 16th

1164: By the summer of this year, Henry II had suffered nearly two years of intransigence from Archbishop Thomas Becket over the question of Canon Law (*see* June 3rd). Consequently, the King was now determined to break him with a series of trumped-up charges. Becket was duly summoned to a hearing at Westminster on this day to answer one of these allegations, but he failed to turn up. It seems he was suffering from a recurring stress-related illness. Other meetings were called, where either the King or the Archbishop didn't show up, culminating in one held on October 13th, where Henry refused to be in the same room as Thomas (*see* November 2nd). (Urry: *Becket: His Last Days*)

◆

1838: The members of the Canterbury Catch and Glee Club met on this Sunday, at the Guildhall Tavern, to elect a president for the ensuing year. Thomas Neame Esq. was chosen unanimously. The business having concluded, the members maintained to its fullest extent the spirit of their motto, by devoting the remainder of the evening to conviviality and harmony. [The Guildhall Tavern, at No. 10 High Street, opposite the old Guildhall, had gone by 1910.](*Kentish Gazette*)

September 17th

1783: On this day, the *Kentish Gazette* reported: 'On Monday night, a man who had been to receive 20 guineas went into a public house in The Borough where, in a public taproom, he impudently pulled it out to tell it over [i.e. in the modern parlance, he flashed his wad!]. As soon as he had drank his pint of beer he left, but had not gone far before he was knocked down and robbed of the whole sum, supposed to be done by two men who saw him tell it over in the pub.'

1798: On this Monday, his Royal Highness George, Prince of Wales, passed through Canterbury en route to his 'temporary' residence at Charlton Place, near Barham Downs. (Hasted: *Kent*, Vol. IX)

1962: Two new business premises opened in Canterbury on this Monday. They were: the Caffyns showroom and offices in New Dover Road, and the Riceman's department store in St George's Lane (*see* March 23rd). The latter opening was celebrated by a costumed pageant through the main street.

2005: On this Saturday, England cricketer and Old Boy David Gower opened a new pavilion at the King's School's Birley's playing fields off St Stephen's Road. (King's School website)

September 18th

1759: At a meeting of his Majesty's Deputy Lieutenants of the County of Kent, held at the Red Lion Inn on August 21st, it appeared that a sufficient number of militia men were enrolled as needed. But there not being a sufficient number of gentlemen to offer themselves for subaltern officers, a further such meeting was held on this Tuesday at the King's Head, Canterbury. [The Red Lion, next to the Guildhall, was demolished in 1806 to make Guildhall Street.]

———◆———

1807: 'A man of shabby but genteel appearance engaged a bed on this Friday night at the George Inn, High Street, Canterbury, and departed early the next morning taking a fine sheet from the bed. He left a parcel in the room which, on being examined, was found to contain a whisp of straw only.' [A 'whisp' was a small bundle of straw or hay used to wipe something dry or clean! The George and Dragon Inn was demolished in 1895 for the Beaney Institute.] (*Kentish Gazette*)

———◆———

1963: Riceman's reopened after the fire (*see* March 23rd). Disc jockey David Jacobs was invited to cut the ribbon and signed many autographs afterwards. (Crampton: *Yesterday's Whitefriars*)

September 19th

1848: The new Jewish synagogue in King Street was consecrated on this Tuesday. The ceremony was attended by the Chief Rabbi, Sir Moses Montefiore. Afterwards, a reception was held at the Guildhall. The new synagogue replaced the one in St Dunstan's Street, demolished to construct an approach road (i.e. Station Road West) to the new Southern Eastern Railway station (*see* February 6th).

———•◆•———

1914: 'Major-General Young, commanding the Home Counties Division, is about to take up his residence on the Dane John. The citizens will be glad to learn that the great advantages of Canterbury as a centre for all parts of East Kent are being recognised, and the city will continue to be used as an important headquarters during the period of "military occupation"(*see* September 4th).' (*Kentish Gazette*)

———•◆•———

2002: A report, looking at the possible expansion of Manston Airport, stated that the effectiveness of a high-speed rail link between it and London might be compromised by the sheer number of level crossings in the Canterbury area. Since this report, however, the line from Ashford to Thanet, via Canterbury West, has been upgraded for the new high-speed 'Javelin' services, including the elimination of all gated crossings.

September 20th

1782: 'Several of the planters near this city have begun to pick their hops, which fall short one half of what was expected. The farmers were obliged to begin (although not ripe) on account of the flea being in them, the sample of course is but indifferent.' [An old Kentish rhyme said of hops: 'First the flea, then the fly, then the mould, then they die'.] (*Kentish Gazette*)

———◆———

1919: Auctioned on this Saturday at the Royal Fountain Hotel in St Margaret's Street was 1,350 acres of land and agricultural properties that made up 'The Milton Estate'. The area encompassed the parishes of Milton, Thannington, Nackington, Petham and Lower Hardres. (Auction poster)

———◆———

1965: In the week ending September 20th, the Kent Coalfield – including Chislet Colliery near Canterbury – broke its productivity record, with an output-per-man shift of 33.8cwt. (Author's archive)

———◆———

2000: On this day, local architect David Coupe won the Canterbury Conservation Advisory Committee's first award, for the conversion and extension of the Old Sessions House at Longport. He successfully married the old and new without resorting to the inevitable 'pastiche'. The building now boasts a superb circular lecture theatre, which serves the whole city.

September 21st

1349: On this day, the citizens elected Thomas Chiche and Daniel le Draper as bailiffs of Canterbury. However, after the victorious candidates had departed, Hamo Doge administered the oath to the losing contender, and previous bailiff, John Dodekere. The deception was revealed when a re-election was held, and Chiche and Draper were unanimously confirmed. (*Canterbury Mayoral Quincentenary*)

1910: The 21st Lancers left the cavalry barracks in Sturry Road for Egypt after a two-year stay in Canterbury. They departed via Canterbury (West) station. (Courtesy of Derek Butler)

1913: The five-year-old son of Albert Waller of the Three Cups, in Broad Street, was knocked down by a motorcar on this Sunday afternoon. The lad, named Cyril, was standing near one of the garden openings in Lady Wootton's Green, when he was struck on the head by the splashboard of a motorcar coming from Monastery Street. He was picked up unconscious and taken to Kent and Canterbury Hospital in a passing milk cart. The motor, which had a London number, contained a lady and gentleman and two little girls, with the chauffeur. [The Three Cups at No. 18 Broad Street was damaged in the Blitz on 1 June 1942 and later demolished.] (*Kentish Gazette*)

September 22nd

1231: On this day, the Lord Chancellor of England, Ralph Neville, was elected by the monks of Christ Church Priory to be Archbishop of Canterbury. However, this was quashed by the Pope, Gregory IX, on the preposterous grounds that he was illiterate and unlearned. The same Pope would reject two further consecutive Archbishop elects (*see* March 16th).

1938: An American tennis tournament will be held in aid of the Kent and Canterbury Hospital at the Hillside Hardcourts Tennis Club, Cherry Drive, on this Thursday and during the following weekend. A silver cup with replicas will be represented to the winners by the Mayor, Councillor H. Harrison, with prizes for runners-up and semi-finalists. (*Kentish Gazette*)

1999: On this day, Canterbury Archaeological Trust signed an agreement with Land Securities plc for the excavation of the eleven-acre Whitefriars site. A financial deal was also struck with Channel 4's *Time Team*. [All the buildings on the area were about to be demolished with a view to comprehensive redevelopment and, as the new scheme would have underground servicing facilities, this would be a once-only chance to record 2,000 years of Canterbury's past before it was destroyed.] (Lyle: *Tall Oaks*)

September 23rd

1815: Master of Eastbridge Hospital and Vicar at Blean, Allen Fielding, was appointed a Six Preacher on this day. He was the son of novelist Henry Fielding, and also connected with the well-known firm of Canterbury Solicitors. He has been described as a great wit, a dignified man with a clear and distinct utterance, but so slow in his pronunciation that he was called the 'Minute Gun'. (Derek Ingram Hill)

1939: 'As the third week of the anti-Hitler war draws to a close, it is to paraphrase the official communiqués: "all quiet on the home front". Nothing is very much different from last week. A few more evacuees have arrived, and some citizens are in revolt against the ARP measures being carried out in the cathedral (*see* September 10th). The Civil Defence department is still quietly functioning, prices are beginning to rise, and streets continue to provide risks during the blackouts. Presumably though, the screening of lights in the city has been very effective for, unlike other towns, Canterbury has yet to have its first "too much light" prosecution'. (*Kentish Gazette*)

1957: The new St Mary Bredin Church was consecrated on this day by the Archbishop of Canterbury, Geoffrey Fisher. (Courtesy of Derek Butler)

September 24th

1732: 'An Announcement': 'John Brames, in the Borough of Staplegate, Canterbury, will sell all sorts of linen-drapery goods as cheap, if not cheaper, than the person at the Blue Boar – or any Scotsman that comes to Canterbury, provided they pay 20s in the pound'. [The Borough of Staplegate was in the area immediately surrounding Knotts Lane. Indeed, the Blue Boar Inn could once be found in Knotts Lane. Later reopened as the Lord Nelson, the pub finally closed in 1910.] (*Kentish Post or Canterbury Newsletter*)

1932: The curator of the Beaney Institute reported that a collection of over 4,000 British and foreign beetles had been sent on loan by Mr Walter A. White of Edward Road, Canterbury. (*Kentish Gazette*)

1955: On motorcycle patrol in Littlebourne Road this Saturday, PC Randall saw an ice-cream van overtaking all other traffic, and he accordingly followed it for half a mile at 50mph. The driver was later summoned at Canterbury Magistrates Court for exceeding the speed limit. In his defence, he claimed to be used to driving a heavier vehicle and found it difficult to judge the speed. It hadn't dawned on him to look at the speedometer. (Author's archive)

September 25th

1934: On this Tuesday evening, two young lady employees of William Lefevre Ltd found they had been inadvertently locked in the arcade. Through the iron gates, they explained their predicament to passers-by and a constable was fetched. He eventually secured a key and the girls were released after an hour's imprisonment. (*Kentish Gazette*)

———◆◆———

1940: 'Second World War Notebook': '2.45 a.m., many oil bombs dropped at Thannington. One woman killed and five injured. Six houses and one shop destroyed; twenty houses damaged by a Heinkel.'

———◆◆———

1959: 'The hop oast in Dover Street, built during the Napoleonic War, is being demolished. The date of its erection (1811) can be seen on two bricks either side of the entrance. However, its eastern end is much older, as the lower part of the wall is constructed from Caen stone, probably taken from the ruins of St Augustine's Abbey'. [This wall, which also included early post-medieval bricks, had clearly survived from the previous oast – *see* September 15th. In the event, much of the old wall escaped the 1959 demolition, becoming incorporated into one of Martin Walters' garage buildings. It finally disappeared in the early 1990s when the garage was pulled down.] (*Kentish Gazette*)

September 26th

1803: The painter, Thomas Sidney Cooper, was born in St Peter's Street, Canterbury, on this day. His early years were comparatively humble, being brought up in a single-parent household. William Cooper, a military surveyor, had deserted his wife, Sarah, and their five children when Thomas was only five. The young Cooper spent much of his youth sketching in the cathedral grounds, where other artists noticed his talents. (Stewart: *Thomas Sidney Cooper*)

———— •◆• ————

1908: A work of much importance in the renovation of the drainage of Canterbury is now on the point of completion, in that the old main trunk sewer between Northgate, St Stephen's and the Irrigation Farm [a respectable euphemism for the sewage works in Sturry Road], besides others in the neighbourhood of the river – all of which were in a very leaky condition – have now been entirely supported by watertight piping. (*Kentish Gazette*)

———— •◆• ————

1939: On this day, *The Times* reported that interesting archae-ological finds were unearthed during the construction of an underground air-raid shelter for the Simon Langton Schools at the Whitefriars. These included amounts of worked stone, no doubt from the dissolved friary, and a skeleton lying east-to-west, thus indicating a hitherto undisturbed Christian burial. (See Crampton: *Yesterday's Whitefriars* for a picture)

September 27th

1167: Prior Wibert of Christ Church Priory died on this day, after fourteen years in harness. His final months were troubled by the dispute between Henry II and the exiled Thomas Becket, but he managed to maintain a balance between the two factions. His achievements at Canterbury Cathedral were considerable, particularly his waterworks system, the best visual remains of which is the water tower (often called 'The Baptistery') in the infirmary cloister.

1459: On this day, Pope Pius II granted a licence to Thomas Cok, Friar Minor of Canterbury (i.e. the Greyfriars), to hold a benefice and to wear his habit under a mantle of decent colour! (Cotton: *The Greyfriars of Canterbury*)

1784: 'On this Monday morning, a desperate battle was fought in the borough between twenty sailors with bludgeons, when a number of constables were ordered out and several of the local inhabitants interfering. Eleven of them were taken and lodged in the New Gaol [in Longport]; the others got off.' (*Kentish Gazette*)

1850: Edward Tomlin, an in-patient, left the hospital without permission yesterday evening and returned again this morning, and left yet again today. His name was placed in the 'Black Book'. (*Archaeologia Cantiana*, 1988)

September 28th

1838: On this Friday, a man named Lee, in the employ of a horse-dealer in Canterbury, 'was driving a horse and cart furiously through the village of Sturry and knocked down a poor old man named Richard Barron, fracturing a shoulder-bone, hurting his head and other parts of his body. Barron, who is about eighty years old, was immediately conveyed to the Kent and Canterbury Hospital. We hope this unfortunate occurrence will act as a warning to persons driving too fast through public thoroughfares and villages – the latter generally thronged with aged people and children.' (*Kentish Gazette*)

———•◆•———

1880: A Royal Commission sat at Canterbury on this day to enquire into corrupt election practices, specifically those surrounding former Conservative MP, Henry Butler-Johnstone who, it was alleged, bribed electors to keep his son – also called Henry, and also a Conservative MP – in the local Parliamentary seat. One witness talked of half-sovereigns being handed out at the Rose Hotel, many of which were promptly spent at the adjacent Rose Tap pub. (Bateman: *Hail, Mother of England*)

———•◆•———

1938: This day saw the beginning of the removal of the cathedral's medieval stained glass in response to the Munich Crisis (*see* September 10th). (Cathedral Chronicle, 10/38)

September 29th

1376: The funeral of Edward, the Black Prince, took place at Canterbury Cathedral on this day. Having lain in state at Westminster Hall for over three months, his body was brought to Canterbury with due ceremony. His elaborate tomb, probably designed by Henry Yvele, was positioned close to that of Thomas Becket in the Trinity Chapel, doubtless due to his fame, but this was in defiance of the Prince's own last wishes (*see* June 8th).

———◆———

1938: On this Wednesday afternoon, from 4 p.m., gas masks were issued from ten depots across the city, and it was stated they were being distributed at a rate of 100 an hour. By the next morning, the central respirator fitting station in St George's Street had dealt with some 7,000 citizens. Also on the Wednesday, all the city's elementary schools, and also the Simon Langton Schools, closed indefinitely. [*See* September 10th for the background to this crisis. However, the threat of war was lifted by the signing of the Munich Agreement in the small hours of the following day. This settlement effectively gave the Sudetenland to Nazi Germany, provided Hitler made no further territorial demands.] (*Kentish Gazette*)

September 30th

1896: On this day, Thomas Sidney Cooper sold Abbott's Mill, in St Radigund's Street, to a Mr Denne. The well-known painter had inherited both this and the Westgate (Hooker's) Mill from his late father-in-law, but both mills were in decline, and finally left unoccupied, because of the cheaper price of imported flour from America. (Stewart: *Thomas Sidney Cooper*)

❦

1933: Ronald Baker, a small boy of St Peter's Lane, Canterbury, fell into the river near the floodgates at Hooker's Mill (The Causeway). Hearing cries for help, Lewis Wellings (aged fourteen-and-a-half) of No. 5 Turnagain Lane, Palace Street, jumped over the railings and, wading into the water, brought the boy ashore. [The 1934 *Street Directory* lists a Mr J. Baker at No. 87 St Peter's Lane, near its top end, and only yards away from The Causeway. It was demolished in a slum-clearance scheme in 1938.] (*Kentish Gazette*)

❦

1940: A Messerschmitt 109, escorting enemy bombers en route to London, exploded whilst under attack by RAF fighters over Canterbury. Wreckage was scattered over a wide area, debris falling at Canterbury Artillery Barracks, Honey Wood and Old Park Farm, near Tyler Hill. The pilot was killed. (*The Blitz Then and Now*)

October 1st

1186: On this day, the Archbishop of Canterbury, Baldwin, obtained permission from the Pope to establish a new college of secular Canons. The 'College of St Stephen's and St Thomas Becket' was to be established at Hackington, effectively becoming the Archbishop's administration centre and taking all secular matters away from Christ Church Priory. The cathedral monks immediately felt threatened by this, fearing a diminution of their status, and fought the idea bitterly. Work was at an advanced stage when the project was halted (*see* November 27th). As to what happened to the unfinished building: some say the material was used to expand St Stephen's Church at Hackington. (Sparks *et al*: *Canterbury Cathedral*)

———•••———

1733: 'An announcement': 'Stolen or strayed from Mr William Fox at Nackington, near Canterbury – during the night of 30th September and 1st October – a black horse, about thirteen hands three inches high; five years old, a cut tail (but not lately); all black except a small white spot where the saddle lies, and small feet. He pads, and was bought at Chilham Fair. Whoever gives intelligence of the said horse; to as to be had again to Mr Fox, aforesaid, shall have all reasonable satisfaction.' (*Kentish Post or Canterbury Newsletter*)

October 2nd

1884: A statue of Canterbury artist Sidney Cooper was proposed on this day. Sadly the idea was never acted upon. (Courtesy of Brian Stewart)

———◆———

1937: 'We understand that in response to a unanimous petition from the members of Canterbury Corporation asking him again to take office as Mayor, Alderman Charles Lefevre has expressed his regret that he cannot again undertake the duties.' [Finally bowing to popular pressure, he became Mayor of Canterbury during the difficult period of the Blitz: he was a much-respected man who became a local Churchillian figure.] (*Kentish Gazette*)

———◆———

1957: People living in Littlebourne Road and Warwick Road have complained to the Council about the nuisance and damage caused by Teddy Boys and other older youths using the adjacent children's playground, and have asked that steps be taken to restrict the use of the playground to younger children. (City Council records)

———◆———

2009: On this day, a topping-out ceremony took place to recognise completion of the first stage of the repairs to the stonework of the Corona Tower at the cathedral. Begun in 2006, the work to replace stones subject to corrosion was deemed essential. Suitable material had to be obtained from northern France and Dorset.

October 3rd

1742: A monumental inscription inside St Dunstan's Church: 'Near this place lieth the body of Daniell Hall, twice Mayor of the City of Canterbury. His first wife was Leah Rigden who, with her three children, lye buried near this place... He departed this life Oct 3rd 1742, in his 81st year'.

◆

1938: This Monday night's gale, with its rain and 70mph gusts, sent thousands of apples falling to the ground at Chartham Hatch. In the Cathedral Precincts, workmen were using axes and saws on a tree that could not stand the wildness of the night, and from all parts of Canterbury came similar stories of havoc. A man propped his bicycle up on the kerb and a gust of wind blew it under a stationary car. The motorist, returning in blissful ignorance, slowly drew away, passing right over the unfortunate bike. (*Kentish Gazette*)

◆

1979: A man who left Canterbury Woolworth's without paying for a Parker pen had suffered from an 'uncontrollable urge' to go to the lavatory, magistrates at Canterbury were told on this day. A female store detective stopped him outside, with the pen concealed inside a comic. The forty-six-year-old man was fined £50. (*Kent Herald*)

October 4th

1644: On this day, Richard Culmer became a Six Preacher. Known as 'Blue Dick', this infamous Puritan and iconoclast liked nothing more than to scale a ladder high inside the cathedral and, with his pike, smash out 'inappropriate images' from the cathedral's ancient stained glass (*see* December 13th). In his own words, he was 'rattling down proud Becket's glassie bones'. (Ingram Hill: *The Six Preachers*)

───◆───

1783: During this Saturday morning, at about three o'clock, 'an uncommon flash came out of the sky in the north, which for about two seconds was as light as noon-day. It seemed to strike a great heat on the earth and never moved from the place where it made its first appearance. It left a long train of fire, which increased, and within five minutes afterwards, both ends joined together to form a circle, which continued for the space of a quarter of an hour and then vanished.' (*Kentish Gazette*)

───◆───

1903: Born at the Blean Workhouse on this day: an illegitimate son to Eva Burrows and Stephen Garlinge of the parish of Staplegate. The child was baptised William Garlinge Burrows: a rare example of both the father and child's name appearing on record. (Author's archive)

October 5th

1539: On this day, work began to convert the dissolved St Augustine's Abbey into a Royal Palace (*see* December 30th). Most of the massive former abbey church had already been demolished for building materials – much going to strengthen the defences at Calais – but the core of the new palace would be formed from the surviving, largely domestic buildings around the courtyard immediately behind the Findon Gate.

———◆———

1838: An accident befell an individual named John White, of the 'railroad establishment', on this Friday evening. 'In propelling one of the train carriages in an elevated shed, he fell through an aperture called a "hopper", used for the purpose of discharging coals into wagons below, and severely hurt himself, but we are happy to say without injury to his spine. He was promptly conveyed to hospital, and great hopes are entertained of his recovery'. [This was on the Canterbury to Whitstable railway. The 'Canterbury West' main line didn't arrive until 1846, with the 'Canterbury East' line following in 1860.] (*Kentish Gazette*)

———◆———

1955: Parents on the Martyr's Field housing estate were told to keep their children under proper control, following numerous complaints of hooliganism and damage. (City Council records)

October 6th

1832: William Spain was convicted before Richard Halford on this Saturday, and sentenced to one calendar month's hard labour at St Augustine's Prison, on the complaint of the guardians of the poor of the parish of Harbledown, for having run away and left his wife and family chargeable to that parish for upwards of six months. (*Kentish Gazette*)

———•◆•———

1870: On this Thursday, and for the following night, a musical was performed at St George's Hall, next to St George's Church, in the main street. W.S. Woodins, on his farewell tour, appeared 'with his celebrated and original Carpet Bag, character and entertainment'. (*Living in Victorian Canterbury*)

———•◆•———

1954: The Town Clerk, John Boyle, promised he would do his best to obtain a liquor licence for the new Cattle Market at St Stephen's, there being no public houses in the vicinity. (City Council records)

———•◆•———

1959: On this Tuesday, work began to demolish the 130ft-high chimneystack at the Kingsmead Road Electricity Works. Initially it was hoped to fell the stack, but fear of damage to adjacent buildings forced a decision for the work to be done by hand, from the top down. The task was expected to take five weeks. (Author's archive)

October 7th

1913: Dramatic circumstances were narrated at an inquest conducted at the Municipal Offices, Guildhall Street, on this Tuesday afternoon by the City Coroner, Mr John Plummer. Evidence revealed that the deceased's wife, while riding from Canterbury to Sturry in an omnibus, witnessed her husband, a Sturry labourer, fall from a cycle he was riding and pass under the wheels of a traction engine. (*Kentish Gazette*)

1959: On this Wednesday, tenders were invited for the demolition of the old Simon Langton Boys' School buildings on the Whitefriars site. Although most of the original 1881 establishment had been lost in the June 1942 Blitz (*see* April 6th), substantial ranges of later buildings existed along the St George's Lane and Gravel Walk frontages, as well as numerous prefabs. All buildings were pulled down during the following summer, and the area turned into a large car park. (Crampton: *Yesterday's Whitefriars*)

1964: On this day, the Canterbury Sanitary and Licensing Committee reported on the following food complaints: a ham and egg pie with extensive mould; dirty lemonade powder; a fruit pie containing dark-coloured objects; a loaf containing a half-inch metal bolt; and corned beef with a large fly embedded in it. (City Council records)

October 8th

1835: Thomas Sidney Cooper's second wife, Mary Cannon, was born on this day. When she married the Canterbury artist in 1863, Mary was twenty-seven years old and he was nearly sixty. By all accounts, the marriage was not a happy one and the couple separated in 1874, when their son Nevill was only ten (*see* January 9th). (Courtesy of Brian Stewart)

———◆———

1933: At the annual meeting of the North Kent Coalfield, it was reported that during the present year that Chislet Colliery, near Canterbury, had been the victim of a lightning strike. The chairman said the results at that date were not satisfactory as at the equivalent date the previous year. On the other hand, the Chislet company thought sufficiently well of the life of their company not only to have put down a considerable amount of new machinery, but to contemplate installing further machinery. (*Kentish Gazette*)

———◆———

1965: Planning permission for a new dance hall for the city was approved on this day. It was to be an extension of the ABC cinema in St George's Place, which lost its ballroom in the October 1942 Blitz (*see* February 22nd). In the event, the scheme never went ahead. (Author's archive)

October 9th

1592: On this day, a case against playwright Christopher Marlowe, for an assault on his friend, William Corkine, was dismissed. On September 10th, whilst walking near the Westgate, a discussion between them became heated and turned violent. Then, on the 15th, they met again at the same location, but this time Marlowe had a dagger. However, he did no more than cut the buttons from his friend's coat. This case is the last record of Marlowe in Canterbury. (Urry: *Quatercentenary Book*)

———◆———

1807: The sum of £5 has been paid into the Canterbury Bank for the benefit of the Kent and Canterbury Hospital, being compensation for a misdemeanour committed by James Steed and William Keen, in wantonly mutilating the ears of some sheep belonging to Mr Champion of Wickham (probably Wickhambreaux). (*Kentish Gazette*)

———◆———

1923: On this Tuesday, the First World War memorial at St Edmund's School was unveiled.

———◆———

1940: 'Second World War Notebook': 'Afternoon, ten high-explosive bombs were dropped on Canterbury. One dropped in front of two semi-detached houses in St Augustine's Road, which completely wrecked them but nobody was at home. Many other houses damaged.' [This is likely to have been bombs jettisoned from a Dornier 17 returning from a raid on London.]

October 10th

1361: On this day, Edward, the Black Prince, married his half-cousin Joan, the 'Fair Maid of Kent'. In gratitude, he financed the remodelling of a chapel in the cathedral crypt, known thereafter as the Black Prince's Chantry.

1814: On this Michaelmas Day, Canterbury's traditional Michaelmas Fair was held at the Cattle Market for the first time. For centuries it had been held in the cathedral 'Church Yard', being the paved part of the South Precincts between Christ Church Gate and the cathedral's south-west porch. (Sparks: *Canterbury Cathedral Precincts*)

1921: The city's memorial to the fallen of the First World War, in the Buttermarket, was unveiled by Field Marshall Earl Haig in a gesture seen by some today as bitterly ironic. The County Memorial is in the Cathedral Precincts' Memorial Gardens.

1984: The City Council leader has been challenged to spend a Saturday in a wheelchair to find out the problems of the disabled in Canterbury. But Councillor Jim Nock ignored the challenge, made at this Wednesday's Council meeting by a Labour councillor. He said that he was already sympathetic to the problems of the disabled and would investigate ways of improving consultation over projects that could effect them. (*Kentish Gazette*)

October 11th

1896: Archbishop Edward White Benson died on this day from heart disease after an incumbency of fourteen years. He had six talented but troubled children, some of whom were thought to have suffered from bipolar disorder. Amongst them were: Edward (author of *Mapp and Lucia*); Arthur, lyricist to 'Land of Hope and Glory'; and Margaret, an artist, author and amateur Egyptologist. Allegedly, after the Archbishop's death, his widow Mary set up a 'lesbian household' with Lucy Tait, daughter of the previous Archbishop (*see* December 3rd).

———◆———

1940: 'Second World War Notebook': 'Friday at noon, Canterbury attacked twice within fifteen minutes, by Me. 109s. First three [high-explosive] bombs burst with terrific crashes, completely demolishing six shops in Burgate Street and severely damaging others. Irving Williams' [furrier at Nos 18-19] shop got a direct hit and killed him [together with his] shop assistants and customers. Lydia Hill killed. Two [KCH] nurses killed [Staff Nurse Gwendoline Bragg and Nurse Fairfax-Brown]. In the bookshop next door [Carver & Staniforth at No. 20] one of the sisters was killed [Miss Gertrude Carver] and the other seriously injured. Nine killed altogether. Cathedral 19th century window glass blown out. Canon Crum's house [No. 13 The Precincts] got a direct hit.'

October 12th

1782: 'Mary Hopton, alias Upton, for entering the dwelling house of Anne East of the Borough of Staplegate, and stealing a black "callimance petticoat", one cloth apron, one muslin apron and other things: to be privately whipped.' (*Kentish Gazette*)

1886: At a recent Council meeting, Mr Furley said that on Sunday evenings the smell from the Cattle Market was most filthy and obnoxious. He wondered how the people in St George's Terrace could live. The surveyor stated that the market was cleaned every Saturday night and he had not had a single complaint as to the smell. [Back in 1991 Joyce Cozens, formerly of Nos 1 and 13, told me that the smell could indeed be overwhelming, making it impossible to open any windows in summer. Conversely, Kenneth Pinnock of No. 10 insisted he'd never noticed any such problem in ten years of living there.]

1940: This Friday was the last day of a successful *Kentish Gazette* campaign to raise £5,000 to buy a Spitfire. To help with the fundraising, Barrett's put a Messerschmitt 109 on display that had crash-landed intact. [It was probably the one forced down at Blean, *see* September 6th.] (Barrett's archive)

October 13th

1733: 'On this Tuesday, Thomas May Esq., one of the candidates for this city was presented with his freedom, and as an acknowledgement of that favour gave a hundred pounds for the clothing of four-score poor children nominated by the Mayor, Alderman and common men of the said city.' (*Kentish Post or Canterbury Newsletter*)

---◆---

1889: On this Sunday, Hilda Holdstock, an unmarried woman from the parish of St Gregory's, Canterbury, who was resident in the Blean Workhouse (at Herne), delivered a stillborn female child who was unnamed. Residents with the surname 'Holdstock' could be found in Edwardian Canterbury in St Radigund's Street and Broad Street. (Author's archive)

---◆---

1940: Boys from the adjacent King's School were called in to finish moving the vast piles of soil that had been deposited in the cathedral nave (see September 10th). The Dean and Chapter continued to defend their use of the crypt as an air-raid shelter, but did agree to a compromise. The soil would now only be placed in the choir aisles, thus allowing the main part of it to continue in use. Moreover, the soil would be boarded over so that the aisles could still be used for access.

October 14th

1170: Henry II and the exiled Archbishop Thomas Becket met in France for the last time in an attempt to reconcile their differences. As a result, Henry agreed to reverse some of the sanctions against the Archbishop (*see* October 15th) and Becket declared his intention to return to England (*see* December 2nd). (Urry: *Becket: His Last Days*)

———◆———

1884: James Wood, a young man, was charged with assaulting PC Hewett in the execution of his duty. Hewett said that on the previous night he was called to a passage near Ruttington Lane, where he found Wood brutally striking an old man, whose face was covered in blood. He took the prisoner into custody, but en route to the station, Wood knocked him against a wall. (*Kentish Gazette*)

———◆———

1940: 'Second World War Notebook': 'Before warning in the afternoon, four heavy oil-bombs were dropped. One landed in Station Road West, almost exactly where previous bombs had dropped, and completely demolished all the remaining shops round the corner. A car was blown on top of a single-storey shop. Another fell on Barrett's premises and ignited, damaging two ambulances, private cars and the Me. 109 previously on display [*see* October 12th]. In total, four killed and twenty-nine injured.'

October 15th

1170: Henry II sent a writ from France to his son, Prince Henry, in England ordering restitution (the return) of all the property and possessions that had been seized from Archbishop Thomas Becket upon his fleeing into exile, back in 1164. [This move would greatly upset Rannulph de Broc, occupant of Saltwood Castle, near Hythe, who had materially benefited the most from this confiscation.] (Urry: *Becket: His Last Days*)

———◆———

1799: On this day, the Canterbury Burghmote (City Council) considered a proposal from Alderman Simmons to demolish the unused King's Mill and build a house for himself on the site. The house had been completed by 1802. [Substantial remains of the King's Mill still exist, absorbed into the fabric of the house, particularly the side wall adjacent to the River Stour – visible from the King's Bridge. Today, the house is a pizza restaurant.] (Panton: *Canterbury's Great Tycoon*)

———◆———

1932: The following letter appeared in the *Kentish Gazette* on this day: 'Can nothing be done to shorten the duration of cathedral bell-ringing competitions or practises at one time? On Saturday last, we had four consecutive hours of it, which was almost unbearable.' It was signed 'Another sufferer'.

October 16th

1822: At about 5.32 a.m., the south and west sides of the 'Ethelbert Tower', once part of St Augustine's Abbey, suddenly collapsed 'with a dreadful crash'. In 1765, the ancient structure had been weakened by the demolition of its north side, in order to salvage stone for re-use, but this work became so laborious that it was abandoned. All that was left following the accident was the tottering east wall, then still standing some 100ft high (*see* October 24th).

◆

1933: While a bullock was being driven along Beer Cart Lane on this Monday, it suddenly ran into the builder's office of L.T. Dadds. After causing some damage, it was persuaded to leave the occupants in peace. [Dadds' premises, adjacent to No. 2 Beer Cart Lane, were demolished in around 1970 to make way for the Council office block.] (*Kentish Gazette*)

◆

1986: This was the morning of the Great Hurricane that devastated much of South-East England. In Canterbury, part of Holter's Mill collapsed, as did the parapet of the Roper Chapel at St Dunstan's Church. Vast trees were also torn up in the Dane John, Westgate Gardens and on Miller's Field. (Crampton: *Before and After the Hurricane*)

October 17th

1909: Through the kindness and generosity of Mr Alfred Slater of Tyler Hill House, Blean, a handsome organ has been placed in the little parish church of Blean, St Cosmos' and St Damian's. Hitherto, the church has been dependent for music on the efforts of the choir, augmented by an 'American Organ', kindly lent by Mr A. Price. [An 'American Organ', or melodeon, was a small portable organ with foot-operated bellows, similar to a harmonium.] (*Kentish Gazette*)

———•◆•———

1933: A massive fire in Abbott's Mill, St Radigund's Street, began on this Tuesday and lasted for some three days, completely destroying this six-storey landmark. Designed by John Smeaton, the watermill was built in 1792.

———•◆•———

1940: 'Second World War Notebook': '01.35 pm, a formation of Messerschmitts dive-bombed Canterbury and made a deliberate attack on the cathedral. In all, thirty-eight bombs were dropped; three round the cathedral: one in the [front] garden of The Deanery [resulting in] dangerous, wide cracks in the fabric, and Hewlett Johnson had a lucky escape. Another bomb on Canon Banks' house [No. 12 The Precincts], demolishing a corner of it, but he and his family also escaped. The third landed near Canon Shirley's house [No. 15].'

October 18th

1783: Following the great improvement in the road leading from the Green Court Gate to the Red Pump – undertaken and completed by a very liberal subscription from John Monins Esq. and others – it was the desire of many city inhabitants that the same improvements might be continued from the Red Pump to the Buttermarket. [At this time, the Mint Yard Gate was situated further down The Borough, and Palace Street effectively extended right up to the Green Court Gate. The Red Pump, at the junction with Orange Street, can still be seen today.] (*Kentish Gazette*)

———◆·◆———

1915: The funeral of Lieutenant Alan Hardy, who died following a fall from an aeroplane, took place at Chilham on this Monday. The young officer, who belonged to the East Kent Yeomanry and was attached to the Royal Flying Corps, was the son of the late Mr C.S. Hardy of Chilham Castle. (Author's archive)

———◆·◆———

1944: From the list of 'Big Ben' incidents, 'October 1944: On the 18th, at 06.32 a.m., at Chislet, near Canterbury'. 'Big Ben' was the codename for the wartime V2 rocket. This was the eighty-fifth recorded V2. Another rocket landed near Whitstable. (*The Blitz Then and Now*)

October 19th

1804: On this day, it was reported that the proposed Canterbury Canal (*see* June 6th) be linked to the Royal Military Canal on the South Coast via another proposed canal, called the Weald of Kent Canal. The last-named project envisaged a canal from Yalden Lees and Ashford, running northwards to Canterbury, linking up with the first project. This network was seen as desirable commercially and for defensive purposes. Subsequently, only the Royal Military Canal was constructed. (*Archaeologia Cantiana*, 1988)

————•◆•————

1873: Born at the Blean Workhouse on this day: an illegitimate daughter to Ann Boodle of the parish of Blean. The child was baptised 'Ann' at the workhouse. (Author's archive)

————•◆•————

1934: 'The 700th anniversary of the granting of the charter by Henry III to the City of Canterbury will be celebrated on this Friday. It is stated that a cathedral service will be held.' [By the charter of 1234, the citizens of Canterbury were allowed to elect their own tax-collecting bailiffs, as opposed to having them appointed by the King.] (*Kentish Gazette*)

————•◆•————

1964: On this day, the Council approved plans for the construction of the new College of Art in New Dover Road. (City Council records)

October 20th

1868: A city-based Catholic priest, Father Peter Van de Voorde, was charged with indecency. He was accused at the County Police Court, Canterbury, of indecently exposing himself in the sight of Sarah Reed and Mrs Warner – the wife of a police constable! The alleged offence was committed on the footpath near the bottom of Tyler Hill at Hackington, after which the accused is said to have run away. In his defence, Van de Voorde's doctor said he had heart disease and could barely walk, let alone run. This, and glowing character references from several priests, resulted in the defendant being discharged. (Christopher Buckingham archive)

1986: On this day, the Green Cross man came to Canterbury to bring home the road-safety message to local primary-school children. During the afternoon, he visited Canterbury's Parkside School. (*Kentish Gazette*)

1990: A mystery vandal struck at the King's School and burnt an obscene word into a wooden floor. The two-word message was discovered in Shirley Hall, the school's main assembly room, in the Precincts on this Monday morning. One of the words used was 'Duck', which is understood to be a nickname used by pupils for the headmaster, Canon Anthony Philips. (Author's archive)

October 21st

1188: The Christ Church Prior, Honorious, died of the plague on this day. He had been chaplain to Archbishop Baldwin, but as Prior he vigorously opposed the Archbishop's scheme for founding a College of Canons at Hackington (*see* October 1st). For this purpose, he went to Rome to lay the appeal of the priory before Pope Urban III, but died of the plague en route at Velletri. (Woodruff and Danks: *Memorials*)

———•———

1747: Thomas Herring, a staunch anti-Jacobite, was nominated Archbishop of Canterbury on this Saturday. (Wikipedia)

———•———

1887: On this day, an archaeological investigation began on part of the Bifrons Estate at Patrixbourne, near Canterbury. Some Saxon graves had been discovered whilst planting trees, and noted local antiquarian Thomas Faussett of Heppington House, Nackington, was granted permission to investigate further. A total of 100 graves were found, with weapons and jewellery. (Pearson: *Ghost Houses*)

———•———

1939: 'Registration of all persons staying at your premises will, from now onwards, be compulsory. Registration forms, when completed, must be kept by you in a safe place, and would be open to inspection and, if necessary, removal by the police. These instructions come into force forthwith and failure to comply with them will lead to severe penalties.' (*Kentish Gazette*)

October 22nd

1802: On this day, the Corporation was presented with a bill of £2,237 for the demolition of St George's Gate, which had taken place the previous year. This excessive amount may have been a contributory factor in saving the Westgate (*see* June 21st). (*Archaeologia Cantiana*, 1988)

◆

1965: On this Friday, a police car chase took place in Canterbury. PC Hover noticed Mr B. from Nunnery Fields speeding through Sturry, and then chased his Ford Consul along the 40mph limit of Sturry Road at around 60mph. He entered the city, overtaking another car near Burgate at 50mph. Mr B. finally pulled over in Castle Street when he noticed the police car behind him. He was fined £6. (Author's archive)

◆

1984: Canterbury's new Marlowe Theatre, in The Friars, is a big success – even though it will still cost ratepayers more than £50,000 this year. Shows have been selling out and income is on the up and up, the City Council's Amenity Committee heard on this Monday. Losses are less than expected and takings last week were over £30,000. 'Things are looking very rosy', said a delighted Councillor Peter Lee, the committee's chairman. (*Kentish Gazette*)

October 23rd

1769: 'William Francis has died holding one messuage called the "Sign of Dover", one other messuage and a smith's forge adjoining and six acres of land belonging to said messuages… [This is a reference to Nos 79, 81 and 81a Old Dover Road.]'. (Courtesy of John Farrar)

1845: The *Kent Herald* reported an accident on the Canterbury to Whitstable Railway: 'We understand that an accident occurred on this line to the late train on Tuesday afternoon. A light carried by the conductor was mistaken for a signal and a collision took place, by which a wagon was thrown over the embankment. The passengers in the van were much alarmed, but fortunately none were hurt, although several ventured to leave the carriage ere it was stopped'. (Courtesy Brian Hart)

1936: While walking in Sun Street, Canterbury, on this Friday, Florence Baldock of No. 19 Artillery Gardens tripped and fell, striking her head against a passing car. She received a cut to the face, but was able to continue on her way after treatment. [Florence had lived at No. 19, with her husband Edwin, since the early 1920s. By 1937, however, she was listed as living there alone.] (*Kentish Gazette*)

October 24th

1822: On this day, the remaining east face of the 'Ethelbert Tower' was pulled down following the major collapse of October 16th. Although tottering, the remains proved substantial enough for a battering ram to be fashioned for the purpose. 'The descent was awfully grand, and to the lovers of antiquity, grievous!' Today, a stump of this early twelfth-century tower still survives.

———◆———

1883: As Dr Johnson's horse and carriage was standing outside his house in St George's Place on this Wednesday morning, the horse suddenly started and came in contact with a lamppost. The carriage was considerably damaged. Dr Johnson, who ran after the horse, was caught by one of the carriage wheels and thrown down, but was not hurt seriously. (*Kentish Gazette*)

———◆———

1940: From an official war diary: 'The cook, Gunner Ramsey, with assistance from Sgt Glover, picked up a 5th columnist suspect in the grounds of Barton Court. He was dressed in civilians and when questioned by Major Thackray, was unable to show any identification, having left his papers at home. On being taken to the Canterbury Police Station, he was readily identified as Inspector Jones of the City Police. He took the incident in good part.'

October 25th

1782: 'An Announcement': 'Thomas Goff has been taught by His Majesty's rat-catcher to take alive or destroy those pernicious vermin in dwelling houses and elsewhere, with the greatest safety. Those who please to employ him in the City of Canterbury may depend on being punctually waited on.' (*Kentish Gazette*)

1842: Clare Luckhurst was refused admission to the Kent and Canterbury Hospital. Mr Denne declared that she had already spent seven months in the hospital with an ulcerated leg, and the condition proved to be incurable. (*Archaeologia Cantiana*, 1988)

1940: Passenger services on the Elham Valley Line were suddenly suspended so that passing loops could be installed prior to the railway's takeover by the military. A massive mobile gun would soon arrive on the line. (Hart: *Elham Valley Railway*)

1961: On this day, a public enquiry was held to hear objections to the compulsory purchase of all the old houses in Rosemary Lane and Church Lane, St Mildred's. Sadly for the occupants, the result was never in doubt. The public health inspector testified that the properties were damp and insanitary, with 'no properly ventilated food-stores'. Re-housing was offered on the Spring Lane Estate. Demolition took place the following year. (Author's archive)

October 26th

1535: Whilst staying in lodgings at Christ Church Priory, Dr Richard Layton discovered a fire and immediately summoned help from the town. And then, being fearful of the safety of the Becket shrine, he alerted all the monks and readied them should the holy relics and treasures need moving out of the cathedral. Luckily, the fire was successfully controlled. Ironically, within three years, Layton would play a quite different role regarding Becket's Tomb (*see* September 7th). (Butler: *The Quest for Becket's Bones*)

1941: On this Sunday, Canterbury held an anti-invasion exercise, which included role-playing 'Nazi parachutists' attacking the East and West railway stations.

1944: On this day, Archbishop William Temple died suddenly after only two-and-a-half years in office. He was sixty-three. Temple suffered from a rare, lifelong gout problem, and this contributed to his early death. He was a socialist, and his approach to religion was broadmindedly ecumenical. He also championed the repatriation of Jews escaping Nazi Germany. Temple was no pacifist, but supported a negotiated peace once it was clear that the Allies would win the Second World War. He was the first Archbishop to be cremated, and his ashes are buried in the cathedral corona (*see* April 23rd).

October 27th

1837: On, or very near, this day, hoaxer and fantasist 'Sir William Courtenay' was released from Barming Asylum into the care of Mr Francis of Boughton-Under-Blean, near Canterbury, a lifelong supporter and friend. In October 1833, Courtenay had been transferred from gaol to the asylum, not long after his perjury trial. (Rogers: *Battle in Bossenden Wood, see* July 1st)

1882: 'As proof of the mildness of the season, we may mention that a few days ago Alderman Linom gathered some ripe strawberries in his garden.' (*Kentish Gazette*)

1940: A Messerschmitt 109, escorting bombers en route to London, was damaged by Spitfires from No. 74 Squadron and crashed at Upstreet, near Canterbury. The pilot baled out and was captured slightly wounded. (*The Blitz Then and Now*)

2005: On this day, the *Guardian* reported: 'If plans for a "house of poetry" are successful, Canterbury could be home to a vibrant community of poets sharing their thoughts over a cup of coffee or glass of wine, before leading a workshop or giving readings of their work to the public. Michael Curtis, manager of the Words Unbound project hopes to gather support for a permanent building based on the French idea of "maisons de poesie".'

October 28th

AD 994: On this day the Saxon Archbishop of Canterbury Sigeric 'the Serious' died, probably in the city. Prior to becoming Archbishop, he had been Abbot of St Augustine's Abbey. In the same year as his death, Archbishop Sigeric paid 'tribute' (sort of medieval 'protection money') to the Danes to prevent them sacking and burning the cathedral. Sigeric was buried in the building he had personally saved.

———◆———

1884: During this morning, John Thomas, an elderly man, was charged with stealing sprouts from the garden of Major Plummer at North Holmes. Joseph Hoar, a labouring man, deposed that he saw the defendant in Major Plummer's garden that morning. (*Kentish Gazette*)

———◆———

1955: This Friday was a bad day for accidents on the roads of Canterbury. In the morning, a seven-year-old girl was run over near the junction with Littlebourne Road and Querns Road. She sustained severe head injuries. In the afternoon, an Army lorry hit a bicycle at the junction of Castle Street and Gas Street; the male cyclist received a cut to the head. And then in the evening, a car and motorcycle collided at St George's Gate. The rider and pillion passenger sustained slight injuries. (Author's archive)

October 29th

1701: A Six Preacher of Canterbury Cathedral, Arthur Kaye, died after thirty years in the role. He was also Vicar of the united parishes of St Andrew's, in The Parade, and St Mary Breadman, in the High Street. He was buried in St Andrew's Church. When it was demolished in 1763, his memorial tablet was moved, probably to the replacement St Andrew's Church, and then moved yet again when that was demolished in 1956 to St Margaret's Church. (Ingram Hill: *The Six Preachers*)

———•♦•———

1806: Alderman James Simmons was nominated by the Freeman of the city as one of the two MPs for Canterbury. The other was the incumbent, John Baker. There being no other candidates submitted, both men were elected unopposed. (*Archaeologia Cantiana*, 1988)

———•♦•———

1965: A Utopian vision of the future Canterbury has been announced: 'In 1981, the city could well have a population of 50,000. It will be ringed by a new road and have at least four multi-storey car parks; its central area would become a traffic-free haven for shoppers and tourists; its beautiful old buildings and monuments will stand shoulder-to-shoulder with new Modernist offices; new houses and flats would shoot up like mushrooms.' (*Kentish Gazette*)

October 30th

1830: On this day, *The Times* reported rioting around Canterbury in response to the arrival of threshing machines, which had put many out of work. Troops were called out from the city, such was the concern, and from the top of the Dane John blazing farms could be seen all around.

------◆◆------

1934: The splendidly appointed new church of the Spiritualist Society in St George's Terrace was opened on this Tuesday evening. Mr A. Lander presided over a large attendance, supported by Mr Vyvyan Deccon, one of the leading mediums in the country. [The church, part of the 'Sun Buildings' complex, was destroyed in the Blitz on 1 June 1942. Today, the Spiritualist Church is situated in Kirby's Lane.] (*Kentish Gazette*)

------◆◆------

1942: On this Friday, Canterbury played host to the wives of the two leaders of the free world, namely Mrs Churchill and Mrs Roosevelt. In the company of Alderman Lefevre, they spent some time in the city and then took a special train along the Elham Valley Line to Barham. There, they visited the Barham Women's Institute. The following day, a newspaper carried an uncensored headline reading: 'Barham, Kent' (*see* October 31st). (Crampton: *The Blitz of Canterbury*)

October 31st

1568: On this day, the second son, and fourth child of John and Katherine Marlowe was baptised at St George's Church. No name was recorded and the child lived only for a few days, being buried on November 5th. A few months earlier, on August 28th, they had also buried their first-born, a daughter named Mary, in the same graveyard. She was six years old. Christopher Marlowe, their second-born child, would have been four at the time. (Urry: *Christopher Marlowe and Canterbury, see* August 7th)

———— ◆ ————

1942: During this afternoon, Canterbury's barrage balloons were down for essential repairs. And then, at 5 p.m., twenty Messerschmitt 109 fighter-bombers made a low-level attack on the city. Shoppers in the main street were ruthlessly strafed, whilst twenty high-explosive bombs were dropped across the east of Canterbury, destroying many houses in Northgate, Wincheap and Watling Street. The Regal cinema in St George's Place was also hit. The aircraft went as quickly as they'd arrived, leaving thirty-two people dead in their wake. (Crampton: *The Blitz of Canterbury*)

———— ◆ ————

2002: Archbishop George Carey resigned on this day after an incumbency of eleven years. Some sources say that he was the 'most excoriated' (criticised) Archbishop since Laud.

November 1st

1066: It is likely that on, or near, this date, Canterbury submitted to William the Conqueror without bloodshed. This was on William's journey from Dover to London, along the route of today's A2. It is also likely that on this journey he decided on the siting of his first three major castles at Dover, Canterbury and Rochester, as well as some minor ones, such as that at Tonge, near Sittingbourne.

———◆———

1762: On this day, John Wesley came to Canterbury to visit the recently formed 'Methodist Society'. A letter from him afterwards demonstrates that he was far from impressed. He did not like several people singing, speaking and praying all at once; their using improper expressions in prayer – sometimes too familiar, sometimes too pompous; their screaming, even to the point of making their words unintelligible; and their using poor, flat, bald hymns. (Taylor: *The Free Churches of Canterbury*)

———◆———

1936: A 310-year-old tawny owl's egg has been presented to the museum at the Beaney Institute by Mrs Bartlett from Canterbury. One of four, it was found in 1887 in the middle of a wall in Queenborough church tower, which has been filled in after a subsidence in 1626. (*Kentish Gazette*)

November 2nd

1164: This Monday was the first day of Thomas Becket's self-imposed exile in France after a furious Henry II had dubbed him a traitor at Northampton Castle on October 13th. Since then, he and his entourage had been fleeing in secret, clearly fearing for their lives. (Urry: *Becket: His Last Days*)

❖

1937: 'Tory Tirade': A warning against the dangers of Communism and Fascism was issued to the women of Canterbury by Mrs R.S.I. Friend, when she presided at a meeting of the Canterbury Divisional Women's Conservative Club on this Tuesday: 'Communism and fascism are dangers to our Empire, and particularly to us women in Canterbury, because living here, almost within sight of these windows, we have someone whom we know is very much in sympathy with, if not actually being, a Communist,' she declared. [This is clearly aimed at the Dean, Hewlett Johnson, popularly known as the 'Red Dean': a much-respected figure who saw no dichotomy between the ideals of Communism and the teachings of Christ.] (*Kentish Gazette*)

❖

1955: 'Tory Trees': The Council reported that trees in the disused St Margaret's churchyard were to be felled because they excluded light from the Conservative Club next door!

November 3rd

1349: On this day, the adjacent parishes of St Edmund Riding Gate and St Mary Bredin were united under the authority of the Prior of Christ Church. This was because the former church had fallen into ruin. Built into the back of the Riding Gate in Watling Street, nothing remains of St Edmund's Church today. (Hasted: *Kent*, Vol. XI)

———◆———

1813: On this day, Jane Austen wrote of a visit to Canterbury with her brother: 'Edward and I had a delightful morning for our drive… He went to inspect the gaol and took me with him. I was gratified and went through all the feelings, which people must go through, I think, in visiting such a building. We paid no other visits, only walked about snugly together and shopped. I bought a concert ticket and a sprig of flowers for my old age'. (*Written City*)

———◆———

1954: A cash crisis was discussed by the Council on this day. One solution suggested was to sell off the undeveloped freeholds already purchased, as part of the Post-War Redevelopment Plan (*see* February 13th). This would then pay off the loan taken out for the building of the new shops in St George's Street. (City Council records)

November 4th

1790: 'David Pares, late pupil to David Mendoza, the celebrated pugilist, informs the public that on this Thursday he intends to open up a school to learn the art of boxing at the King's Arms. Mr Pares, zealous to afford pleasure to the public in this manual art will, between the hours of ten and one, display a series of "sparrings", equal to those exhibited in London'. [The inn – at No. 49 St Peter's Street – closed in 1935 and, for the next fifty-seven years, became Longley's pork butcher.] (*Kentish Gazette*)

1861: On this Monday, Charles Dickens gave a reading of *David Copperfield* at the recently completed Theatre Royal in Guildhall Street. The reading took about two hours. Afterwards, Dickens remarked on the theatre's admirable acoustic qualities. (Stewart: *Thomas Sidney Cooper, see* January 30th)

1946: On this Sunday, a memorial service was held in the school chapel at Kent College to remember the thirty-eight Old Boys who had been killed in the Second World War. A War Memorial Fund was inaugurated and, two years later, this resulted in the installation of the Memorial Organ in the chapel. It was purchased from the redundant Congregational Church in Guildhall Street. (Wright: *Kent College*)

November 5th

1811: On this day, future Canterbury painter Thomas Sidney Cooper – then eight-years old – was shot in the face by a young boy with a horse pistol. The wound nearly proved fatal and some pellets remained embedded under his skin for the rest of his life. (Courtesy of Brian Stewart)

———•◆•———

1914: 'About half a mile of the carriageway in Sturry Road has recently been reconstructed upon the "Gladwell" system. This form of carriageway dries quickly after rain, it is mudless and practically dustless. The Road Board has now agreed to this form of road surface being laid upon three of the main roads in the city, viz: Sturry Road, New Dover Road and Thannington Road.' (*Kentish Gazette*)

———•◆•———

1957: A dispute between two Canterbury businesses, over some smelly drains, was finally settled on this day. The complainant was Mr Siminson, optician, at No. 9b The Parade, and the alleged nuisance was being caused by the Pilgrim's Tearooms in St Margaret's Street. In June, the judge in the case inspected the drains at the back of the tearooms, but the claimant's solicitor claimed they had been 'dolled up' especially for the inspection. Consequently, the judge made a second, unannounced visit, and the settlement was agreed shortly afterwards! (Author's archive)

November 6th

1795: 'Last night and early this Friday morning, the wind blew from the W-N-W a tremendous storm, accompanied with very black clouds and sharp lightning. In Canterbury, many large trees were torn up, and several chimneys, walls and fences blown down.' (*Kentish Register*, courtesy of Tina Machado)

1884: 'That's gotta hurt, 1': 'A serious accident occurred in the engine shed of Mr Kingsnorth's Brickfield on this Thursday night. Thomas Arnold (aged sixty) was sent up by the engine driver, Robert Harris, to remove the strap from the bucket wheel when he slipped against a large flywheel and was carried part of the way round, becoming jammed in the 9in gap between the wheel and a brick wall.' (*Kentish Gazette*)

1939: 'That's gotta hurt, 2': 'There was an exciting scene in Canterbury Cattle Market during this Monday morning, when a man was attacked by a bullock. Arthur Bax (aged fifty-three) was trying to drive the animal onto the weighbridge when it suddenly charged him, knocked him down and gored him on the upper part of his right leg. With others, PC Castle finally managed to get Bax – a heavy man – free, and taken to Kent and Canterbury Hospital.' (*Kentish Gazette*)

November 7th

1808: 'The anniversary of the Historical Society was held on this Monday at the City Arms, Northgate, Canterbury, and was attended by nearly seventy persons who partook of an excellent supper. The evening was conducted with that distinguished hilarity and good order, which the occasion never fails to produce.' [With all that 'distinguished hilarity', it sounds more like the 'Hysterical Society'! The inn, at No. 60 Northgate, closed in 1892.] (*Kentish Gazette*)

1956: At a Council meeting on this Wednesday, it was reported that traders in the Westgate and St Dunstan's area had suffered since the bus station was moved to St George's Lane earlier that summer. In response, the Council promised to lobby for the proposed coach park to be sited on a vacant plot in Roper Road. [In the event, the coach park continued to remain at Longport.] (City Council records)

1960: The consequences of the recent serious flooding in Canterbury were reported on this Monday. The only houses significantly affected were those in St Peter's Place, although water in cellars elsewhere was reported. At the Hales Place Estate, a barrage of sandbags, laid by the fire brigade, had proved very effective. (Author's archive)

November 8th

1755: A court of lieutenancy was held on this Saturday, to consider the ways and means for immediately putting the militia of Canterbury on a useful footing. [This was at a time when England was at war with France in Canada.] (*Kentish Post*)

— ◆ —

1887: Whilst Mr Gammon and other workmen were sitting at dinner, on the building in course of erection by Mr Thomas Sidney Cooper at Tyler Hill, they were alarmed by a report from a gun, followed by the whiz of a bullet, which passed between two of them, striking the brickwork and rebounding some distance. Soon afterwards, another shot was heard and, on searching the neighbouring fields, it was found that Mr Hambrook of Shelford Farm was out scaring rooks! [The house would become Allcroft Grange, named after one of the painter's patrons, *see* September 3rd.] (*Kentish Gazette*)

— ◆ —

1920: Rupert Bear made his first-ever appearance in the *Daily Express* on this Monday. Created by Canterbury-born artist Mary Tourtel (*see* January 28th) Rupert was the paper's response to the popular Teddy Tail character who had appeared in the *Daily Mail* since 1915. (Stewart: *The Rupert Bear Dossier*)

November 9th

1896: Archbishop of Canterbury Frederick Temple was elected on this day. He was a passionate advocate for unity in the Church of England. He was also the first Archbishop to be able to reside in the city for many years, the new Old Palace being completed in 1900. Temple was taken ill during a speech in the House of Lords on 2 December 1902 and died on the 23rd. His second son, William, would also go on to become Archbishop (*see* April 23rd).

1960: The Library and Museums Committee reported that many of the folding-type chairs in use at the Slater Lecture Hall required replacing. One of them suddenly collapsed under the weight of an elected member during the last Council meeting. (City Council records)

1984: The city will be lit up for Christmas this year with the best streetlights Canterbury has seen. Thanks to the Chamber of Trade and traders in St Margaret's Street and Palace Street, the whole city centre will be ablaze. The new lights, costing £6,000, will stretch from the Longmarket to the Westgate Towers. They go up during the next few days and will be switched on in a week's time. (*Kentish Gazette*)

November 10th

1356: William de Apuldrefeld was appointed Keeper of Canterbury Castle Gaol on this day. During his tenure, a prisoner named William de Rothwell escaped and took sanctuary in nearby St Mildred's Church. He had been incarcerated for 'abducting' Maud, the wife of William de Lenegor, and also much of his property. However, it is more likely that Maud went willingly! Rothwell was later released 'because the King is informed he was indicted by the malice of enemies'. (Gardiner: *Story of Canterbury Castle*)

---◆·•---

1882: Hannah Goodall was summoned for neglecting to send her daughter regularly to school. The clerk to the School Board said it was a case of persistent neglect. The child was growing up in utter ignorance, and the defendant also failed to send other members of the family to school. The bench imposed a fine of 5s, including costs. (*Kentish Gazette*)

---◆·•---

1933: An appeal for a sum of £2,000 to enable the Canterbury Churches Housing Fellowship to begin work in the city – which will make for the betterment of people's housing conditions – was made at a well-attended meeting at the County Hall on this Friday, when the subject of housing was reviewed by the Mayor, Alderman Frank Hooker. (City Council records)

November 11th

1939: The message of Her Majesty the Queen, broadcast to the women of the Empire on this Saturday night, was successfully relayed to the audience at the Friars Cinema, Canterbury, by means of a Burndept radio, supplied and installed by Messrs Gouldens. [Established in about 1840, Gouldens traded from Nos 39 and 40 High Street for well over a century.] (*Kentish Gazette*)

———◆———

1959: The following articles have been found in Canterbury and district, and taken to the City Police Station: high-heeled blue shoes; a parcel of chicken and bacon rashers; a red lorry wheel; a shopping basket with meat; a grey beret for Wincheap School; and a pair of lovat green trousers. (City Police records)

———◆———

1960: The once-banned novel *Lady Chatterley's Lover*, by D.H. Lawrence, was now on sale in Canterbury and local bookshops reported pre-publication interest in it as 'fantastic' and 'completely unprecedented'. Orders for the unexpurgated edition of Lawrence's book – complete with its now famous 'four letter words' – had been flowing ever since Penguin Books were found not guilty of publishing obscene literature. Several booksellers had enquiries from young children. A schoolboy marched into one shop and ordered a dozen copies! (Author's archive)

November 12th

1720: Interesting monumental inscription inside St Dunstan's Church: 'Burial place designed for ye family of Mr Claude Rondeau, Merchant (silkweaver) of Canterbury, refugee in England, for the Protestant Religion (Huguenot). Here lieth the body of the said Claudius Rondeau, who departed this life 12th November 1720, aged 72 years.' [Records show that he had been churchwarden for St Dunstan's.]

———•◆•———

1833: 'There has been lately erected at the tannery of the Messrs Keen at St Stephens, near this city, a hydraulic water wheel attached to a bark mill. The wheel was composed wholly of bar and sheet iron, and in the construction of which, no other artificers were employed than the labouring tanners of the yard.' [A 'bark mill' is a small building that was once used for processing tree bark, used in the dyeing and tanning industries. Many small tanneries could once be found on the banks of the River Stour.] (*Kentish Gazette*)

———•◆•———

1940: 'Second Worl War Notebook': 'Nine bombs dropped, but only a few houses were damaged on the outskirts, near St Stephen's Hill.' [They were likely to have been jettisoned by a Luftwaffe bomber returning from a London raid.] (*The Blitz Then and Now*)

November 13th

1419: Cristine Beneyt (or Benet) by her will, proved on this day, gave to the Friars Minor (Greyfriars) 6s 8d. She was the widow of Robert Benet, Bailiff of Canterbury, who lived in Stour Street. Both were buried in the nearby Church of St Mildred. (Cotton: *Greyfriars of Canterbury*)

———◆•◆———

1758: 'For the benefit of Mrs Midnight, at the playhouse in Canterbury on this Monday evening, will be presented her concert and oratory, in which will be introduced her rehearsal after the manner of Boys in Petticoats. With the garden scene in *Romeo and Juliet*: in which the several voices of Mrs Cibber, Mrs Bellamy, and Miss Nossiter will be imitated by Mrs Midnight.' [This is a reference to the Buttermarket Theatre, which occupied the central position, from 1734 to 1789, before being replaced by the covered market building – *see* September 5th. Later theatres would be situated in Orange Street and Guildhall Street.] (*Kentish Post*, with thanks also to David Manners)

———◆•◆———

1795: On this Friday, Mr William Baldock, brewer, of Canterbury, gave 200 sacks of potatoes to be distributed to the poor of Northgate, St Mildred and other parishes in the city. (*Kentish Register*, courtesy of Tina Machado)

November 14th

1882: Arrangements have been made for the nave and choir of Canterbury Cathedral to be lighted by electricity. The architect and engineer have devised a plan by which the cathedral can be effectively illuminated by just six lights. If the results of the experiments are satisfactory, the Deanery and other residences in The Precincts will be supplied with the electric light (*see* November 21st). (*Kentish Gazette*)

———•◆•———

1955: Three people escaped unhurt when the roof and front bedrooms of two old houses at Nos 19 and 20 New Town Street collapsed during this Monday evening. Brick, tiles, timber and furniture crashed into the road, as residents Mrs Payne and Mr and Mrs Palmer dashed to safety through the back doors. Firemen were quickly on the scene and, with the aid of searchlights, had to demolish the upper party wall, which was swaying dangerously in the high wind. Evidently, the residents had been expecting this for months after telltale cracks began to appear: 'We told the landlord about it, but nothing was done!' (Crampton: *Canterbury Suburbs and Surroundings*)

———•◆•———

1962: 'Should you want the Canterbury Public Health Department to exterminate a wasps' nest, it will cost £1 in future.' (City Council records)

November 15th

1244: 'A gift from Henry III to Canterbury Cathedral: To make 1,000 tapers each of half-a-pound of wax, and place them about the shrine of St Thomas the Martyr… for the preservation of the health and for the delivery of the Queen, who is with child.' (Friends Report, 1946)

———◆◆———

1842: On this day, the *Kentish Gazette* reported: 'Queen Victoria visited Canterbury, accompanied by Prince Albert and their two infants, one of whom was Edward, heir to the throne. The streets were absolutely in motion, and the windows peopled with many human heads. The first carriage contained the Royal couple. However, the glass on the Queen's side was up, and the anxious spectators were not able to view and greet the sovereign, as they seemed to desire.' [Audrey Bateman's book *Victorian Canterbury* adds: 'One local citizen caused deep offence. Rushing forward, with a cry of "Bless 'is little heart", a woman planted a kiss on the brow of the infant Prince, who was being held by his nurse'.]

———◆◆———

1954: On this day, Minister of Housing William Deedes inspected some new 'experimental houses' on the London Road estate. Unlike other newly built terraced houses nearby, these included some pre-fabricated elements.

November 16th

1458: Canterbury Cathedral master mason Richard Beke died on this day. He was responsible for rebuilding the vast majority of the south-west tower, which became the new Belfry (*see* May 21st), as well as the new crossing piers under Bell Harry Tower and the new Lady Chapel. (Blockley: *Canterbury Cathedral Nave*)

1638: William Dunkyn was appointed a cathedral Six Preacher on this day. Being of the High-Church persuasion, when the Civil War began he fell out of favour with local Puritans. In fact, Dunkyn faced several charges. These included: frequenting alehouses; drinking Prince Rupert's health (a Royalist leader); and bowing before the altar. He is also said to have had unmistakably recognisable handwriting that was very difficult to decipher. (Derek Ingram Hill)

1832: 'Mrs Levy, an aged woman whose name will be familiar to our readers in connection with the late deplorable fire at St Thomas' Hill, near this city, and who was recently sentenced to transportation for seven years, has received His Majesty's gracious pardon. She was liberated from St Augustine's Gaol the same day. However, the son-in-law of this woman is paying the penalty of his crime in a convict settlement abroad.' (*Kentish Gazette*)

November 17th

1558: The Archbishop of Canterbury, Cardinal Reginald Pole, died on this day, thus ending the brief Catholic renaissance at Canterbury Cathedral. He had been appointed by Mary Tudor (*see* March 22nd) and was her willing vassal in the attempt to stamp out the Protestant religion in England. Ironically, he died on the very same day as Queen Mary I, and was buried in the cathedral corona.

———◆———

1809: Last week, as John White – servant to Messrs Read & Co., brewers in Canterbury – was assisting a blacksmith in shoeing one of the horses, the animal kicked him on the leg, by which accident it was broken in a shocking manner. He was taken to Kent and Canterbury Hospital. (*Kentish Gazette*)

———◆———

1965: Under the Canterbury Northgate Improvement Scheme, the following properties were subject to a compulsory purchase order: Nos 137-140 Northgate (early Victorian terraced houses), and part of the forecourts of Nos 125/127 (Bishop's Taxis), No. 136a (the Prince of Wales Youth Club) and Nos 141/146 (County Electrical), also in Northgate. This was largely to effect street widening. Demolition of the houses, with others, occurred in late 1966. (See Crampton: *Canterbury Suburbs and Surroundings* for a complete photo survey of the Northgate area)

November 18th

1833: During this Monday evening, as the express coach – en route from London to Dover – was within half-a-mile of this city, the horses took fright and, bolting across the road, the coach was dragged up the bank and overturned. Luckily, the passengers escaped unhurt, with the exception of one who was slightly confused. [This accident is likely to have occurred on the descent through Upper Harbledown which, even to this day, is steeply banked on one side.] (*Kentish Gazette*)

———•———

1941: During this Tuesday evening, at about 7 p.m., two enemy parachute mines were jettisoned above the village of Sturry, destroying much of the old High Street. In all, fifteen people were killed (including four children), and forty were injured. (Butler: *Village Views*)

———•———

1991: On this Monday, Terry Waite, the special envoy of the Archbishop of Canterbury, was released by Shiite Muslims, after more than four years of captivity. Prior to his kidnapping, he had secured the release of missionaries in Iran, British hostages in Libya and American hostages in Lebanon. Terry came home to a different Archbishop – George Carey – than the one who sent him out on that fateful last mission, Robert Runcie.

November 19th

1932: At a private meeting held in the city on this Saturday, in connection with the Canterbury Dramatic Society, it was decided to call a public meeting in order to appoint trustees to receive funds for the establishment of a Marlowe Memorial Theatre for Canterbury. After Alderman Frank Hooker had proposed the setting up of a committee in March 1933, plans were drawn up by local architect H. Campbell Ashenden. These included an imaginative sketch showing the proposed T-shaped theatre at a riverside setting on the outskirts of the city. In the event, these plans were never 'acted' upon.

———◆———

1937: While employees of the Canterbury Electricity Department were excavating under the pavement outside Holy Cross Church during this Friday morning, in order to make a cable junction, they unearthed the skeleton of a man about 2ft below the surface. [Up until 1825, the only way to negotiate the Westgate was through the central arch – *see* June 21st. The churchyard for Holy Cross also extended right up to the Westgate, hence the discovery of this burial. Are there more deceased parishioners, or executed prisoners, yet to be discovered under the flagstones?] (*Kentish Gazette*)

November 20th

1175 and 1240: On this day, future Archbishop of Canterbury, Edmund Rich, was born in Abingdon. On the same day sixty-five years later, he was buried at Pontigny Abbey, Burgundy, France, having died on November 16th. He had been made Archbishop in 1234 and, like Becket before him, immediately began picking fights with the King (in his case, Henry III). As a result, also like Becket, he was forced into exile in France. Edmund was canonised as a saint in 1247. St Edmund's School, on the outskirts of Canterbury, is named after him.

———◆———

1914: On this Friday afternoon, Princess Clementina of Belgium visited the hospital in the Dane John to see the wounded officers and men of her native land. Special efforts had also been made on November 15th so that the Belgian wounded could celebrate King Albert of Belgium's birthday. (*Kentish Gazette*)

———◆———

2007: On this day, a live concert by the Canterbury Scene group Gong was recorded in Brazil, and later made available on DVD. The line-up featured founder member and ex-Soft Machine guitarist Daevid Allen. At the time, he was only a couple of months away from his seventieth birthday.

November 21st

1444: William Byllynton, of the parish of All Saints', died on this day. In his will, he left money towards the construction of the Dorter (dormitory) at the Greyfriars. [There is only one building surviving today from the Greyfriars friary complex, being a charming little building of late fourteenth-century date that spans one branch of the River Stour. As the original purpose of this building remains unclear, it could well be the structure that Mr Byllynton helped to finance.] (Cotton: *The Greyfriars of Canterbury*)

———◆———

1882: 'In all probability, Canterbury will be one of the first towns in Kent in which the electric light will be used on a large scale. The local electric light company intend to apply to the Board of Trade for the power to produce and store electricity, as well as that for the digging up of streets in the city to make such illumination possible.' [The City Council proved somewhat resistant to the arrival of electricity, the Electric Light Works finally being built in 1898, just off Northgate Street.] (*Kentish Gazette*, see September 11th)

———◆———

1940: Second World War Notebook: 'Three land mines dropped [probably jettisoned] during the night on Chislet Marshes.'

November 22nd

1694: The Archbishop of Canterbury, John Tillotson, died on this day after only three-and-a-half years in office. However, before the 'top job', he had been both a Canon and the Dean at Canterbury Cathedral. He also possessed the special confidence of William of Orange and Queen Mary II. (Wikipedia)

◆

1732: On this Saturday, one Philip Giles, upwards of seventy years of age, blind of his left eye and an inhabitant of Axe and Bottle Yard, and George Baker, aged about forty, also blind in his left eye, were apprehended and taken to His Majesty's gaol at St Dunstan's, near this city, charged upon oath with playing cup and balls and betting and laying wagers with intent to defraud and cheat people of their money. (*Kentish Post or Canterbury Newsletter*)

◆

1928: The East Kent Regional Planning Scheme envisaged a number of new roads for the Canterbury area. As well as the proposed northern bypass (*see* March 11th) there was also a link road to the east of the city, running from St Augustine's Road to Littlebourne Road (of which Warwick Road would later form part), and a link road from Summer Hill to Wincheap Green (an early version of the Rheims Way).

November 23rd

1854: On this day, the Auditor of the Canterbury Dean and Chapter, Daniel Finch, made one of many pleas for funds to the Ecclesiastical Commissioners. As is still the case today, the prime concern was to finance essential repairs to the cathedral fabric. The cost of restoring the nave roof alone was estimated at some £2,000. Limited finance was subsequently forthcoming. (Sparks *et al*: *Canterbury Cathedral*)

———◆·◆———

1937: 'A half-pint of milk a day, fruit and barley sugar are included in the dietary fibre of the 200 under-standard recruits who are at the Recruits Physical Development Depot, which began its work at Canterbury this week of bringing potential soldiers up to the Army standards of physical and medical well-being.' (*Kentish Gazette*)

———◆·◆———

1965: Objections to the demolition of prefabs in New Dover Road were made by Alderman Tom MacCallum at a Council meeting on this Tuesday. He said that the tenants were quite happy living in them, particularly as they were warm and cosy. He was a lone voice, however, and the rest of the Council agreed to press on with a five-year plan to clear away the 400 late-1940s pre-fabricated houses that could be found across Canterbury. (City Council records)

November 24th

1170: Thomas Becket was preparing to return to England and, hopefully, to the resolution of disputes with Henry II. However, he had already written to the Pope asking for three bishops, who were close to the King, to be sanctioned (*see* July 22nd). The letters from the Pope duly arrived, authorising excommunication of Gilbert and Jocelin and the suspension of Roger. But Becket hesitated, not wishing to jeopardise the new understanding he had with Henry, and wrote again to the Pope asking if their publication might be issued at his own (Becket's) discretion. On 24th November, the Pope wrote back in agreement (*see* November 29th). (Urry: *Becket: His Last Days*)

1914: On this day, the Chislet Colliery Ltd came into being and continued to sink boreholes towards the coal seam. By 1919, saleable quantities of coal were being brought to the surface. Other boreholes even nearer Canterbury, at Sturry and Bekesbourne, proved unsuccessful. (Llewellyn: *Hersden*)

1934: On this Saturday, two Canterbury boys, aged fourteen and thirteen respectively, admitted stealing an electric bicycle lamp on November 15th. The chief constable said that PC Cripps saw the boys standing in a doorway with the lamp they had pulled to pieces. (*Kentish Gazette*)

November 25th

1882: Feeling the importance of securing an improved attendance at school – under the new regulations contained in the Mundella Code – the local Teacher's Association convened a conference of managers and teachers, which was held at St Paul's School, Canterbury, on this Saturday, for the purpose of discussing the present unsatisfactory method of enforcing regular attendance in local elementary schools. [The code, named after Anthony Mundella, ensured that English literature became more firmly established in the curriculum, and important writers such as Shakespeare and Milton were included.] (*Kentish Gazette*)

———◆———

1897: The Mount Hospital in Stodmarsh Road was opened on this day. Originally called the Canterbury Sanatorium, it later became known as the Fever Hospital. With the decline of fever cases in 1951, the hospital was closed. A proposal to reopen it for tuberculosis patients was dropped. The hospital eventually reopened in 1958, dealing with nurses' training and cases of pneumoconiosis; a chest disease suffered by coal miners. (Marcus Hall *et al*: *KCH 1790 to 1987*)

———◆———

1960: At a Council meeting, it was confirmed that Canon de Laubenque was to be allowed to install a Christmas crib beneath St George's Church tower, as in previous years. (City Council records)

November 26th

1333: The Archbishop of Canterbury, John de Stratford, was consecrated on this day. He had previously been Treasurer and Chancellor of England. As was often the case, the Archbishop had a volatile relationship with the King, Edward III, but on this occasion, an understanding between the two was reached. His brothers, Robert and Ralph, were also both bishops. John died in August 1348.

------◆------

1833: 'On this Tuesday morning, a labouring man named John Patterson (aged fifty) was killed at Oaten Hill in this city. The poor fellow was drawing a truck along the road when he observed a team of horses coming towards him at rapid speed, and he drew to the side of the embankment to avoid contact with the wagon. It, however, caught the truck, Patterson was dashed to the ground and one of the wheels passed over his neck and killed him on the spot.' (*Kentish Gazette*)

------◆------

1960: The Service Authorities asked the Council to help increase the strength of the regular Army. Statistics showed that Canterbury was falling behind in this respect. To date, twenty-two men had gone to the Army Information Office in Roper Road, which was only two per month. (City Council records)

November 27th

1189: On this day, King Richard the Lionheart came to Canterbury to arbitrate in the dispute between Archbishop Baldwin and the Christ Church monks, over the former's intention to establish a separate Secular College (*see* October 1st). In the end, Baldwin backed down and agreed to the dismantling of the college, and also to the deposition of Prior Norreys. Earlier, the Christ Church Prior had defected to the Archbishop's cause, escaping the Cathedral Precincts by crawling along the 'Great Drain' that discharged from the monastic 'Necessarium'. (Woodruff and Danks: *Memorials*)

1807: On this Friday afternoon, 'a fire broke out in the officers' room of the front infantry barracks in Northgate, Canterbury, owing to some workmen leaving a pitch-pot on the fire unattended. This was soon got under by the exertion of the soldiers and inhabitants without doing any material damage, except slightly burning the floor.' (*Kentish Gazette*)

2009: Canterbury City Council has agreed to loan the Kent Cricket Club £4 million to help towards the redevelopment of the St Lawrence Ground. The club will meet the full cost of the loan over the next twenty-five years, so there will be no costs to local taxpayers. (England and Wales Cricket Board)

November 28th

1914: 'Your Country Needs You': 'It is regrettable to have to record a falling off during the past week of recruits for Lord Kitchener's Army, and we would point out to the young men of Canterbury that a continued slackness in this respect will assuredly lead to some form of conscription in the near future.' [The names of those 'Young Men of Canterbury' who fell can be read on the war memorials all over the city.] (*Kentish Gazette*)

———◆———

1940: 'Second World War Notebook': '11:15 a.m., I was going onto the roof [Telephone Exchange?] when I heard an enemy plane diving. Rushed up the iron stairs to the roof, in case I was blown off the stairs and down into the Post Office yard. As soon as I'd landed on the roof, I heard the swish of bombs and two were dropped: one in St Mary's Street, damaging four houses; the other in front of the Maternity Home in the Dane John. It blew a monument off its pedestal.'

———◆———

1980: Mike Leigh's *Grown-ups* was first shown on BBC Playhouse. It was largely filmed around two houses in Nunnery Road, but also featured various locations across Canterbury. (Author's archive)

November 29th

1170: By this Advent Sunday, Thomas Becket was en route back to England and had reached the French port of Wissant, near Boulogne. The Archbishop had with him the letters of sanction he'd requested from the Pope (*see* November 24th) but hadn't yet received Alexander's reply permitting him to issue them at his discretion. However, contrary to his earlier caution, Becket now changed his mind and decided to send the letters across the channel – in the care of a trusted servant – to be immediately served on the three bishops whom he knew were in Dover (*see* December 2nd). (Urry cites both mental and physical exhaustion to explain this seemingly self-defeating move in *Becket: His Last Days*)

1787: On this Thursday, the Canterbury Pavement Commissioners ordered that an archway be cut through the staircase turret of St George's Church for foot passengers (*see* August 4th). This was an experiment, about which the Archbishop himself had been consulted, so that a pavement could be provided for this part of the main street without having to demolish the turret, which projected out into the street from the south-east corner of the main tower. Other intruding structures were also affected (*see* June 25th). (*Archaeologia Cantiana*, 1988)

November 30th

1648: The Alderman of Canterbury, Avery Sabine, was buried in St George's Church on this day. Of Puritan leanings, he was a member of the County Committee for Kent under Parliament. Sabine successfully mediated in the Christmas Day Riot in 1647 (*see* December 25th) but this did not win him any favours with the ultra-Puritans. As a result, he was imprisoned, and this injustice turned him into a Royalist. He died shortly afterwards. (Urry: *St George's Church*)

———◆◆———

1887: During this Wednesday afternoon at about three o'clock, a fatal accident occurred on the Elham Valley line at Bridge. A navvy named Bristow was sitting at the side of the cutting, but he incautiously sat forward, mindless of the trucks that were running to and fro. Consequently, he was struck by the buffer of a truck, which smashed his chest. In total, there were three deaths on this stretch of the line during its construction. The other two victims were caught in an earth slip near Bourne Park tunnel.

———◆◆———

1955: On this day, sections of North Lane were purchased compulsorily in order to widen the road. This included the surviving Blacksmith's shop at No. 51, and a small oast house. (City Council records)

December 1st

1840: 'Railway Opening': 'A bill will be introduced into Parliament in the next sessions for a 'branch line' from the South Eastern Railway to the Isle of Thanet. The line will commence at Ashford, running through Canterbury withoutside the wall near Westgate to the terminus at Ramsgate'. [The line was opened in 1846, joining the existing 'Crab & Winkle' line at what would become Canterbury (West) station.] (*Kentish Gazette, see* February 6th)

———•◆•———

1952: 'Railway Closure': On this Monday, the old Canterbury & Whitstable Railway – popularly known as the 'Crab & Winkle Line' – officially closed. This was the date given 'for the withdrawal of freight facilities' on those ominous posters put up along the line, but, in truth, the last train had run two days before. However, this was not quite the end of the old line (*see* February 6th).

———•◆•———

1986: On this Monday, Her Royal Highness Diana, the Princess of Wales, came to lunch with Archbishop Robert Runcie (who had officiated at her marriage to Prince Charles) at the Old Palace, in Canterbury. In the afternoon, she attended a spectacular Advent carol service in the cathedral. (Canterbury Cathedral Chronicle, 1987)

December 2nd

1170: On this day, Archbishop Thomas Becket arrived back in Canterbury to a rapturous reception, thus ending his six-year-long exile in France (*see* October 14th). On the previous day, he had landed at Sandwich, deliberately avoiding Dover, where trouble was waiting for him in the shape of Rannulph de Broc and the three prelates who had, by this time, received their letters of excommunication or suspension (*see* November 29th). (Urry: *Becket: His Last Days*)

1732: 'This is to give notice that none may presume to take or destroy any fish within the liberties of the City of Canterbury, without leave first obtained in writing; and whoever shall give notice of any offender shall receive a reward of 10s upon their conviction.' (*Kentish Post or Canterbury Newsletter*)

1959: 'I said scrag-end; not fag-end!': During this day's Council meeting, the chief public health inspector reported that some minced meat recently bought in Canterbury had been found to contain a quantity of shredded tobacco, some of it charred. (City Council records)

1964: An application from the Canterbury Fund for the Blind, for permission to display a small plastic wishing-well in the Buttermarket for fundraising purposes, was refused. (City Council records)

December 3rd

1170: By now settled in his Palace at Canterbury, Thomas Becket received a deputation from the three disgraced bishops – still waiting in Dover – asking that the letters of excommunication and suspension be reversed and their bishoprics restored. Becket refused, saying that it was the Pope who had signed the letters, so he could do nothing about it. Rannulph de Broc, also in attendance, made threats against the Archbishop's life as a result (*see* December 9th). (Urry: *Becket: His Last Days*)

———•◆•———

1657: On this day Brother Storr, of the ruthlessly-disciplinarian Congregational Church in Canterbury, was admonished 'because he had in him much that is the root of all evil, i.e. the love of money'. (Taylor: *The Free Churches of Canterbury*)

———•◆•———

1882: Archbishop Archibald Campbell Tait died on this Sunday. The life of this Scots-born Primate was beset by tragedy. In 1856, five of his children were carried off by scarlet fever in as many weeks. Becoming Archbishop in 1868, his final years were plagued by illness and overshadowed by the deaths of his wife and only surviving son. News of the Primate's passing reached Canterbury early on the same morning, and from 9 a.m. until 11 a.m. Bell Harry was tolled.

December 4th

1835: On this day, Mary Felicity Hales was born in Boulogne. She was the last from an indirect branch of the once mighty Hales family. Almost straight away, Mary was made a British subject and her family took up residence in the ancestral mansion at Hackington, Hales Place. She was baptised at the nearby St Stephen's Church, but educated at a French convent. (*Victorian Hackington*)

———◆———

1909: 'During the heavy wind storm on this Saturday morning, a large stone was dislodged and fell from the roof of the Congregational Church in Guildhall Street. On striking the ground, it rebounded and broke a large plate-glass window at Messrs Deakin & Sons. Several hoardings were also blown down in various parts of the city and tiles and slates dislodged from houses.' [The upper parts of this, by now, redundant church were demolished in about 1949, but its lower section survives today as part of Debenham's.] (*Kentish Gazette*)

———◆———

1957: On this Wednesday, the Council decided that St George's Clock Tower wasn't interesting enough to have one of the Chamber of Trade's 'Places of Interest' notices positioned near it, nor one of the Council's own street maps. (City Council records)

December 5th

1815: On this day, convicted robber Nicholas Nolan was hanged at the gibbet outside the Westgate. The unhappy convict ascended the platform at 8.30 a.m., prayed for an hour, and then turned to the surrounding multitude to declare his innocence. Soon afterwards he dropped without convulsive movement. (*Bygone Kent*, Vol. 5)

——◆——

1939: 'An Announcement': 'Every Thursday afternoon from 2.30 p.m., a demonstration and test of civilian respirators in a gas chamber will be given at the Canterbury ARP headquarters in Palace Street. Members of the public are invited to attend in order to test the efficiency of their gas masks, as any leakage is immediately discovered without harmful effects.' [Fear of gas bombs was very real and quite understandable, given the terrible experiences of troops in the trenches of the First World War.] (*Kentish Gazette*)

——◆——

1940: 'Second World War Notebook': '4 p.m., two bombs were dropped in Mount Road... Six other bombs fell, one directly into, or right on top of, the chimney stack of Stone House Asylum at the back of Little Barton Estate. Another bomb fell in the asylum grounds. Four injured and two killed, including Cork the Chimney Sweep.' (1940 Kelly's: Herbert Cork of No. 4 Church Lane, St Mildred's)

December 6th

1759: 'On this Thursday, James Homersham, a boy of about thirteen or fourteen years of age, was convicted before the Mayor of Canterbury, George Knowler Esq., of firing a rocket in the streets and was fined 20s. This, the boy's father immediately paid to Mr Mayor: one moiety [a half] to the use of the prosecutor, and the other moiety to the use of the poor of the parish where the offence had been committed.' (*Kentish Gazette*)

———— •◆• ————

1788: Richard Harris Barham was born on this day at No. 61 Burgate Street. He would grow up to become an ordained priest of the Church of England, but was more famously known as the author of the anthology *The Ingoldsby Legends* using the pen-name of Thomas Ingoldsby.

———— •◆• ————

1875: On this cold Monday morning at 7.15 a.m., a train left Canterbury West for Whitstable but came to a standstill in a cutting at Tyler Hill having just negotiated the tunnel. The locomotive was embedded in a snowdrift, and had to be dug out by a gang of men. Much later, when another train attempted the six-mile journey, it came to grief at exactly the same location. (Hart: *Canterbury & Whitstable Railway*)

December 7th

1533: Elizabeth Barton, the so-called 'Holy Maid of Kent', did penance outside Canterbury Cathedral in a plea for mercy following her death sentence. Elizabeth had gained notoriety for receiving holy visions, in which she was warned of dire consequences for Henry VIII should he marry Anne Boleyn. She had received support from the likes of Sir Thomas More, as well as the Convent of St Sepulchre's in Canterbury. (Neame: *The Holy Maid of Kent, see* February 16th)

1887: 'The subject of the telephone is under the consideration of the Canterbury Town Council. Nearly the whole of the meeting held on this Wednesday was devoted to its discussion and a strong opinion was expressed that 'a little stationary town like Canterbury did not need the telephone'. The forceful reply of Mr Alderman Hart was that if Canterbury was little, it was because there were little-minded people in it! A vote was taken, showing a majority against progress and the telephone.' (*Kentish Gazette*)

1960: 'Health Inspector's Report': Complaints included: a chocolate-flavoured sponge mixture infested with the larvae of the cocoa moth; a portion of New Zealand cheese containing a bolt head; and a pin found in some fudge. (City Council records)

December 8th

1832: 'During this Saturday morning, an inquest was held at the King's Arms (*see* November 4th) on the body of William Turner, foreman in the employ of Mr James Bell, carpenter. The deceased went home on Friday night last, with a female, to a house in King Street where, after supper with her and the landlord, he retired to rest having drunk very hard. In the morning, he caught her in his arms, but made a strange noise and soon after expired. A bottle of laudanum was found under his bed, but the surgeon detected no sign of the drug in his stomach. The people of the house were examined and the jury, perfectly satisfied, returned a verdict of "died by the visitation of God".' (*Kentish Gazette*)

———————— ◆ ————————

2008: Pacifist, writer and children's television creator Oliver Postgate died on this day at Broadstairs. He was eighty-three. Amongst his best and most-loved creations were those in collaboration with artist Peter Firmin. The two men formed Smallfilms and, based at Peter's home in Blean, near Canterbury, created such characters as Ivor the Engine, Noggin the Nog, The Clangers and Bagpuss. In 1987, he was awarded an honorary degree by Canterbury University.

December 9th

1170: After a week back in Canterbury, things weren't going well for Thomas Becket. The three sanctioned bishops had pressed him hard to absolve them, without success, and the de Broc family continued to occupy the Church's lands and property (*see* December 3rd). Unable to appeal to Henry II, who was still in France, Becket set off to see his former pupil and prodigy: the fourteen-year-old crowned Prince Henry at Winchester. Travelling with a modest retinue, Becket received much adulation en route, but was denied access to young Henry. Concurrently, the three bishops set sail for Normandy, to lobby Henry II and tell exaggerated tales of Becket parading round the country with a private army (*see* December 24th). (Urry: *Becket: His Last Days*)

◆

1939: Because of the recent declaration of war, it was decided to stop restoration work on the cathedral's Bell Harry Tower.

◆

1984: South African anti-apartheid activist Bishop Desmond Tutu preached in Canterbury Cathedral on this Sunday before flying to Oslo to collect his Nobel Peace Prize. The bishop spent the weekend in Canterbury with his wife Leah and two of their daughters as guests of the Archbishop, Dr Robert Runcie, at the Old Palace. (*Kentish Gazette*)

December 10th

1835: 'Guildhall Good News': 'The frontage of the Guildhall in this city will, we hear, be completed in the course of a few days. The scaffolding will be removed on Saturday next.' [The new façade was in the popular Regency style and resembled that of the Corn Exchange and Longmarket building in nearby St George's Street.] (*Kentish Gazette*; see Crampton: *Canterbury's Lost Heritage* for pictures of both buildings)

———•◆•———

1947: 'Guildhall Bad News': On this Wednesday, City Architect L. Hugh Wilson published a report on the structural condition of the Guildhall, which had been causing concern for some time. His initial examination revealed some alarming problems: the flank wall on Guildhall Street was badly fractured near the south-east corner and also leaning out. Dry rot had also affected the rafters. Subsequent investigations uncovered further structural problems. (Courtesy of Anthony Swaine)

———•◆•———

1968: On this day, at a meeting of both management and unions, it was learnt that the National Coal Board had declared Chislet Colliery in Hersden, near Canterbury, to be in jeopardy. Three reasons were given: falling output, falling manpower and a fall in the price of coal. At this stage though, they insisted it was only a warning. (Llewellyn: *Hersden*)

December 11th

1882: On this Monday at the City Police Court, a boy named Gann, in the employ of a sweep, was charged with throwing snowballs. He was discharged with a caution, as he'd been locked up since the previous evening. It appeared that he had thrown snowballs at several persons including two clergymen. (*Kentish Gazette*)

———◆———

1940: 'Second World War Notebook': 'Wednesday night at about 8 p.m., parachute flares were dropped in a circle around Canterbury and it was a wonderful sight. Everybody thought that Canterbury was going to have a proper Blitz, and the flares were seen from Whitstable, Tankerton and Herne Bay. Incendiaries were dropped on Old Dover Road and Nackington; two fell on the hospital and one crashed through a skylight into a ward. I saw one burnt-out close to Pinnock's Coal Yard by the hospital [Canterbury South Station]. For some reason, the attack was broken off, probably by RAF fighters, who were intercepting'. [No date was given, but evidence points to the 11th.]

———◆———

1966: Van driver Ronald Gray failed to stop at the traffic lights at the Guildhall Street Junction on this day. Gray later admitted he hadn't noticed the red light, having been talking to his passenger. (Author's archive)

December 12th

1470: In his will, signed on this day, twice former Mayor of Canterbury William Bygge, of St Peter's parish, left to his wife, among much other property throughout the city, his 'tenement called the Steere [Star Inn] and one called The Forge, in the parish of Holy Cross, Westgate'. A bequest of £10 was also made towards the completion of St George's Gate. (*Archaeologia Cantiana*, 1942)

• ◆ •

1884: 'A young woman named Seaward, employed at the buffet at the South Eastern railway station [Canterbury West], died on this Friday after a short illness. It is stated that tight lacing was the primary cause.' [The decade's most popular corset was the 'oval-chest' horizontal-waist corset, which raised and compressed the chest, and also produced a long, concave waist. This particular design, although undeniably fashionable, was not considered to be very healthy, as it restricted breathing, and also flattened the liver!] (*Kentish Gazette*)

• ◆ •

1940: 'Second World War Notebook': 'About 6 a.m., high-explosive bombs were dropped in Old Park, missing the Old Barracks, but the New Barracks were hit, one bomb directly on the quartermaster's stores, but no one was killed'. [No date was given, but evidence points to the 12th.]

December 13th

1538: On this Tuesday, the three friaries at Canterbury, the Greyfriars, the Blackfriars and the Whitefriars were dissolved. The Deed of Suppression demanded that the newly appointed Bishop of Dover, Richard Ingworth (himself a former Black Friar) sequestrate and catalogue all their goods and properties. Afterwards, the Blackfriars became a weaving factory, whereas Whitefriars and Greyfriars both became private houses.

———◆———

1643: On this Sunday, Protestant zealot, iconoclast and, ironically, Six Preacher Richard Culmer smashed much of the stained glass in the 'Royal Window' situated in the martyrdom transept (*see* October 4th). 'Idolatrous' glass broken by him on this occasion included images of Thomas Becket, the Virgin Mary and a large crucifix. However, he left those panes depicting Edward IV and other Royal subjects. The remaining glass was rearranged in the eighteenth century.

———◆———

1787: 'Notice is hereby given that the commissioner will meet at the Guildhall in Canterbury on this Thursday morning, at eleven o'clock, to receive proposals for contracting to pave the foot and carriageways of Burgate Street, and of such other streets and places within the City Walls of the said city as they shall think proper to have paved in like manner.' (*Kentish Gazette*)

December 14th

1592: Sir Roger Manwood died on this day. In his lifetime, he had the reputation of being a ruthless but corrupt judge. He lived in 'Place House' at Hackington: a large mansion that used to stand in front of St Stephen's Church. [This would later become the residence of the Hales family.] Sir Roger established a family vault in the church, where his rather elaborate tomb can still be seen. He also financed the construction of the almshouses on St Stephen's Green. (Rogers: *Sir Roger Manwood*)

———◆———

1741: The lead coffin of Mrs Catherine Strickland (née Henshaw) was the last one to be buried within the family vault beneath the Roper Chapel at St Dunstan's Church. Hers was one of the five lead coffins observed in 1837 when the vault was opened.

———◆———

1984: Angry businessmen from the Canterbury Chamber of Trade have stepped up their fight to prevent massive increases in parking charges. During a meeting with two senior City Council members on this Friday, delegates from the chamber made it clear that they were wholly opposed to the increases. And they suggested that the Council should improve the efficiency of facilities before taking any drastic steps. (*Kentish Gazette*)

December 15th

1809: 'The barracks in St George's Place, in this city, lately occupied by the Horse Artillery and which were in part taken down, are to be immediately rebuilt. They will be re-engaged for the reception of 800 of the sick soldiers expected from Walcheren.' [During the French Revolutionary Wars – 1793 to 1802 – a number of temporary barracks were built in Canterbury to supplement those off Sturry Road. The new, undeveloped turnpike road of St George's Place, built in 1790, made an ideal location. The partial demolition was probably due to the Treaty of Amiens, which brought peace between England and France in March 1802. However, this proved short-lived for on 18 May 1803, hostilities were renewed and the Napoleonic Wars began in earnest. The Walcheren Campaign of 1809 was an unsuccessful British expedition to the Netherlands.] (*Kentish Gazette*)

———————◆———————

1894: John Williams was charged with begging on this Saturday. Sergeant Jackson said that at 6.50 p.m. in the evening, he was on plain-clothes duty in St George's Place where the prisoner stopped and asked him for a 'copper' for a night's lodging. He was sentenced to seven days' hard labour. (*Kentish Observer*, courtesy of Tina Machado)

December 16th

1867: On this day, Mr Thomas Holman signed an estimate for the dismantling of St Martin's Hill, Black Mill, and using parts of it to build one at Blean. [This windmill once stood on the opposite side of the road to the surviving Quern's Mill.] (Finch: *Watermills and Windmills*)

———◆———

1894: Rosetta Pile, who was summoned for keeping a brothel in Kirby's Lane, St Dunstan's, pleaded guilty to having soldiers at the house. Sergeant Dunk deposed that on this Sunday at 2.10 a.m., he visited Pile's house with PCs West and Stone and found several soldiers with girls. The chairman said it was clear she had been keeping a disorderly house. [Because Rosetta came from Faversham, and had only been in Canterbury for three weeks, she could be forgiven for not noticing that the County police station was also in Kirby's Lane.] (*Kentish Observer*, courtesy of Tina Machado)

———◆———

1946: On this Monday, classical musician Trevor Pinnock CBE was born in Canterbury. He is the son of local historian and publisher Kenneth Pinnock, who died in October 2008. Trevor is probably best known for performing and recording music of the Baroque period.

December 17th

1538: Pope Paul III issued a Bull of Excommunication against Henry VIII for ordering the destruction of the elaborate shrine to Archbishop Thomas Becket in Canterbury Cathedral (*see* September 7th).

1894: 'On this Monday, Walter Larkin, a farmer's son from Staple, on bail, was charged with being drunk and disorderly whilst in charge of a horse. PC Lockey said that about 3.30 p.m. on Saturday he saw the prisoner riding in Longport Street. The horse went backwards and forwards in the road and onto the pavement, where children had to run to get out of the way. Upon being approached, Larkin galloped away towards St Martin's Hill.' (*Kentish Observer*, courtesy of Tina Machado)

1939: 'Everyone during this first Christmas when we are all at war should stop waste in every possible way, including the needless consumption of food. If every single individual in this country saved 1lb of imported food stuffs every week, there would be a saving of about 1 million tons of imported food a year, occupying vital cargo-space that could be used to bring actual armaments of war to this country, or some vital raw materials on which our final victory may turn.' (*Kentish Gazette*)

December 18th

1770: On this day, a petition to pull down 4ft of the City Wall 'by Wincheap Gate' was allowed in order to widen the street. It appears that the city gate itself had already perished earlier the same year, having been demolished 'upon the petition of the inhabitants of St Mildred's'.

1894: On this Tuesday, Henry Cozens was summoned by the School Board for not sending his son to school regularly. Mrs Cozens appeared and pleaded guilty. It was shown that her son had made only nine attendances out of a possible ninety-six, and when he did show up the boy was so covered in vermin that he had to be sent back for fear of contaminating other pupils. (*Kentish Observer*, courtesy of Tina Machado)

1909: 'The County Committee have decided to carry out some alterations at the St Lawrence Cricket Ground for the convenience of the public. In order to prevent the congestion caused during the past few years, the present passenger entrance, which now adjoins the entrance for vehicles, will be moved a distance of about 30yds further up the Old Dover Road, thus greatly reducing the present risk of accident.' (*Kentish Gazette*)

December 19th

1741: On this day, a 'parhelion' [bright spots on either side of the sun, formed by refraction] was observed at Canterbury. It was described as 'being two mock suns and an inverted rainbow of the most lively colours'. The appearance ended about noon. (Hasted: *Kent*, Vol. XI)

———◆———

1807: The show of fat beef and mutton, which of late years has been customary in Canterbury in this period of the year, was very good on this Saturday and attracted much attention. Among the many fine carcasses exhibited were two three-year-old South Down Wethers, fed on grass only. (*Kentish Gazette*)

———◆———

1921: This day saw the unveiling of the King's School War Memorial adjacent to the Norman Staircase in the Green Court. Surrounding the cross, a new paved courtyard was made at the lower medieval level, allowing the steps of the Norman Staircase to be restored to their former glory. The actual names of the 147 Old Boys who fell are on a nearby plaque.

———◆———

2003: On this day, the Canterbury Archaeological Trust's 'Big Dig' at the Whitefriars came to an end. This massive excavation attracted the attention of thousands, as well as bringing Channel 4's *Time Team* to the city. (Author's archive)

December 20th

1553: This day was the deadline set for the resumption of the Latin service in Canterbury Cathedral following the accession of the Mary Tudor. A new Catholic Archbishop was also appointed, Cardinal Pole, to replace the Protestant Cranmer, who was burnt at the stake (*see* March 21st and 22nd).

———•◆•———

1782: At Canterbury sessions was tried Thomas Stokes, charged with robbing Bernard Astley Esq. in the St Mary Bredin parish of the sum of 7s. In the course of the trial, it was proved that Stokes had not only robbed the young man, but also threatened that if he disclosed the robbery he, Stokes, would swear that Mr Astley had come into his company with an intent to commit an 'unnatural crime' on him. After the jury brought the prisoner in guilty, the Recorder advised Stokes to make best use of the short time he had to live, and assured him he had so exceedingly aggravated his offence by an abominal attack on the character and reputation of the young gentleman that he could have no hope for mercy, which probably might have been extended to him had he been guilty of the robbery only. Sentence – death. (*Kentish Gazette*)

December 21st

1120: Thomas Becket was born on this day, being St Thomas the Apostle's Day. It is likely that he had three older sisters. His parents, Gilbert and Matilda, were both Norman. The family name is thought to have originated from the hamlet of Becquet, on the Le Havre peninsula. (Urry: *Becket: His Last Days*)

———◆———

1959: All was quiet in Canterbury High Street on this Monday evening: a city almost deserted under the twinkling Christmas lights. 'Silent Night, Holy Night' was being sung by children carollers in a nearby side street. However, inside the Post Office, the night was far from silent as eighty men and women furiously struggled to cope with the peak of the Christmas mail. (*Kentish Gazette*)

———◆———

1962: On this day, an enterprising individual arrived at the Treasurer's Department in the Municipal Offices, Dane John, and announced that he'd come to collect the wages for the Beaney Institute staff. Apparently, as he bore some resemblance to the usual messenger, £83 was handed over without question and a receipt was duly signed. It was not until later, when the genuine messenger arrived, that the trick was exposed and a further £83 had to be found. (Author's archive)

December 22nd

1939: 'A Canterbury man walking in the blackout was using his umbrella as a walking stick when the point stuck in the grass verge. He pulled it out and hooked the crook on his arm. When he got home, he found that he was carrying just the handle. He is still out looking for the rest of the gamp!' (*Kentish Gazette*)

———•◆•———

1965: On this Wednesday, Somerset Maugham's ashes were buried in the grounds of his old school, the King's School, Canterbury, in accordance with his wishes. A metal gate with his symbol was made, and leads to the burial place, just north of the Norman Staircase. World-renowned writer and Old Boy Somerset Maugham contributed to the cost of the King's School boathouse, and another gift helped to establish the Maugham Library. (Hinde: *Imps of Promise*)

———•◆•———

2002: On this Sunday morning, the newly appointed Archbishop of Canterbury, Dr Rowan Williams, appeared on Radio 4's *Desert Island Discs*. Amongst the inevitable selections from Bach, Handel and Vaughan Williams could be found 'The Hedgehog's Song' by folk hippies The Incredible String Band. In addition to the ubiquitous Bible, he chose a collection of W.H. Auden poems and his luxury was a piano! (BBC website)

December 23rd

1752: Archbishop Herring wrote to Dean Lynch concerning a request to have the remains of Archbishop Anselm removed from the cathedral: 'I would get rid of them all, if the parting with the rotten remains of a rebel to his King, a slave to Popedom and an enemy to the married clergy would purchase ease and indulgence to one living Protestant'. (Sparks *et al*: *Canterbury Cathedral*)

———◆———

1824: Thomas Sidney Cooper won a place at the Royal Academy Schools. Cooper's Uncle Elvey, a strict Dissenting minister, had been encouraging, but did not approve of his twenty-one-year-old nephew working as a scene painter at the theatre in Orange Street. Thomas duly resigned and moved into his uncle's London house, but soon fell out with this Puritan and was sent back to Canterbury. (Stewart: *Thomas Sidney Cooper*)

———◆———

1884: Thomas Applin was charged with being a deserter from the 1st Middlesex Regiment at Dover. PC Holder said that at 3.45 a.m. he was on duty in The Parade. He saw the prisoner, who had no pass, and was told he'd come to Canterbury for a holiday. The bench ordered Applin to be taken back to Dover, and granted Holder a 10s reward. (*Kentish Gazette*)

December 24th

1170: Over in Normandy, Henry II simmered with rage, having been lobbied by the three sanctioned bishops, and although he may not have said the words: 'Will no one rid me of this turbulent priest?' the phrase nonetheless summed up his mood. Moreover, the knights in his presence were growing ever more restless to resolve the situation. Back in Kent, Becket was suffering more intimidation. Robert de Broc, nephew of Rannulph, cut off the tail of a donkey that was transporting Christmas foodstuffs to the Archbishop's palace kitchen. (Urry: *Becket: His Last Days*)

1676: The Canterbury Cathedral Six Preacher, Shadrach Cooke, was ordained on this day. He was popularly known as 'Absolution Cooke' because, in 1696, he was present on the scaffold at the execution of Robert Channock and Thomas Keyes, involved in a plot to assassinate William III, and absolved them both. (Ingram Hill: *The Six Preachers*)

1914: 'Limited leave only has been granted for the Christmastide to the territorial units stationed in Canterbury. This procedure has occasioned some surprise so far as it affects men who are unequipped and, as yet, not efficient. However, efforts are being made for those 'on service' to spend as happy a time as possible.' (*Kentish Gazette*)

December 25th

1170: During a service in Canterbury Cathedral, Becket told his congregation that he feared his imminent death. He also publicly excommunicated both Rannulph and Robert de Broc. Over in Normandy, Henry II authorised three senior barons to go to England and arrest Becket. However, four knights in the King's court decided to take more drastic action: William de Tracey, Richard le Bret, Reginald FitzUrse and Hugh de Morville. They quietly slipped away, intending to reach Becket first (*see* December 28th). (Urry: *Becket: His Last Days*)

———◆———

1647: In this year, the so-called 'Christmas Day Riot' took place. Canterbury's Puritan Mayor, Michael Page, tried to prevent people attending Church for the Christmas Festival. He met with much resistance and anti-Commonwealth cries of 'for God, King Charles and Kent' preceded many scuffles.

———◆———

1937: Half an hour after he received the King's shilling, the latest recruit at the Buffs Depot, Canterbury, was sitting down in a festoon-decorated dining hall to a Christmas dinner of roast turkey, Christmas pudding, mince pies and drink. This is an example of the comforts of modern Army life. There was no time to fit him out with a uniform, but they managed to find him a mug. (*Kentish Gazette*)

December 26th

1773: St Andrew's Church, in The Parade, was opened by licence of the Archbishop on this day and consecrated in the July following. The Church was formerly seated on a spot called The Parade, in the middle of the High Street, but was taken down in 1763 and the new one built in a more convenient situation (*see* August 19th). (Seymour's *Survey of Kent* and Crampton: *Canterbury's Lost Heritage*)

1886: At six o'clock on this Sunday morning, there were cries of 'Murder!' and 'Police!' in St George's Street, and on a police constable turning up he was directed to a house in Canterbury Lane, the occupier of which had been frightened by the behaviour of a drunken barber whom he had been entertaining over Christmas. (*Kentish Gazette*)

1927: On this Boxing Day, the River Stour burst its banks after a sustained period of heavy rain. Some 400 families were affected, the worst area being in St Peter's Lane, Pound Lane and North Lane. In response, the Mayor of Canterbury, George Barrett, set up a 'Mayor's Fund' to help the victims. Indeed, he could empathise as his own house in Linden Grove had also been flooded. (Barrett's archive)

December 27th

1539: On this day, an Augustinian Friar named John Stone was executed at Canterbury. Like Thomas More before him (*see* June 3rd), John Stone had refused to sign the Act of Supremacy. This occurred when the Whitefriars friary had surrendered to Richard Ingworth (*see* December 13th). A year later, Stone was tried at the Guildhall, Canterbury, and following the inevitable guilty verdict, he was taken to the Westgate Towers to await his fate. John Stone was hanged, drawn and quartered on a scaffold specially erected on top of the mound in the Dane John.

◆

1626: Izaak Walton, author of *The Compleat Angler*, married on this day at St Mildred's Church, Canterbury. His bride was nineteen-year-old Rachel Floud. They had six sons and one daughter. Sadly, all died young and Rachel followed them in 1640.

◆

1782: 'At this season of universal festivity, let the opulent reflect on the miseries of the indigent; let not the honest and industrious father, the weeping mother and the helpless infants be deprived of their little possessions; let every creditor temper justice with mercy; and let all this be done in honour of him whose heart abounds with benevolence, love and charity.' (*Kentish Gazette*)

December 28th

1170: In the continuing Becket saga, the four knights from Henry II's court in Normandy had become separated whilst crossing the Channel. Therefore, it wasn't until this day that they were able to re-group near Dover, and then ride on together to Saltwood Castle. Here, they were welcomed by Rannulph de Broc, who played host to the men for the night. Elsewhere, the garrisons of other castles (Canterbury, Dover and Rochester) were being alerted in case Becket were to barricade himself in Canterbury Cathedral and a siege ensue. (Urry: *Becket: His Last Days*)

1880: On this day, it was reported that the famous 'House of Agnes', at No. 71 St Dunstan's Street, had been sold for £1,300. (*Bygone Kent*, Vol. 1, No. 12)

1939: The Mayor, Mrs Catherine Williamson, in the course of her tour of Canterbury schools – for the purpose of distributing her voucher tickets to local and evacuee children – was presented with numerous gifts in appreciation of her generosity. The presents included a calendar made by the children of St George's School (Canterbury Lane), and an ornament made by one of the teachers at the Payne Smith Infants' School (Lower Chantry Lane). (*Kentish Gazette*)

December 29th

1170: Late this afternoon, Archbishop Thomas Becket was brutally murdered in his own cathedral. The four knights responsible had ridden up from Saltwood Castle that morning and then dined (and drank heavily) at St Augustine's Abbey with the corrupt Abbot Clarembald. They then rode to Palace Street and entered the Archbishop's Palace precincts through the gatehouse. Here they met Robert de Broc, who had occupied the palace during Becket's exile. Leaving their weapons under a mulberry tree, the four knights confronted Becket in his chambers, trying to entrap him with accusations. Unsuccessful but angered, they went back outside to take up arms. Becket's entourage tried barricading him in, but de Broc, knowing the palace well, soon gained access. Becket was then compelled to go to the cathedral for sanctuary, but he refused to hurry. The knights caught up with the Archbishop in the north-west transept and matters soon became violent. Becket was struck down by a series of sword blows, the last one slicing off the top of his skull. As he lay dead, his brains were scooped out onto the flagstones, to ensure death, and the knights withdrew, looting the palace in the process. (Urry: *Becket: His Last Days*)

December 30th

1170: Late on the previous day, the anguished Christ Church monks had carried Thomas Becket's bloodied body to the high altar in the cathedral choir, and here it stayed for the night. However, at dawn, Robert de Broc entered the choir and demanded they bury Becket immediately or he would drag the corpse through the streets of Canterbury behind his horse. This the monks duly did, using a tomb already prepared in the eastern chapel of the crypt. (Urry: *Becket: His Last Days*)

1539: The future Queen, Anne of Cleves, spent the night of the 29th/30th in the newly completed Queen's Lodgings at the Royal Palace of St Augustine's (formerly the abbey). And then, during the day, she travelled up to meet Henry VIII at Rochester. (Tatton-Brown: *Canterbury: History and Guide*)

1882: 'Attention has been called to the state in which the clock at St George's Church, Canterbury, is being kept. At present, it is very far from reliable and often stops.' (*Kentish Gazette*)

1963: Derek Ingram Hill was appointed a Canterbury Cathedral Six Preacher on this day. A former King's School pupil, he was also Vicar of St Gregory's Church at the time. In 1976, he was installed as a Residentiary Cathedral Canon.

December 31st

1750: An account of a meteor observed on this day by the Revd Mr W.M. Gostling, a Minor Canon of Canterbury Cathedral: 'About one in the afternoon, I found my house violently shaken for some seconds of time, as if several loaded carriages had been driving against my walls; and heard a noise, which at first my family took for thunder, but of an uncommon sound. For my own part, I concluded it an earthquake; and, going immediately to the top of my house, found the sky cloudy, but nothing like thunder cloud in view; only there was a shower of rain from the eastward presently after, and the coldest that I have felt.' He later discovered that many had observed a 'ball of fire': a shooting star leaving 'a train of light' in its wake. William Gostling was the author of *A Walk in and about the City of Canterbury*. He died in 1777, aged eighty-one, having been a Minor Canon for fifty years.

—◆—

2009: Canterbury City Councillors claimed £404,500 in expenses and allowances over the last financial year. Each member receives £4,710 in basic allowances, with only Councillor Michael Steed not claiming the full amount. (*Kentish Gazette*)